Cleveland's West Side Market

100 Years & Still Cooking

To Carolyn
Treasure the Memories

[signature]

12/25/12

To Carolyn,
 I've shared 10 times more
than can be written with you
over our time together. The
stories will never end.

Your best friend eve, love,

[signature]

Cleveland's West Side Market

100 Years & Still Cooking

Laura Taxel & Marilou Suszko

with photographs by Barney Taxel

Ringtaw Books
Akron, Ohio

All inquiries and permission requests should be addressed to the Publisher:
The University of Akron Press, Akron, Ohio 44325-1703

17   16   15   14   13   5   4   3   2   1

LIBRARY OF CONGRESS CATALOGING IN PUBLICATION DATA
Taxel, Laura.
Cleveland's West Side Market : 100 years and still cooking / Laura Taxel & Marilou Suszko.
—1st ed.
    p. cm.
Includes bibliographical references and index.
ISBN 978-1-931968-94-2 (hbk. : alk. paper)
1. West Side Market (Cleveland, Ohio) 2. Cleveland (Ohio)—Social life and customs. 3.
Cleveland (Ohio)—Biography. 4. Grocery trade—Ohio—Cleveland—History—20th century.
I. Suszko, Marilou K. II. Title.
F499.C68W486 2012
977.1'32—DC23

2012026764

The paper used in this publication meets the minimum requirements of
American National Standard for Information Sciences—Permanence of Paper
for Printed Library Materials, ANSI Z39.48–1984. ∞

Cover Design: Christina Matijasic, Edgewater Graphics, Vermilion, Ohio
Book Design: Christina Matijasic, Amy Freels, and Zac Bettendorf

WE WENT LOOKING FOR THE FACTS AND FOUND SO MUCH MORE. Nothing would have been possible without all the West Side Market vendors and employees, past and present, who shared their stories, memories, and photos with us. We are infinitely grateful for your generosity and openness—this book is for you. We hope we've told your story well.

CONTENTS

ACKNOWLEDGMENTS

FOR THEIR BELIEF IN THE VALUE OF THIS PROJECT, plus unstinting support and infinite patience, we thank University of Akron Press Director Thomas Bacher and Editorial and Design Coordinator Amy Freels. Thanks are also in order to Marketing Manager Julie Gammon and Print and Digital Production Coordinator Carol Slatter.

Barney Taxel's photographs capture the heart of the Market through the building, the people, and the food. They are more than special and we are so glad he has been part of this project.

Christina Matijasic of Edgewater Graphics had a special vision for this book and demonstrates it beautifully throughout the pages. We are grateful for the talent she has shared.

Many people helped with our research and we appreciate each and every one of them. We are especially thankful to Lynn Duchez Bycko, Special Collections Associate, Michael Schwartz Library, Cleveland State University; Michael Ruffing, Research Collections and Services Coordinator for the Cleveland Public Library; Elaine Herroon, Public Administration Library, Cleveland Public Library; Don Petit, Cleveland Landmarks Commission; and Martin Hauserman, Chief City Archivist, City Council Archives. Although he passed away in 2006, long before we began our work, Walter Leedy, Cleveland State University Professor of Art, provided important assistance. In his passionate pursuit of local architectural history he amassed a file of newspaper articles about the West Side Market, now held in Cleveland State University's Michael Schwartz Library, that was invaluable.

We want to recognize Joanne Lewis, author of *To Market, To Market, An Old-Fashioned Family Story*, John Szilagyi, the book's designer and photographer, and his son Steve Szilagyi, who searched out some of his father's original prints.

Others who have earned our gratitude for the role they played in bringing this project to fruition include Eric Wobser and Amanda Dempsey of Ohio City, Inc.; and Christine Zuniga-Eadie, Manager of Markets.

Finally, we thank the Market goers—regular shoppers, occasional visitors, and wide-eyed children—who shared their memories to help us tell this story. They are the source of all the wonderful anecdotes scattered throughout the book that didn't come from vendors and employees, and are acknowledged by name.

FOREWORD
MICHAEL SYMON

WHEN I WAS YOUNG MY DAD USED TO WORK MIDNIGHTS AT FORD MOTOR COMPANY. Because of his crazy hours I would sometimes spend weekends with my grandparents in Cleveland Heights. It was always a blast. My greatest memories were cooking with my Pappy and Grandma. My Grandma worked in sales at Higbee's in the Terminal Tower. After we dropped her off at work, my Pappy and I would head over to the Market to gather food for dinner.

I can still remember the smells of the Market the first time I walked in. The aromas of pastries and breads filling the air, and of course, the enticing scent of smoked bacon and kielbasa everywhere. We would buy some jerky from J & J to enjoy during our day of shopping. Pappy was a master of soups and stews, so we would go from counter to counter searching for the perfect soup bones, then head over to Dohar's for his amazing smoked pork. I would gaze into the glass looking at all the ribs, loins, and sausages smoked to meaty perfection. After we gathered our meats we would head outside to rustle up some produce from Nate Anselmo. We would load up on carrots, celery, and parsnips. All of this would soon be on the stove and simmering for my Pap's amazing split pea soup. I would always get a big slice of juicy pineapple from Nate and our day would always end with a stop at Johnny Hot Dog. It is amazing I ever had room left for dinner!!!

I took the Market for granted as a teenager. I just assumed that most cities had an amazing market like ours. As I got older and began to travel, I realized how truly special and unique it was. The West Side Market is among the last of its kind in the US and one of Cleveland's greatest gems. When I bring famous chefs from around the country there I can literally hear them gasp in amazement as we walk through the front door. The architecture and magical smells just take them to another place. I can't tell you how many times they say "I wish we had this in my city" or "I haven't seen anything like this since last time I was in Europe." My response is always "Welcome to Cleveland, baby...the best location in the nation!"

Like so many Clevelanders it is my childhood memories that will always make the Market so special to me. But it is the travel and experiences I have had as an adult that makes me understand that the Market is not only a local but a national treasure. Here's to another hundred years of memories.

Introduction
The Opening

OVER THE PAST HUNDRED YEARS, millions have shopped the West Side Market. They arrive in the thick of it, when everyone is already in place and things are working smoothly, just as they should. Customers crowd the aisles, merchants bag or wrap their orders while making small talk or telling a joke, and food, wonderful food, catches the eye no matter where one stands. It all blends together for a truly memorable experience, much different than simply shopping for groceries.

Few witness the ritual awakening of this century-old market in the hours before the doors open to the public. The West Side Market is not just one of the most famous and beloved landmarks in Cleveland, it's the keeper of tradition, holding tightly to some of the ways people have done business, shopped, and eaten for a century, even as the world and neighborhood surrounding it changes. It still takes a strong back, hard work, and a special passion to make the Market come alive in this Ohio City neighborhood—long before the sun comes up.

It's 4 AM, the middle of the night for most of Cleveland. For the butchers, bakers, and produce peddlers—anyone who makes a living at the city's West Side Market—it's the start of another day. The movement around the neighborhood is thin but steady on this seasonally warm mid-summer morning. A few pedestrians move along the sidewalks and cars proceed in all directions on W. 25th and Lorain. RTA's No. 20 bus travels north on W. 25th, crossing paths with the No. 22 heading south on Lorain, tracing the same routes street cars and horse-drawn wagons followed to get here long ago. Each bus carries a few passengers, taking them to or from their shifts at the city's hospitals or factories. More than one rider glances up at the Market's lighted clock tower, which pierces the dark sky. The hands of the clock have not always served as the most reliable indicator of time over the century, yet the tower itself has always confidently announced the presence of the West Side Market on this corner. A familiar and welcoming sight, it says this is a place of importance that deserves special attention.

Memories

"I can remember when I was a little guy in the 1940s, my mother would take me at 5 AM to go to the Market on the streetcar. She left me with my father who had a produce stand outside the Market. I would stay all day with him. He would put me in a banana box to go to sleep. I remember once when he woke me, I was looking up at the big clock that was all lit up. It was midnight. "Come on, honey boy," he said. "It's time to go home."

—**Mario Rini, former vendor**

The lots behind the Market host a few cars parked in the spaces furthest from the doors. The workers know to save those closest to the Market for paying customers. Snagging one later in the day will be a constant source of competition among patrons and during the busiest times finding any parking space, let alone a prime one, is considered a small victory.

Light shines from inside the Market hall, but the brightest comes from the produce arcade that wraps around the north and east side of the exterior. It hints that this is where the Market begins to wake up. The overhead lights cast a harsh glow on the empty aisles and whitewashed wooden stands, painting a scene void of color. The hanging scales, some that have weighed produce for generations of vendor families, hang motionless from the rafters, all arrows pointing straight up. They suggest that in this place, it's okay to hold onto some of the old ways of doing business, including adding up orders in their head or on scraps of paper.

Standing where the two corridors meet, it's easy to see the Lorain Road and W. 25th Street entrances in the distance. Nothing blocks the view now, yet in a few hours it will be impossible to walk even a few feet without bumping into someone with a folding shopping cart or tote bags filled with food.

A few colorful tarps and tablecloths help break up the stark look of the aisles. They protect potatoes, onions, and garlic, produce that prefers the warm night air to the refrigerated coolers beneath the Market where tender lettuces and delicate fruits stay cool and crisp overnight. Emery Bacha is already adding color to his stand, creating orderly stacks of green, red, and yellow peppers and arranging bright orange carrots still sporting their frilly fronds. A few stands over, George and Samia Harb work quietly unpacking figs and mangos and standing pineapples upright so their firm, spiky crowns get noticed. In the hours leading up to opening of the Market, more merchants arrive. Tom and Anita at the Basketeria add a few more hand-printed signs above their bins, calling attention to what's good, special, or a bargain—Russian Fingerlings, $1.50 a pound; Lacinato Kale, $2 a bunch; local tomatoes, the first of the season, are $2.50 a pound, priced to sell fast today. Another

 emories

"I get here at 4 AM, I put in fourteen hours and go to bed early. One thing about a job like this—I never have trouble falling asleep."

—**Steve Rose, employee**

"It's been said on a good day, you can hear, 'How much?' spoken in twenty different languages."

—**Plain Dealer**, *July 4, 1979*

Above, from top: Joe Tieri of Nonno Joe's;
Joe DeCaro at the scale

vendor leans tall stalks of sugar cane against a pillar, a curiosity for a tourist and a statement that this Market caters to the tastes of ethnic customers.

This morning two vendors, friends now, competitors when the shoppers arrive, talk across the aisle as they ready their stands. It's a lively conversation in Arabic that would have been in Italian eighty years ago. Their animated chat suggests something important has happened. It's hard to say what it's about until one blurts the name of a local sports figure who announced his plan to leave the team just hours ago. This will certainly dominate the conversations throughout the Market today—in more than one language.

The alley that separates the arcade from multiple entrances to the Market building has always served as a walkway for shoppers and a staging area for produce vendors. Later in the day, customers will sit on benches and overturned buckets eating bratwurst, falafel, or pastry while getting a behind-the-scenes look.

Empty boxes and wooden crates are stacked behind the vendors' stands, waiting to pack large orders or hold vegetable trimmings. A forklift sits idle next to a bin that held melons the previous market day. Workers who pedaled to the Market in the dark prop their bicycles against the sides of the building, knowing that they might find themselves pedaling home in the dark as well—working at the Market has never been a nine to five existence.

A truck is backed up to the loading dock with the earliest delivery of the day. It won't be long before the platform will rumble with the comings and goings of vehicles and vans. For now, big men with muscle and small, wiry guys work side-by-side, quickly unloading one truck to make room for another. Flats of tomatoes, mushrooms, and avocados; trays of cakes and pastry; bricks and wheels of cheese and cases of sausage disappear through the doors of the Market or are whisked into the arcade.

Inside the Market hall the lights are low and it feels peaceful and calm, even though there is plenty of movement and energy on the floor. Only one stand is brightly lit, as if ready to take customers' orders. "You're late!" says Diane Dever to a fellow vendor just arriving. It's 5 AM, but she means it. It says a lot about this lifestyle.

The quiet in this great hall echoes off the walls and arched ceiling, feeling like the near silence of swimming under water. With the arrival of every worker, every "hello," each "morning" the noise will build, but it will still be a few hours before conversations between merchants and customers and among shoppers blend into one gloriously busy sound as the clatter and bang of doing business commences.

At the back of Market, below the clock, is a large Toledo platform scale. In its time, it has weighed countless bushels and boxes of produce, meats, dairy, and poultry. It has also weighed generations of visitors, entire families and children who can't resist stepping on and marveling at the results.

Near the scale, the freight elevator arrives from the basement and the doors part, like a giant yawn. Brian Foster emerges wearing a butcher's coat over a bulky sweatshirt. He wheels out two whole lamb carcasses. Butchers like Gordon Fernengel, Bruce Tayse, and Grant Lance are glad to start their day in the chilly cooler, a respite from the heat that is already present on this particular morning.

As Foster pushes his load to his stand, the clacking of the wheels over the tiled floor keeps a steady rhythm. It's the music of the Market. Those who have worked here for a lifetime know the personality of this floor, the dips and bumps that rattle and shake the carts. It's impossible to guess how many pork chops, rib roasts, bricks of cheese, and slabs of butter have traveled these aisles over a century.

He could have broken down the lamb into choice cuts in the cooler but doing his work in plain sight of customers is part entertainment and part marketing plan. Foster will draw a small crowd that lingers to watch as he cuts chops, shoulder steaks, and whole legs, and frenching a rack of lamb for a regular customer who doesn't want them any other way.

Workers make their way up and down the aisles; some heft trays on their shoulders that are stacked with stew meat or layers of steaks. Larry Schade, a longtime poultry vendor, wheels a cart of fresh, whole fryers to his stand at the opposite end of the Market. He nods to Tom McIntyre, the "kid" who works at his mother's fish stand. Bent far into the case laying a glistening bed of crushed ice for the incoming snapper, mackerel, and trout, Tom returns the nod.

Ⓜ emories

"I remember when people used to line up early in the morning waiting for the doors of the Market to be unlocked. We'd get a lot of cops and hookers at that time. The first group was starting their shift and they'd stop here for breakfast. The ladies were just getting off work, if you know what I mean, and came to pick up some groceries before heading home. But it's not like that anymore."

—Don Whitaker, vendor, D. W. Whitaker Meats

"There are times I don't get out of here until 1:30 AM. Then I have to be in at 5:30 AM. But we do it for our customers. We don't tell them we do this. We just do it!"

—Vince Bertonaschi, vendor, Vince's Meats

Outside more trucks and vans back into the loading docks, generating a constant parade of dollies and carts into the Market. Breads just out of the ovens a few blocks away, cases of eggs, tubs of pickles and olives, and more come down the ramp.

The aroma of freshly brewed coffee drifts through the air from the opposite end of the building, the signal for vendors to come and get their first fix of the day. Carafes, not cups, are filled to carry back to the stands. Hot dogs are already spinning on the roller grill in a corner of the Market. The smell may seem out of place at this time of the morning, but for some it announces breakfast.

This great hall begins to light up one stand at a time, like a theatre production revealing different scenes. Daylight creeps through the large palladium windows that face one another from opposite ends of the building and the sounds of the Market begin to change. Conversations are now loud, lively, and animated, peppered with laughter and excitement. Some of the butchers run their knives across sharpening steels or chop at the beds of ice where freshly dressed chicken, ducks, geese, and rabbit will lay. More aromas fill the air—smoked sausage, vanilla-scented cakes and cupcakes, pizza bagels, roasted meats for gyros, and warmed cashews and peanuts.

Ⓜ emories

"When you stand behind the counter, you are like a bartender. We hear stories about people's lives. You learn a lot about your customers here."

—Karen Curiale Torreiter, employee

"When I opened my stand at the West Side Market, Larry Schade took me under his wing. We would walk around the Market at 7 AM eating chunks of goose liver from Czuchraj's and fresh bread with butter. He's trying to show me the ropes and give me advice on how to survive the lean months but the whole time, I'm thinking, 'This is the best breakfast I've ever had!'"

—Patrick Delaney, former vendor

Tim Jeziorski is at a meat slicer, turning a large salami into thin slices. He's done this countless times and knows the feel of a pound before it hits the scale. He builds stacks of lunch meat, all teetering on parchment paper—bologna, roast beef, turkey, and ham—which will eventually make it into someone's sandwich next week. Two aisles over, Ed Meister, a cheesemonger, artfully displays countless varieties and shapes, while one of his workers squeegees the glass front of the case, erasing smudges, fingerprints, and children's nose prints from the previous market day.

The tops of the cases begin to fill with stacks of cookies, crocks of pickles, jars of salt and spices, and more, all at eye level. One of the last stands to light up before shoppers arrive is the popcorn and candy counter in the corner. Jeff Campbell knows he has something to tempt everyone or stir a childhood memory—fat candied apples; chocolate-covered pretzels and marshmallows; popcorn dusted with sweet and savory flavors. For parents shopping with children in tow, this might be their last stop—as part of a bribe or a reward for good behavior.

Outside, the produce arcade has transformed from a drab scene to a panorama of amazing color. The cloths and tarps are gone, replaced by brilliant displays of produce—red raspberries, mounds of yellow lemons and orange oranges, deep crimson beets with the leafy greens still attached, rippled bunches of sturdy spinach, and tall fresh stalks of aromatic dill, fennel, and basil. Merchants greet early-arriving customers, calling attention to their products. "Grapefruits, six for two bucks," or "Sweet melons, try some," offering a taste off the tip of a knife.

The energy of the Market builds as if everyone is waiting for the starter's gun. Merchants ready their ears, too. Customers have stories to share—about cooking, a recipe, their family, or their health. There's not only a lot of talking at the Market, there's a lot of listening, too.

At 7 AM the Market is officially opened. That's what the lettering on the entrances says, but some vendors have already taken care of customers who routinely arrive and leave before the crowds—because that's the way it's always been done.

Tony, the night security guard walks down the aisles one last time as his shift ends. He makes small talk as he goes, saying "good morning" to a scattering of shoppers and "goodbye" to vendors, stopping to share a handshake and a word with Jimmy Traynor, the patrolman arriving for duty. Before he walks out of the arcade to his car, Tony greets an arriving customer with, "Welcome to another day in paradise."

With that, another day in the history of Cleveland's West Side Market begins.

CHAPTER ONE

THE BUILDING
of the Market

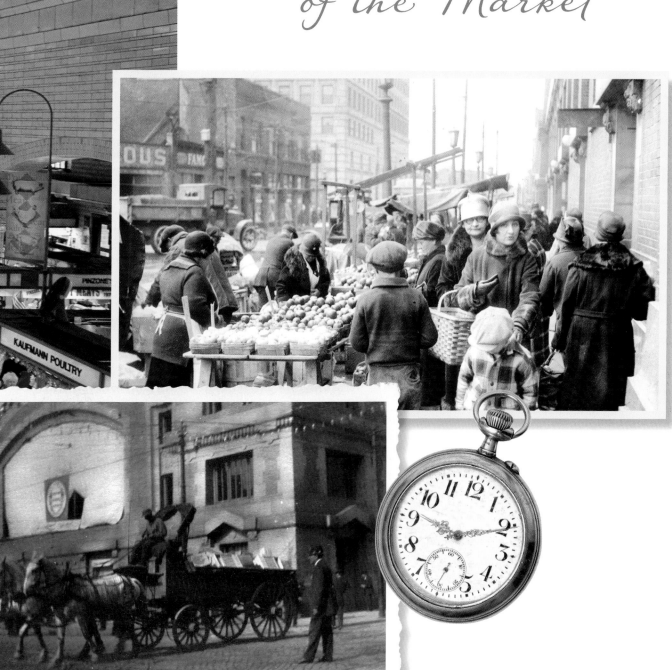

THE SIXTH CITY

Cleveland became an industrial powerhouse in the nineteenth century. Immigrants were coming in large numbers, attracted by jobs in the factories, steel mills, and foundries. A boomtown requires infrastructure—there were bridges, roads, sewers, and schools to build, which meant work for anyone willing and able to wield a shovel. The Germans, Irish, and Hungarians arrived first, followed by Italians, Jews, Poles, Russians, Ukrainians, Slovaks, Slovenians, and people from many other Eastern European ethnic groups. By 1901, Cleveland was the country's seventh most populous city, with approximately 380,000 residents. The census of 1910 pushed Cleveland to sixth place, with a population of 560,663.

Previous pages, clockwise from top: The main hall of the West Side Market, present day; Produce hucksters on the sidewalk, 1927; the nearly-completed Market, 1911

A PUBLIC BOON
A Market for the West Side

MARKET SQUARE WAS a gathering spot for farmers and shoppers even before 1840, the year two of the community's founding citizens, Josiah Barber and Richard Lord, gave the parcel of land at what is now W. 25th Street and Lorain Avenue to the City of Ohio. More gifts of property followed and in 1868 a one-story shed was built to provide shelter for goods and the people who brought them there to sell. This was the Pearl Street Market, also referred to as the West Side Market, and many of the first vendors who rented space at the grand new building when it opened in 1912 started doing business here. Among them was H. P. Schenk, who sold freshly ground horseradish.

> "My father's first stand was across the street when the old market was on the northwest corner of Lorain and W. 25th (then Pearl St.). It was on the curb, as we are now.... The old pole on which my dad hung his kerosene lamp Saturday nights is still there. The old market house was a square wooden building painted a brownish red, with a sloping roof.... I remember the double door and the sawdust on the floor.
>
> In those days families walked to the market with a basket on their arm or pulled a little express wagon behind them on which they put their purchases.... it was the custom of a lot of families to go to market on Saturday night.... They chatted with everybody, met their friends down there and did their weekly shopping. My dad said that was the big event of the week..."
> —Myrtle Chappell, The Horseradish Lady[1]

A newspaper reporter touring the city's markets in 1880 described them as "a public boon in many senses." He noted that they made food from the

farm available to urban residents at the lowest possible cost, and so had a modifying effect on prices for similar provisions at other shops in the surrounding neighborhoods.

> **Added to all this—the nearness of producer and consumer and the general lowering of the cost of all necessaries of life—the markets are a source of large revenue to the city…the West Side Market [*i.e.* the Pearl Street Market] brings in $9,500 in round numbers.**
>
> **In point of construction the West Side Market is nearer what a market should be than many of the others, which are too low for thorough ventilation or to give them an air of coolness and freshness.**
> —*Plain Dealer*, January 2, 1880

Looking back on the neighborhood's early years, *Cleveland Press* writer George Davis described a pharmacy and soda fountain next to the original market house. "In a rear room was a potbellied stove where farmers dried their red woolen mittens when they drove in to the West Side Market." He mentions hotels where they could spend the night, a bar and vaudeville theater, blacksmith shops, and a feed store. The Market House Tavern, built in 1862, must surely have been a popular watering hole for Pearl Street vendors.[2]

Cleveland's population grew rapidly and in the final years of the nineteenth century, the Pearl Street Market was deemed inadequate for the community's needs and too small and primitive for a modern city on the move. A committee formed under the auspices of the Western Improvement Association, a sort of area chamber of commerce, considered plans and sites for a new public market. In 1898, they reported to city officials that they'd secured options on several potential parcels, prepared drawings of what they dubbed the Cuyahoga Market, and urged them to pass the necessary legislation and issue bonds to fund the project.

In response, an official City of Cleveland commission was appointed and empowered to acquire land and go forward with erecting the building, but Mayor Tom Johnson didn't actually name members of the commission until August 1901. And thus began what was to be a pattern of decision followed by delay, which would plague the venture for the next decade.

The first bonds were authorized in November 1901 and the site was chosen in 1902. All the necessary land was purchased or legally appropriated, and

WHAT HAPPENED TO THE PEARL STREET MARKET?

In 1902, when land had been purchased and it seemed certain there'd be a new market, there was talk of putting a greenhouse or a playground on the Pearl Street Market site. In 1905, there was a proposal to link the old and new markets with an underground tunnel. After the completion of the building across the street, the old structure was briefly occupied by seasonal flower vendors and the basement was used to store plants and bulbs from city parks during the winter. In the spring of 1915, the city was ordered to tear it down by the state fire marshal, who proclaimed it a menace.[3] Happy to see the aging edifice removed and replaced by the modern new mart, the community celebrated the demolition with a carnival, concerts, and parades.

Opposite: The completed West Side Market
Above: The Pearl Street Market

Memories

Mother and I walked to the [Pearl Street, circa 1900] market at least once a week.…On the left as one entered the market's broad diagonal corner entrance, was the dried fruit stand with its huge cubes of dates, figs, raisins, and prunes, all generously exposed to the public gaze and the elements. On the right hand was the stall of the butter and egg man. Great tubs of butter, dairy, creamery, and unsalted, cheeses of various shapes, colors, and smells, and eggs, white or brown.…It wasn't the still life of the market that enthralled me nearly so much as the real life: the pleasant rosy German faces, the strange headgear, and the puzzling, fascinating broken English on all sides.

—Plain Dealer, March 5, 1967

THINK BIG

Tom Johnson, a Democrat, was
elected Mayor of Cleveland in 1901
and held the office for three terms.
A businessman and self-made mil-
lionaire, he was a civic reformer and
a proponent of social justice. Johnson
aimed to make Cleveland a more
beautiful and humanized place to live
and was especially concerned with
the plight of the poorest residents,
which made him a populist hero.
Describing Johnson's way of thinking, author and newspaper columnist
George Condon wrote, "…Cleve-
land's idealistic chief executive
refused to 'make little plans' because
he knew instinctively that such low
level concepts 'have no magic to stir
men's blood.'"[6] Johnson's support for
building a magnificent new market
house on the west side grew out of
his belief, shared by other adherents
of the Municipal Reform Movement,
that city governments had an obligation to provide people with public
amenities that improved the quality
of their lives. The idea was that this
would lead to a productive citizenry,
civic pride, and a cohesive society.
Johnson lost the 1909 election and
died on April 10, 1911, never seeing
the project brought to completion.

Above: Early drawing of proposed market
house, from *Cleveland Leader,* March 2, 1898
Opposite: F. E. Cudell, from *Cleveland Press,*
November 17, 1906

existent structures removed or razed by March 1903. From the start, the vision
was for a magnificent structure, something both functional and beautiful.
There was to be an upper level promenade and an auditorium for concerts,
meetings, and conventions. Newspaper headlines announced that construction would begin soon.

But in June 1903, Mayor Tom Johnson disbanded the commission over a
dispute about how funds were to be handled, transferring control of Market
planning to the Board of Public Service. Commission members, led by Albert
Daykin, protested, arguing that the mayor had exceeded his authority. Daykin
called the reasons "purely political" and was quoted in the *Cleveland Leader*
on October 25, 1903, "Without any authority of law we were displaced and
had the expense of a suit in court to be reinstated." A Cleveland judge agreed.

Although the idea of building a new market house on the west side was
proposed before he took office, Mayor Johnson is remembered as a strong
advocate for the project. Yet, at the time, Daykin blamed him and his Democratic administration for undermining the project. Partisanship may have
motivated the accusations, since Daykin went on to urge citizens to vote
Republican in the upcoming elections. They did not heed his advice. Johnson
won and in December, the ruling in favor of the Commission was overturned
on appeal, the judge affirming that the city's action was legal.[4]

Opposition, real and imagined, was eventually overcome. In 1905 the Board
of Public Service appointed the prominent architectural firm of Hubbell and
Benes to submit sketches. It was expected that a design would be chosen
quickly and the foundation laid that year—but that's not what happened.

In September 1905, Frank E. Cudell (spelled Cuddell in some accounts)
initiated legal action to prevent the project from going forward. His primary
complaint was that the design contract had not been competitively bid. He
couched his argument in economic terms, insisting that Hubbell and Benes'
fee, five percent of the total estimated cost of $750,000, or approximately
$37,500, was excessive and that the city could get the work done much cheaper.
He further contended that the city did not have the authority to spend money
on the auditorium, bathhouse, and other extra facilities in the plan and even
questioned the city's right to build the market house itself.

Cudell was not merely a concerned citizen or a wholly disinterested party—
he was an architect. He'd retired but was nonetheless incensed that the Board
of Public Service had simply handed the job to one firm without allowing
others to submit proposals. Moreover, this wasn't his only dispute with government officials. He was the plaintiff in a similar case pending before the
state Supreme Court in December 1905. That case stemmed from his criticism
of the Group Plan, a vision for a civic hub in downtown Cleveland between
Superior Avenue and Lake Erie, now known as the Mall, featuring a central
open space surrounded by monumental public buildings, including a new city
hall. Unhappy with the selection of the architect for that building, Cudell sued.

Over the next two years, Cudell held the market project hostage. There
were motions filed, hearings held, rulings made and appealed, injunctions
and restraining orders issued, lifted, and issued again. He was censured by
west side businessmen and residents for his obstructionist stance and they

pressured City Council to refuse a piece of land Cudell wanted to donate for a park with his name on it. He ultimately agreed to a compromise, motivated perhaps by a desire to insure his legacy. Though he did not succeed in blocking the contract awarded to Hubbell and Benes, he did get planners to abandon the idea of an on-site auditorium in favor of building it elsewhere and at a later date.

In an interview with Cudell after the agreement was reached a reporter inquired,

> "What if they don't ask for bids? Will you enjoin them?"
> "You just wait and see," and the twinkle in the brown eyes that looked out over his glasses showed that there's fun in a fight for this enjoiner. "I do like to fight," he admitted, "but I'm always willing to meet people halfway."[5]

The need to replace the Pearl Street Market had only increased with the years, and the busy, crowded Ohio City neighborhood, along with farmers who sold goods there bore the brunt of Cudell's crusade.

> The West Side merchants have labored long and faithfully to improve market conditions in their territory. To meet the demand of that section of the city in the way of table necessities vendors have for months been compelled to erect their stands along practically the length of W. 25th-st., from Lorain-av. to Detroit-av., N.W. Not only has this delayed established business on that street, but it has been a source of great inconvenience to the marketers [shoppers], who are compelled when making selections to travel long distances.... Had it not been for legal barriers it is probable that the actual work of bettering conditions would have commenced.
> —*Plain Dealer*, October 7, 1906

The conflict came to a close at the end of November 1906. Money was in hand, ground was to be broken when the spring thaw arrived, and the expectation was that the community would have their new market soon after. No one imagined it would take another six years before the building was ready for shoppers, and two more after that to complete the entire project.

"I AM FIGHTING FOR A PRINCIPAL."

"JUST WAIT and SEE."

CITY ENJOINED FROM MAKING CONTRACT FOR WEST SIDE MARKET

Cleveland Press, September 22, 1905

MARKET HOUSE CAN NOW BE BUILT

Injunction Got By Cudell is Dissolved By Judge Lawrence

Cleveland Press, May 2, 1906

CUDELL BITTER: WON'T STOP SUIT

Plain Dealer, August 31, 1906

TO WAR NO MORE ON MARKET HOUSE

Architect Cudell and West Side Residents Sign a Treaty of Peace Injunction Dropped and Auditorium To Be Built Elsewhere

Plain Dealer, October 6, 1906

MARKET HOUSE PEACE IN PERIL

Negotiations Between City and F. E. Cudell Liable to Be Broken Today

Plain Dealer, November 15, 1906

CUDELL SUIT IS WITHDRAWN

Cleveland Press, November 21, 1906

Benjamin S. Hubbell and W. Dominick Benes

Business partners Benjamin S. Hubbell and W. Dominick Benes were highly regarded local architects. After working together at Coburn and Barnum, they set up their own studio in 1897. They made a name for themselves as masters of the Classic Revival and Beaux Arts styles, popular in America for important public buildings from the late 1800s to the early 1900s. The designs integrated Greek and Roman elements such as columns, rounded arches, massive scale, and open spaces with decorative and sometimes elaborate ornamentation. Before their selection for the West Side Market project, they designed Wade Memorial Chapel at Lakeview Cemetery. Other, later commissions included the Cleveland Museum of Art, along with plans for Wade Park, the central YMCA on Prospect Avenue, and the Illuminating Building on Public Square. Benes died in 1935, but the firm continued to operate as Hubbell and Benes until 1939. Hubbell was eventually joined by his son Benjamin Jr., who maintained an office under the family name until 1953.

WELL PLEASED WITH THE PLANS
From Ideas to Blueprints

THE LOOK AND LAYOUT of the building went through numerous changes. Hubbell and Benes, along with the committee that was spearheading the project, made a study of other municipal markets around the country, investigating both their appearance and method of operation.[7]

> Hubbell and Benes, architects for the new West Side market house, upon request of the board of public service, yesterday exhibited to half a hundred West Side citizens tentative sketches showing different possibilities for a market house. Four plans were shown. These were discussed for nearly three hours.
>
> Upon conclusion of the discussion an expression of sentiment by vote was called for, and the West Siders went on record for an auditorium within the market of 5,000 seating capacity; that there should be a public comfort station, bath, laundry, waiting room and cold storage plant sufficient to provide the rental of space.
>
> —*Plain Dealer*, August 4, 1905

Very popular with the public and the planners at first, that auditorium became a source of much debate. There were concerns about the auditorium—the additional cost, overcrowding and obstruction of traffic, noise, unpleasant odors, and unsanitary conditions. The preliminary concepts continued to be refined, even as the legal imbroglio with Cudell kept actual construction work from getting started. The January 26, 1906 edition of the *Cleveland Leader* reported on a City Hall meeting with west side residents during which the architects presented renderings of the proposed market house and public assembly hall, now a separate structure, as well as an impressive new edifice to replace the Pearl Street Market. "The plan decided on was one of several designs submitted by the architects. Views were shown on a screen by stereopticon. The choice was a set of buildings of classical design."

The plan was further revised over the following year. A brick and granite exterior, rather than the more expensive all granite façade originally envisioned, was approved by Mayor Johnson and the Board of Public Service in January 1907. The new design included another significant alteration from

Memories

"I worked for one of the designers of the West Side Market, Benjamin Hubbell, as a secretary and receptionist. It was 1942 and I just graduated from high school. He was an elderly man [seventy-five years old]. I still remember how much he hated it when people mispronounced his name. He wanted it said Hub-BELL [emphasis on second syllable]. He was very strict about it. His family was originally from France and he was very proud of that and I guess that's the French way. He'd be so pleased if you got it right in your book."

—***Ruth Sitko***

previous proposals—the orientation of the Market had been turned around and would now face W. 25th. This would provide more space for wagons at the north end of the building and entrances on three sides. There were also requests for additional, but minor, modifications, plus an amended estimate of costs, and some very specific language about what was—and was not—acceptable. "…[A] building that is substantial and neat is wanted; that gingerbread [lavish and superfluous embellishment] is not desired and that great care must be exercised to prevent waste of space inside…so arranged that every nook and corner could be reached by hose and water and cleaned at any time…."[8]

In March, council authorized the expenditure of $165,000 for laying the foundation and erecting the shell. Hubbell and Benes submitted completed drawings and it was reported that the Director of Public Service, W. J. Springborn, "is well pleased with the plans."[9] Bids were sought and contracts let. Excavation was to begin that spring. Excited west side residents and business leaders announced "a jollification" with fireworks to celebrate "…the day the first shovel of earth is dug."[10] The architects believed the market house could be "under roof" by late fall and ready for occupancy in the spring of 1908.

A detailed description of the master plan was released to the public. Some of the features listed below are part of the finished structure we know today, but others were altered or totally discarded.

> On the north and east will be a large covered shed under which hucksters [the common term for street vendors] will back their wagons to the curb, thus relieving the congestion in the neighboring streets.
>
> The market house is to be one-story high except at the front and back where there will be offices for the superintendent and his staff and apartments for one family. A 150-foot clock tower will be part of the building at W. 25th-st. and Lorain-av.
>
> Brick with granite and terra cotta will be used for the walls. The foundation will be of concrete. In the basement will be the heating apparatus and a complete cold storage plant.
>
> The interior of the market house is planned to be completely sanitary. It is proposed to use white glazed brick for the interior walls. The floors of the market on the street level will be of concrete and asphalt. The sheds for outside will be fireproof.
>
> The sum of $350,000 was voted for the new market house but it is likely that it will cost nearly $500,000…
> —*Plain Dealer*, May 19, 1907

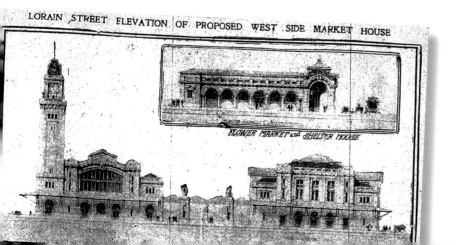

LORAIN STREET ELEVATION OF PROPOSED WEST SIDE MARKET HOUSE

FLOWER MARKET and SHELTER HOUSE

Clockwise from top: Market clock tower, 1912; Drawing of proposed Market design, from *Cleveland Leader*, January 26, 1906

Concerned with controlling costs, the Board of Public Service ordered the architects to shorten the building by twenty-nine feet on the Lorain Avenue side. It was also hoped that it would create more space at the rear for unloading goods and alleviate the possibility of early morning congestion. With this modification made, work finally began in earnest and real signs of progress were soon visible. A fence went up around the site and by early October C. H. Fath & Son had almost completed digging the massive hole. The dirt that they removed was carted a few blocks away and dumped in a ravine known as Wadsworth Run. Five thousand barrels of cement and two thousand tons of crushed stone were delivered for the foundation.

On November 5, 1907, the day before citizens re-elected Tom Johnson as their mayor, a newspaper article announced that the steel and concrete foundation work for the clock tower, "as tall as the ordinary thirteen story building" and "the heavy supports to that are to be beneath the columns…of the great central market room" were both in place. Readers were informed that the architects had integrated many of the most desirable features from other markets into their plans, along with some innovations of their own for lighting and ventilation. There was to be, for example, a separate room for the sale of fish to ensure that the smell would not permeate the entire hall.

"From an architectural as well as a practical standpoint no other public market building in the country will equal the new West Side structure."[11] Stories—and promises—like this continued to keep people excited and raise their expectations. And progress was clearly visible; by the summer of 1908, portions of the steel frame could be seen extending above the fence that enclosed the dig.

In February 1898, the Western Improvement Association, the organization that had originally pushed for a new market house, had hoped to have the official cornerstone laying ceremony on July 4. Ten years later, in 1908, the ceremony was scheduled for the city's birthday, Cleveland Day, July 22. But that event, too, was canceled, because the granite shipped from Vermont would not arrive in time. While citizens voiced impatience with the slow rate of progress, Hubbell made a trip to the quarry. Director Springborn issued a statement soon after, explaining that further delays had been caused by the inferior stone provided and the need to find another supplier. The first shipment of granite arrived in Cleveland on September 10, 1908. The cornerstone was finally put in place on October 27, at a ceremony attended by the Mayor and other city officials.

Above: Market house under construction
Right: The cornerstone is laid, October 27, 1908

THE MOST MAGNIFICENT BUILDING OF ITS KIND

THE YEAR 1909 was a definitive one. Construction was finally moving along at a steady rate; Hubbell inspected the site in April and was happy with both the pace and quality of the work. By June the walls were higher than the temporary wooden barrier surrounding the site. Council approved the expenditure of funds for the roof in July and Director Springborn urged the contractors, John Grant & Sons, to put more men on the job to ensure that there would be no further delay. The Cleveland Architectural Club, whose members included Hubbell, Benes, and other leading local architects, held an exhibition in October. The frontpiece for the catalog was a lovely color rendering of what the Market would like when it was complete, surrounded by throngs of people, horses, and carriages. It seemed the Market would soon be ready for merchants and customers.

Later that month, a reporter spotted ironworkers erecting the steel structure for the roof. Bids were being accepted for installing the 15,000 square feet of red clay roofing tile. The first of five loads of granite needed to finish the exterior was finally on its way from Connecticut, with the rest to follow within three weeks. "Westsiders are taking a more hopeful view now that they can see the tower at the corner of Lorain Avenue and W25th looming up. It's going to be some tower, too—156 feet to the top of the flagpole, and illuminated clocks on all four sides."[12]

The public got some tantalizing details about the interior. "All stalls will be built of white enameled brick with Carrara glass countertops. The floor is to be 6 inch by 9 inch red quarry tile. Side walls are white enameled brick and terra cotta and the ceiling is of Guastavino tile with white raised

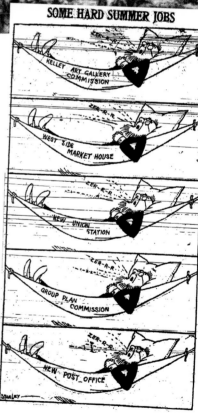

Clockwise from top: Artist's rendering of the new West Side Market, 1909; Political cartoon from *Cleveland Press,* August 18, 1908

joints. In the basement there will be a 5 ton ice making plant and sufficient additional space to triple that capacity. Inside the tower there is a 9 foot diameter steel water tank with a capacity of 16,000 gallons."[13]

The hope was that laborers could focus on the inside features by spring. But it was still just a shell in April when critics began voicing complaints and concerns. Dubbing it a "white elephant" and an "example of poor business judgment," detractors claimed it was unnecessarily extravagant, would be a continuing financial drain on the city's coffers, and could not help but fail to fulfill its intended purpose. Director of Public Service Lea was critical of an apartment on the second floor for the market master and the use of a corner spot on the ground floor for a waiting room instead of for stalls that could be rented. He also opposed esthetic details such as the tower and granite trim on the exterior that, in his view, unnecessarily increased the price tag.

W. J. Springborn, former director of public service under Mayor Johnson, came out in defense of the plans. "'An attractive sanitary structure in a busy locality will draw tradesmen willing to pay good rents,' declared Springborn. '…As to the market master's living suite, we decided that a building of that size needs a man's presence day and night. As to the waiting room, it is simply a question whether the people of Cleveland who get on and off the [trolley] cars at this corner should have that convenience or whether they should stand outside in bad weather and on the crowded curb and street.'" One of the Market's architects, Benjamin Hubbell, reminded the reporter covering the controversy "that the Johnson administration, he knew, had endeavored faithfully to fill the wants of the West Side with the market."[14]

Homer McDaniel, manager of the Sheriff Street Market, a privately owned and operated business, was also a critic, "No city in these days should build a palatial markethouse at public expense.…The project will not only not pay, but will result in annual loss." He argued that the benefit to taxpayers would not be commensurate with the cost because products were coming from middlemen. "In fact, the percentage of producers in all Cleveland market houses put together is very, very small. The overwhelming bulk of goods sold in the market is sold by dealers who have already bought from farmers or commission houses." The result, he predicted, would be increased prices for consumers, not the bargains Market advocates aimed to provide.[15]

Above and right: Market house under construction

IT'S A WASH

Today, few people know that the original designs for the building included public baths. The idea of putting such a facility in the same location as one where food is sold seems unthinkable now. But in 1898, when a new market was first proposed, it made sense.

Many homes did not have running water or tubs, especially the urban poor, a group that included the majority of immigrants. This was the reality not just in Cleveland, but around the country. At the turn of the century, motivated by Progressive era principles and the belief that cleanliness was both a moral and a social imperative, city leaders felt an obligation to provide public bathhouses for their citizens. So there was nothing unusual or unseemly about the 1902 announcement that the commission chaired by A. G. Daykin was "…much in favor of the plan to have a bath house and laundry in the market house."[20] A poll of concerned citizens and neighborhood property owners at a 1905 meeting reaffirmed the idea that both should be features of the new building. The idea was ultimately scrapped but the city put up bath houses elsewhere; there were four in 1918 and three years later Lincoln Park Baths, now converted to condos, opened in Tremont. All were closed by 1954 because there was no longer a need for this kind of municipal amenity.

Above: Market interior in 1912, before vendors move in

McDaniel may have been correct in his observation that public markets were attracting a large number of middlemen. It was inevitable, as rapid urbanization was changing how land was used and the way people earned their livings. However, local growers were still a significant part of the merchant mix. According to Market Master Charles Kamp, there were over 1,300 farmers selling 95 percent of their produce at Cleveland's three municipal markets in 1913. In an article he penned about reducing the cost of food distribution, Kamp noted that "about 150 growers dispose of their goods" at the West Side Market, "an exclusively retail market, and undoubtedly the finest municipal market building in the country." Moreover, rents for stall space were set very low, reducing overhead for merchants. "High rents" wrote Kamp, "destroy the purpose for which markets are intended…the saving of money to the public by minimizing all sources of expense.…"[16] And while the anxiety about the potential future costs were estimable, it's important to remember, as McDaniel and Director Lea apparently failed to do, that the primary function was not to generate profits. Building and operating the Market was viewed as a public service and a governmental responsibility. Moreover, its grandeur was intended as an expression of civic pride and a testament to Cleveland's prominence as the country's Sixth City.

Accusations and finger-pointing continued to make headlines. There was pressure in and out of government to save money. But the penny pinchers and bean counters did not triumph, and Cleveland got the splendid structure that we see today. When Council refused Mayor Baehr's request for an additional $148,000 to cover the cost of completing the building as planned, he announced that the necessary funds would nonetheless be found. He made good on that promise, raising the money by passing an ordinance for yet another bond issue in August 1910.

The building was formally dedicated, with a benediction, speeches, an appearance by the Mayor, and a band concert, and handed over to the citizens of the west side at 11 AM on July 22, 1911. The date was chosen to coincide with the 115th anniversary of the city's founding—there were events all over town highlighting Cleveland's accomplishments.

The Market was very close to completion, but finishing work was temporarily halted in August to prepare for an industrial expo to be held there the first week in September. Reporting on opening night, a writer for the *Cleveland Press* declared, "The market house is an exposition in itself. The most magnificent building of its kind in the world, those who visit the show will find it not the least of the attractions," and noted that those in attendance "were the first to see the market house in the full glory of its beauty."[17] The public was confident that they'd soon be wandering the aisles in search of the freshest meat and eggs. Once again, they had to wait much longer than expected. Summing up public sentiment, a newspaper headline read "Fixtures Nice But When Will Market Open."

> **Everything has been arranged for the housewife's convenience. But there's just one sad feature to the whole affair—no one knows just when the market house is going to be finished. Certainly it won't be completed this winter.**
>
> **"I don't know. Nobody can tell," says Lea [Andrew Lea, Director of Public Service].**
>
> **This dampened the rising spirits of West-siders who had been stimulated by the announcement that there would be a grand opening within two months. The recent exposition decorations had deceived them.**
>
> **"I can't say when it will be finished," declared B. S. Hubbell, architect. "It's been dragging along now for four years. It should have been built in half that time and would have been had the money been forthcoming."**
> **—*Cleveland Press*, September 17, 1911**

Before shoppers could view the interior concourse in all its splendor and take home their first purchases, almost fourteen more months passed, and Newton D. Baker had replaced Baehr as mayor. The Market was officially opened on Thursday, October 31, 1912, and the public welcomed inside on Saturday, November 2. Those who first proposed a new market house in 1898 had called for something that would "present a pretty appearance and make one of the handsomest buildings in the city."[18] And that, after long years of dispute and delay, was what they got.

Memories

"The Market hall was a gift to the community, an outgrowth of the spirit of Progressivism, and a reflection of Cleveland's desire to be modern city."

—*Ted Sande, architect and historic preservationist*

A June 1910 newspaper story, headlined "West Side Market Cost Has Doubled," reported that the slow pace of work, interest accumulating on bonds, and taxes lost had resulted in the structure costing hundreds of thousands more than the original $450,000 estimate. Commenting on the situation A. E. Hyer, secretary of the West Side Chamber of Industry, noted that, "One foolish thing was the tearing down of the old buildings by the market house commission before their place was ready for occupation.... [I]f the city had waited before tearing down the buildings upon the site after purchasing, the rent so gained for future use would have amounted to $30,000–$40,000 per year."[19]

POINT WITH PRIDE
A Detailed Look

Newton D. Baker

Newton D. Baker was a disciple of
former mayor Tom Johnson, serving
first under Johnson as City Solicitor
and Law Director. Elected mayor in
1911, Baker carried on Johnson's
beautification and social reform
efforts, coining the term "civitism,"
by which he meant city patrio-
tism, to express the spirit of civic
revival and public service the two
men championed. "...[T]he work
of humanizing Cleveland which
Johnson had begun reached its peak
during Baker's years as mayor of
the city (1911–1915)....Baker was
elected...by the largest plurality any
candidate for that office had ever
received....During his two terms...a
new market house, considered the
most elaborate structure of its kind
in the country and significantly
located in the heart of a large foreign district, was opened in 1912."[21]

WHAT SHOPPERS SAW that first day may have reminded many of a world they
left behind when they immigrated to America. The tradition of gathering
food vendors together in permanent enclosed markets like this was well
established in European cities. The building's layout resembled a medieval
church. Both were inspired by the Roman basilica—an ancient public gathering place. The model is defined by a rectangular shape, massive scale, and
a central hall—equivalent to the nave—flanked by aisles demarcated with
parallel lines of evenly spaced arches and columns. Strips of windows—called
a clerestory—run along the upper edge of the walls, just under the ceiling.
Because the main arcade is higher than the aisles, there are actually four rows
of these windows, two on each side. The tall clock tower outside, reminiscent
of a campanile, reinforced associations with religious architecture. It's an apt
connection, observes Cleveland architect Paul Volpe, who describes the West
Side Market as "a cathedral for food."

The building was constructed of buff-colored brick. Granite was used for
the base, trim, and bands of dentil molding (a pattern of square tooth-like
cuts). Ornamentation like this was typical of the Classic Revival and Beaux
Arts styles favored by the Market's architects. John Grant & Sons was chosen
to do the stonework. The company was held in high esteem; "It...became an
axiom in business circles here that when John Grant undertook a contract
for a building, the work would be completed punctually, efficiently, and hon-
estly. It has long been rated the leading firm in the city in its line...the list of
fine structures on which they have completed contracts include some of the
most stately and beautiful in Cleveland." In addition to the West Side Market
House, Grant's credits included the Young Men's Christian Association and
the gymnasium on the Western Reserve campus.[22]

The vast high-ceilinged interior space, flooded with natural light and fresh
air, was an impressive sight, a bricks and mortar symbol of progress and
prosperity. In 1912, the majority of stands were occupied by butchers. There
were nine grocers and merchants who sold butter, eggs, and dairy products;
fish; pickles; and baked goods. The roofed outdoor aisles had yet to be erected,
so 176 produce vendors set up temporary curb stands on market days.

Cities could be dirty, smelly, chaotic places. Inside the new market house everything was orderly, hygienic (according to the standards of the day), and organized for the convenience of patrons. The aisles were wide and vendor stands, uniform in size and appearance, were grouped in fours and laid out in a tight grid, each with its own sign and stand number. There were no glass cases then—strings of sausages, wheels of cheese, and loaves of bread were displayed on open counters or hung from overhead racks. Customers liked seeing—and sometimes touching—what they were buying. Glossy white-enameled brick wainscoting on the walls and at the base of every stall projected an image of cleanliness. The goal was to give shoppers a sense of confidence in the new city-run market house. An official year-end summary reported that a total of $734,890.72 had been spent to build the Market. Here's what the city got for the money:

> **Dear Sir**—The New West Side Market is the finest in this country and Cleveland people can point with pride to this beautiful structure opened October 31, 1912.
>
> Sanitary conditions are perfect in every detail, the stands are of glazed brick construction; the counters Carrara glass, and the upper construction is steel. Each section of stands has a separate gutter to drain off the water in the aisles, after tile floors have been flushed. Each stand has twenty feet of counter space.
>
> The lighting is also well arranged; lights being placed in the ceiling arches and over each of the stands.
>
> A receiving station at the rear of the building, and a modern refrigeration plant in the basement are additional features.
>
> Separate departments for fish and groceries are set aside, consisting of two large rooms in the east end of the market. Each one of these rooms has the most modern fixtures necessary for this class of business....
>
> A public comfort station and waiting room, in charge of competent attendants, and open from 6 AM to 11 PM, occupies the southwest corner of the building.[24]

Accounts of the Market's special features often mentioned that Carrara glass was used for stall counters. Not a misprint and or a reference to the costly

Clockwise from top: Stand decorated with plants during 1911 Expo; A woman buying cheese from a vendor, circa 1912
Opposite: Early Market interior, 1912

Memories

"*The building itself is architecturally important. The handsome Beaux Arts design, with its ideal proportions based upon the Golden Mean, draws on classical Greek and Roman precedents and the basilica form. But it is unique and does not replicate another structure.*"

—Ted Sande, architect and historic preservationist

In 1961, when he was seventy-two, Walter Simmelink told a reporter he'd been selling cheese, eggs, and milk his whole life. The family was one of the original tenants when the Market opened in 1912. Before that they had a dairy stand at the old Pearl Street Market, back when customers still came by wagon. According to Walter, the vendors there drew straws for locations in the new building.[23]

"*During World War II, while my mother was buying meat, my job was to check the gutters in front of the stands for precious rationing tokens that were dropped by other shoppers. My reward was broken cookies. Our trip always ended with a glass of cold buttermilk.*"

—Karen Stuart

Above: Sculptures by Matzen and Sinz
Opposite: Ceiling of the market house designed by Rafael Guastavino

marble quarried in Italy, Carrara glass was the trade name for a revolutionary new product from the Pittsburgh Plate Glass Company. Milky white with a smooth, durable marble-like finish, it provided a surface that was non-absorbent, non-staining, and easy to clean. A 1911 *Cleveland Press* article detailed its appealing qualities. "It won't be necessary for the West-side housewife to carry an assortment of germ killers with her when she purchases meat for Sunday dinner in the new West Side Market house. There will be no chance whatsoever for her to bring home meat contaminated by poisonous bacilli from wooden chopping blocks. Every meat stall in the new market house is to be equipped with germ proof Carrara glass tops…[that] will not take up blood as do wooden blocks. 'We're going to have about $15,000 worth of Carrara glass in the new market house,' said Server Lea Wednesday."[25]

The material, technically known as opaque or pigmented structural glass, was also made by other companies and marketed as Sani-Onyx and Vitrolite. Initially it was available only in black and white, but eventually there were other colors. It was especially popular for use in restaurants, kitchens, hospitals, and bathrooms, and became emblematic of the Art Deco and Moderne aesthetic. Carrara glass was also used for the stalls in the basement comfort stations, but these were replaced sometime after 1950.

The wonderful sculptures are still a part of the Market, but few notice them. These reliefs—pig heads, lobsters, rabbits, turtles, cabbages, corn, carrots, and many other plants and animals—are positioned on top of columns inside the Market and out in the produce arcades, as well as above each entrance and on either side of the doorway. Two much larger pieces are found above the big windows at either end on the building's exterior; the cartouche over the loading dock depicts an ox head and the other, facing W. 25th Street, is an American eagle surrounded by cornucopias brimming with fruit and vegetables, a visual reminder that this was known as the land of plenty.

In a 1924 lecture at the Cleveland Museum of Art, Henry Turner Bailey, director of the Cleveland School of Art, identified the ox as "a symbol of patient, devoted service to man," and the eagle as the national emblem of "power and production." Praising these and other aesthetic details he said, "The architects have helped to embody in permanent form, Emerson's philosophy of what art should do for us here in America: namely, to make the things we use every day beautiful and significant, that they may enrich life and thought and promote the higher joys and aspirations."[26]

All the Market castings and carvings were the work of two Cleveland sculptors, Herman Matzen and Walter Sinz. Matzen, born in Denmark, taught design and sculpture at the Cleveland School of Art (now the Cleveland Institute of Art) from 1885 to 1926. When hired to create pieces for the West Side Market, he was already a mature and well-respected artist. Sinz was his student, and became his assistant, as well as a member of the school's faculty after his graduation in 1911. Their designs for "realistic representations of fish, game, and produce ordinarily associated with city markets" were approved by the Director of the Board of Public Service in the summer of 1908.[27]

The public got a peak at them the following year, when several casts were included in an October show hosted by The Cleveland Architectural Club. Matzen and Sinz were both members, along with Market architect Dominick Benes, who helped organize the exhibition at the Rose Building.

The pieces were cast by Fisher and Jirouch Company, a nationally-renowned maker of architectural relief sculpture that also did work on the Palace Theater and Severance Hall. The Cleveland firm, founded in 1902, was still a leading manufacturer when the Market celebrated its centennial.

While built to address practical and pressing issues, the West Side Market house was an expression of something more. The expenditure on nonfunctional features reflected the aspirational vision of the men who had launched the project and shepherded it through years of turmoil to completion. It was meant to stand as a testament to the city's accomplishments and all it hoped to become, affirming the belief that beauty could elevate the human spirit and enrich public life.

Crowning the market house with a spectacular vaulted ceiling designed by the R. Guastavino Company also lent the project prestige and further dem-

HERMAN MATZEN AND WALTER SINZ

Herman Matzen, (1861–1938) had established his reputation as a sculptor with monuments at Lakeview Cemetery, most notably the bronze Collinwood School Fire Memorial, and the figures of Moses and Pope Gregory IX for the Cuyahoga County Courthouse. In an interesting coincidence, he is most famous for his sculpture of Progressive-era Mayor Tom Johnson, the politician responsible for driving the Market project forward. The seated figure on Cleveland's Public Square was unveiled in 1915, three years after the Market opened and four years after the reformist Democrat died. Walter Sinz (1881–1966) had an illustrious career of his own. He did a large piece for St. Lukes' Hospital, another Hubbell and Benes project, and created bas-reliefs for the City Club. His best-known work was the Thompson Trophy, a winged figure in bronze, which he designed for the National Air Races.

onstrated the city's commitment to erect something of aesthetic and lasting value. The patented masonry system, called cohesive construction, was used in a number of important and architecturally significant American buildings in the late nineteenth and early twentieth centuries.

These ceilings could bear heavy loads without the clutter of supporting columns, creating large open floor plans ideal for monumental public spaces such as churches and synagogues, libraries, courthouses, and government offices. The graceful curving structures were elegant and imposing, durable, and remarkably stable. They were also fireproof, a major concern at the time. All this was achieved by setting layers of thin glazed tiles in a special mortar made with fast drying Portland cement and staggering the joints. The technique eliminated the need for an underlying framework.

Like so much else about the Market, the ceiling that has become one of its most distinctive features almost wasn't built. In 1907, it was announced that the "great central market room" would be "surmounted by what is claimed to be the largest vaulted roof in the country" measuring "60x250 feet."[28] But three years later, the steadily rising price tag for the structure prompted Public Service Director Lea to consider a simpler metal ceiling.

But wiser heads prevailed and work went forward as planned. Typically, only trained Guastavino employees constructed the ceilings the company designed. But for the West Side Market, the firm, busy with many other buildings around the country, farmed out at least part of the job to W. B. McAllister, a local contractor. The agreement specified that McAllister would install the terra cotta rosettes and vent panels. Although there is no specific mention in the historical record, it's likely these pieces were the work of the same sculptors—Herman Matzen and Walter Sinz—who designed the other decorative elements for the interior. McAllister's fee was $27,000, but the contractor may have forfeited some of it. According to the terms of the contract, dated March 1, 1911, the arches over the side aisles were to be completed by April 15, 1911, and the entire job on or before July 1, with a $50 a day penalty for failure to meet the deadline. An August 4th letter from a representative of McAllister to the R. Guastavino Company about the purchase of a moving scaffold suggests that the work was not finished on time.

Above: Shoppers at the Market
Opposite: Ceiling of the market house designed by Rafael Guastavino

Memories

"There's no doubt in my mind that Cleveland's West Side Market is the most beautiful building of its kind in the United States. It was built during the early years of the public sanitation movement and is a wonderful example of those ideals. Moreover it has been well maintained and the integrity of the structure with all the original Beaux Arts features is intact. Cleveland is very lucky to have it."

—**John Turnbull, Director of Asset Management and Development for Pike Place Market, Seattle, WA**

"The vaulting on either side of the main hall is lowered to create the aisles and the support piers are very narrow relative to the job they do. Together these features contribute to an open, flowing sense of space, which at the same time is divided into three discrete sections so it doesn't feel cavernous."

—**Paul Volpe, architect**

The lofty vaulted ceiling with its five great arches and signature Guastavino basket weave pattern, like the building itself, was a good investment. It is one of the most memorable and distinguishing features of the Market. Inset lights glow like stars. The difficult task of changing the bulbs, accomplished via a six foot crawl space under the roof, which echoes the curve of the interior ceiling, is virtually the only maintenance required. It has held up well and is as beautiful—and as impressive—as it was the day the building opened, lending an air of majesty to the ordinary everyday activity of buying and selling food.

Rafael Guastavino II, a Spanish architect who came to the United States in 1881, brought this iconic style with him. Also known as tile, timbrel, or Catalan vaulting, the construction method was ancient in origin, used throughout the Mediterranean by medieval masons, and then "lost." The revival he launched and the improvements he pioneered using modern materials and processes would become the centerpiece of his career. He started the Guastavino Fireproof Construction Company in 1889 (later renamed the R. Guastavino Company), collaborating with some of the most renowned Beaux-Arts architects of his day, and opened a factory in Woburn, Massachusetts, in 1900 to produce the clay tiles essential to the system. His son, Rafael III, who was nine years old when they arrived in this country, took over the business when his father died in 1908, partnering with its chief financial officer Will Blodgett. These two would have overseen the West Side Market project and others that followed in the city, including the Cleveland Public Library, the Tifereth Israel Temple, and the Cuyahoga County Detention Home and Juvenile Court Building.

Kathleen Crowther, Executive Director of the Cleveland Restoration Society, thinks of the West Side Market as Cleveland's version of Ellis Island. "It has always been a kind of welcome center and first stop for generations of newcomers to the country and the city. In fact the two look somewhat alike architecturally, with large open gathering spaces under soaring vaulted ceilings where people from different countries came together and became part of America." The similarities are not just a coincidence and are more than symbolic. The R. Guastavino Company was hired to reconstruct the ceiling for the Registry Hall at Ellis Island in 1917, the room where immigrants started to become part of the great melting pot that was America. The Market, with its international foods and shoppers, is Cleveland's melting pot, where those

THE R. GUASTAVINO COMPANY

At its peak, the R. Guastavino Company, which continued to operate until 1962, had offices in New York, Boston, Providence, Milwaukee, and Chicago, and is credited with contributing to more than a thousand buildings. Among the noteworthy landmarks with Guastavino vaults and domes are Saint John the Divine Cathedral and Carnegie Hall in New York; the Lion House at the Lincoln Park Zoo in Chicago; the Peabody Museum of Natural History on the Yale University campus; the Nebraska State Capitol; the Memorial Amphitheater at Arlington National Cemetery; the U.S. Army War College and the U.S. Supreme Court in Washington, D.C.

 Memories

"In the mid-seventies, when I was eight or nine years old, we'd go shopping at the West Side Market. My father would tell me that the ceiling was made of money. Since it was so high and I couldn't see it clearly, I believed him. Then he used to tell me that sometimes the money would fall from the ceiling and when I wasn't looking he'd toss some change over my shoulder and I'd go running after it."

—*Robert Puls*

in search of prasky (summer sausage), plantains, or peanut butter are sure to find what they want. It also seems fitting that these two places represent the achievements of a man who left his home and came to America in search of opportunity.

One of the most enduring myths about the Market is that it was originally a train station. Vendors hear self-appointed guides repeat this fiction almost every week—but there's a good reason for the mistake. The Guastavino company designed tile vaults for more than twenty major railroad terminals, including Penn Station (demolished in 1963) and Grand Central Station, along with its famed Oyster Bar. The look became so closely associated with these places that people just assume a link between form and function. By coincidence, there's another, less obvious, connection between the two: the four-faced clock installed at the top of the tower on the southwest corner of the market building was from the Seth Thomas Company, which also was responsible for the timepiece at Grand Central Station.

The West Side Market tower clock was an eight-day, nonstriking model with four opaque glass faces, each eight feet in diameter, with a set of hands three feet long. It had a weight and pulley mechanical movement that had to be wound manually.

This was the highest clock in Cleveland and it took 335 wooden steps to reach it. In the 1930s, custodian Percy Schuler made the climb weekly, every Saturday between 2:30 and 3 in the afternoon. Schuler told a reporter that he could see his house on W. 74th from a window in a small room near the top of the tower that housed the 800 pound swinging pendulum. "But it's clock winding not sightseeing that Schuler's after, so he dodges the pendulum and wriggles up an iron ladder through a small opening into the clock

Counterclockwise from top: The view, looking east, from the Market's tower; The corner of Lorain Avenue and W. 25th Street, 1930s
Opposite, clockwise from top: "Little Charlie Bisesi," center, with two unknown gentlemen; A commemorative plate featuring the Market

Memories

"The clock is more than just a mechanical device. It's the heartbeat of this public structure and one of the great focal points of the city. It provides comfort and security. If the clock is working, all is well in the world."

—**Charles Barrett**

"I have heard people say the building looks like a train station. I know it's not true. There were never any trains. Even so, a lot of people have passed through here."

—**Tim Ducu, vendor, Ramos Produce**

Dr. Walter Leedy, who died in 2006, was a professor of art, architectural history, and urban environments at Cleveland State University and an expert on the architectural history of Cleveland. He was a valuable resource for author Joanne Lewis. "I'd take Walter to the Market, buy him a bratwurst and listen as he expounded on his ideas and theories about the glory and brilliance of the building's architectural details from the vaulted ceiling and the natural circulation of air to the tile on the walls. He viewed the clock tower as akin to a lighthouse, a beacon for the neighborhood and a dramatic landmark in the urban landscape."

—**Joanne Lewis**

itself. . . . Schuler gets out a big crank and winds up the 1,200 pound weight. He takes out his pocket watch, checks the big clock, oils up a gear here or there and then he's ready for the climb down again. 'And that's the easiest part of it,' said Schuler with a grin."[29]

"Little" Charlie Bisesi was the last clock winder. He started working for the city's Division of Markets in 1934 at the Central Market downtown. After it burned to the ground in 1949, he transferred to the West Side Market. When Joanne Lewis interviewed him in 1980 for her book *To Market, To Market*, he told her that he stopped going up there the day one of the steps collapsed under his feet. Although it was repaired, he never made another trip to the top and the clock didn't keep time until it was electrified in 1954.

More recently the clock was converted to an electronic system. The only part of the original, internal movement that remains is the gear set that interfaces with the dial faces, according to Charles Barrett, a professional restorer of antique clocks and bell towers who volunteered to get it running again in 2003. He replaced a hard-to-find relay and had it working for three years, but in 2006 the installation of new coolers created a problem with the power and the clock stopped.

Barrett, the only person to follow in Bisesi's footsteps, says it's still a daunting trek. "The tower is a dark, empty, cavernous shell. There's nothing in there but an open metal staircase spiraling upwards. You can see right through to the bottom. Then you have to climb a ladder to get into the actual space where the clockworks are located. But once you're there, it's wonderful—clean, bright with daylight, and the numerals are visible from behind, through the dials."

In addition to its function as a signpost and timekeeper visible for miles, the tower had another practical purpose from the start, housing a large steel tank that provided water for washing the floors and for use in case of fire. But it has become something more—the symbol most closely associated with the Market. Over the years the tall, tapering square brick pillar capped with a cupola has appeared in newspaper photos, postcards, ads, aprons, commemorative plates, sweepstake tickets, and countless other promotional items. For many years, neon lettering ran the vertical length of the tower, spelling out the name of the place on one side, and the days of operation on the other.

Now it has the stature of a monument but the tower "that projects high into the air" has had its share of critics and problems. Part of the architect's plans as early as 1907, it was cited in 1910 as one of the "esthetic details" that was too costly and unnecessary.[30] Nonetheless, like the tile ceiling, it was ultimately built, and the copper dome was put in place and gilded in time for the building's 1911 dedication.

TIME AND COIN SAVED AT WEST SIDE MARKET

THE CITY REFRIGERATOR
The Market Underground

BENEATH THE BUILDING is another world, known only to vendors and their employees. The basement, with walls thirty-five inches thick, is a warren of corridors, cubicles, and cooler rooms. There are thirteen refrigerated lockers divided into individual sections, two "dry" locker spaces, and a washroom for cleaning produce. It's busy down there in the pre-dawn hours when everybody's trying to set up their stock, again at the end of the day, and even when the Market's closed, especially on Thursdays when big orders come in for the weekend.

Market merchants prepare and store the things they sell, hauling stuff up and down on four freight elevators. In the old days, boxes, barrels, trays, and sacks were hefted on broad shoulders or pushed around on wooden dollies. Now they've got motorized carts with pallet jacks and fork lifts, but don't imagine that makes it an easy job. It is however, a necessary one. "Having the storage and refrigeration in the basement is hard on the vendors, who have to transport everything back and forth from their stands," explains architect Paul Volpe. "But it enhances the atmosphere for shoppers because the main floor is all selling space. From an experiential perspective that means it's dense, like a city street, interesting and exciting."

Keeping food chilled is essential to the operation of the Market. The refrigeration plant is at the center of all the subterranean activity. The original unit, "a single refrigerating machine, rated at thirty tons of ice a day cooling capacity," was considered the most modern system of its kind when it was installed. It was replaced in 1914 with "a sixty-ton-a-day cooling machine…large enough to furnish refrigeration for the present plant of seven rooms and twenty one counter refrigerators in the market house, and seven new rooms of nearly ninety thousand cubic feet, now nearing completion. The original machine will be for reserve…." Merchants could rent five by six feet cold storage lockers for four dollars a month. "Though it is not apparent, all these lockers are one of the greatest sanitary features of the establishment. The market is only open four days a week. On the closed days, perishable stocks are stored in these lockers instead of being hauled about the city in unsanitary wagons, through dusty streets, to ice boxes of doubtful cleanliness."[31]

A building doesn't get to be a hundred years old without earning a few ghost stories, and this one's no exception. Al Kichak, an engineer who was hired in 2000 to help keep the Market machinery humming, has one. "My favorite part of the building is the basement, that's my turf. I saw a ghost when I first started here. I was on night shift and was making the rounds, checking the coolers, at three in the morning. I hadn't learned where all the light switches were and I had a flashlight with me. I was checking the thermometers and went into cooler #9. This was when the lockers were wooden instead of steel fencing. It looked like the light had been left on.

"It was just a little light," Kichak continues. "I could see someone in one of the lockers, in a smock, and I said, "Oh, I didn't know anyone was in here. I'm the new night engineer." I'm thinking who is this, is he stealing? He came out, almost in front of me. I could see the outline of his face and his hair, pencils in his pocket but the face was in the shadows. Then there was a little twinkling.

I went to turn the light switch on and he was gone. I try to forget about that. But then one of the other engineers told me he saw the same thing."

Another haunting tale comes from Frank Wegling, the Market's former supervisor of weights and measures. "When I was at the Market in the early 1970s, building engineers would have to do their rounds in the middle of the night to check on cooler temperatures and make sure everything was operating correctly. Several would report that they would open the door to cooler #10 (which was in the same grouping as cooler #9) and see a man who was wearing a white coat and black tie. They all swore by the same sighting. It was generally thought that it was Walter Simmelink Sr., one of the original tenants, because that's what he wore all the time. None of the guys who saw the ghost had ever known or met Walter because he was long gone by that time."

Long before talk of apparitions, the public and the planners talked about providing cold storage space in the basement that could be used by vendors, private citizens, and even other commercial enterprises. The idea was mentioned repeatedly in newspaper accounts of the Market's progress between 1903 and 1910.

When the Market finally was completed, there was plenty of refrigerated space to go around. Wholesalers were quick to take advantage of the opportunity the first year, storing thousands of barrels of apples, cases of eggs, and pounds of cheese. We don't think of these foods as seasonal now, since they are available in the grocery store year-round at relatively stable prices. But a hundred years ago things were different. Chickens, kept in unheated unlit henhouses, didn't lay many eggs through the winter. Less cheese was made in the cold weather months when cows produced fewer gallons of milk. Apples were not trucked in from other parts of the country, but came strictly from local growers. Home refrigerators were still uncommon and freezers unknown. So the chance to buy perishables in quantity, especially when prices were best, and keep them cold for later use at a nominal fee was a real benefit. There were private storage facilities in the city but they were expensive or did not accept small lots for individuals. At first, people were not aware that the city provided an alternative. The basement of the Market, 235 feet long and 136 feet wide, had seven cold rooms, the equivalent of almost 50,000 cubic feet, available for public rental.[32]

In a story that appeared in a 1914 issue of *The Technical World Magazine*, editors nicknamed the Market "The City Refrigerator," noting that for a very low fee

Opposite: Market Commissioner shows off the basement cold storage facilities, 1952
Above: Butcher Bruce Tayse at work in the basement

Memories

"Miller Meats was the only place in town selling these special Canadian Maple Leaf Hams. They were very popular. The week before Easter we'd get so many of them in, they had to be packed in our cooler, wall to wall and floor to ceiling. Each one weighed around fourteen pounds. My first year, Don [Miller] took me down there, opened the door, and told me to start loading the cart to bring them upstairs. I was a scrawny wiry little kid. 'How am I gonna do that?' I asked him. If I pulled one ham out they'd all come crashing down. Miller told me to climb to the top of the pile and push them down with my feet. And that's what I did."

—**Joseph Trill Jr., former vendor**

"My grandfather Harvey Hoffman owned a beef stand at the Market from 1930 until he died in 1966. When we were little girls my sister and I would go visit him once a week while our mother bought groceries. We'd ride the elevator to the basement and watch him cutting meat. It was dark except in the coolers and kind of scary to see him with a big cleaver and a side of beef. But he was such a gentle man and we loved him, so we knew it was okay."

—**Elaine (Hoffman) Schaedel, former employee**

Downstairs with the Meat Men

Mark Zarefoss, with Jim's Meats, has spent three decades in the Market basement. He learned the butcher's craft from Arnold Fernengel. Now he and Arnold's son Gordon cut and grind within shouting distance of each other in adjacent cages.

"It's like your second family down here," says Mark. "These guys are my brothers. We fight, we make-up, we help each other out."

"There used to be more cutters and runners," says Gordon. "On a Saturday, they were constantly calling us on the intercom to send stuff up to refill the case because they were selling out so fast. We could barely keep up. But people aren't cooking like they used to and they eat out a lot, so I work by myself now."

"There are fewer of us, doing more," adds Mark. "We were the last of an era. We got to work with a lot of the old timers who taught us the traditional way to take an animal apart."

"We had these 'rodeos,'" Gordon remembers, "competing for the best time to break down a quarter side of beef and trim it out. You can't buy the knowledge we got from people like my father. He'd show you how to do something, then you'd practice till you got it right. That's how skills were passed on."

"Here, in this basement, was the best school," Mark says.

Bruce Tayse, of Tayse Meats, also got his training on the job and in the basement. "I came to get a haircut at the barber college down the street," Tayse says, "and decided to stop in and say hello to my brother who was working at the Market. I left with a job, cleaning up at Larry Kovalcsik's meat stand after school and on Saturdays. That was 1980 and I was fourteen. There were five kids in the family and never enough money. I dropped out of school two years later so I could work there full-time. I watched and I learned. By the time I turned eighteen, I was cutting meat, first for Ehrnfelts, and then almost twenty years for Pinzone's."

In 2007, Tayse got his own stand, but he prefers to leave sales and customer relations to his wife Karen. His domain is downstairs where it's always cold, even on the hottest summer days. So his uniform is a heavy long-sleeved flannel shirt under a white coat and a ski cap on his head. The brightly-lit room where he works,

really a kind of oversized refrigerator, is outfitted with a big wooden butcher block full of dips and grooves from decades of use. There's a table saw at one end. Hacksaws hang on the wall over a long white cutting board. A radio, usually blasting heavy metal music, keeps him company. Wielding blades so sharp they cut through bone as though it were butter, Tayse turns sides of beef into the steaks, roasts, and short ribs his customers want.

Like many of the meat men, he gets in whole animals that have been cut in quarters. Called "swinging beef," it arrives by truck at the loading dock. Each piece usually weighs between 175 and 200 pounds. He picks them up, puts them on a cart, and takes them downstairs on the freight elevator. Because he doesn't purchase select parts in boxes, he has soup bones and cheaper cuts that, he says, appeal to his ethnic clientele. Nothing goes to waste. Everything he can't sell—fat, scraps, and bones—is tossed in a bin and hauled away to be used in gelatin, dog food, make-up, and even perfume. It's a traditional form of recycling, he explains, that's been around since long before the word became popular.

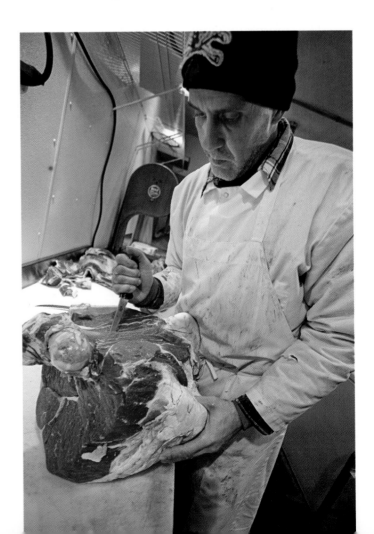

the municipality would "store any citizen's butter, eggs, cheese or apples, from the period of low prices in spring and summer far into the fall and winter." At first, Joseph M. McCurdy, superintendent of the plant, had little success getting people to take full advantage of this great resource in their midst. His initial efforts, he told the writer, were "met with indifference" and people "did not flock to us as we had hoped." Then in early April 1913, a woman who knew him asked if, as a favor, he would store a case of eggs for her. "I could not convince her that the warehouse was designed for just such people as she.... That was our first family lot. As a result of that call the women of the neighborhood combined and stored one hundred and fifty dozen eggs with us." This led to interest in putting away butter in June, when it was plentiful. "The big difficulty was educating prospective consumers to buy butter in tubs and repack it in crocks or to buy one-pound bricks. These were then crated and received as packages which could be removed one or more at a time.... Apples were next in season. A woman who had no way of keeping a barrel of apples in her home was our first customer in this line.... She repacked them in three boxes and sent them in."

The city charged 40 cents to store a crate of eggs (30 dozen) from April 1 to January 1; 15 cents for a hundred pounds of butter from June 1 to February 1; 10 cents a month for one hundred pounds of cheese; and 40 cents for three bushels of apples from October 1 to April 1. The logistics were complicated—from devising proper packaging to prevent spoilage and finding the most efficient way of organizing crates to tracking every individual's merchandise. "Each article must be kept at a certain temperature," explained McCurdy, "and no two kinds of food can be stored in the same room. We have only seven rooms, but as the plant is enlarged we shall be able to extend our facilities. In the meantime we are experimenting, learning, and educating. Eventually we hope to be closer to the public than the corner grocer and of infinitely more benefit."

Participation slowly grew, encouraged by word of mouth, newspaper coverage, and promotional efforts initiated by the Merchants Board of the Chamber of Industry. McCurdy had high hopes of attracting more customers for the winter of 1914–15. "...[T]he glad word has been spread and consignments of family supplies are coming in most gratifyingly."[33] After 1954, as home refrigeration became affordable and vendor needs increased, the practice of leasing basement cooler space was abandoned.

Above: The cooler, circa 1987
Opposite: Bruce Tayse breaks down beef quarters

Memories

"The walls are concrete but the ceilings in the coolers are lined in cork, the best natural insulation in the world. How do I know? I stuck a broom handle in the ceiling to make a little round spot. [According to a 1950 appraisal report both the walls and the ceilings of the cooler rooms were insulated with a three-inch layer of cork.]

Another thing about the basement—when Muny was operating as a light company, and not an electrical distribution company, the electricity went out frequently. Every stand owner had candles in the coolers since you were NEVER in such a dark place in your life. Plus it was quiet since none of the equipment was working."

—*Tom Nagel, employee*

"Little Charlie Bisesi worked at the Market for the city. He helped his son Donny get a Saturday job there. We always arrived at 5 AM to start loading up these big four wheel flat bed carts in the basement and bringing them up to the stands. It was really busy—everybody was doing the same thing—and you had to wait in line for a spot on the elevators. Charlie had keys to the building. He'd let Donny in early, before 5 AM, so he'd be first in line. The vendor that hired Donny always got his stuff first."

—*Joseph Trill Jr., former vendor*

ENTIRELY COMPLETE
The Outside Arcades

A BUILDER SHOULD have been chosen for the outdoor produce arcades at the same time the contractor was selected to install the expanded refrigeration plant in 1914. But instead, the covered sheds, always part of the master plan, got caught up in yet another round of overheated rhetoric and debate.

A few weeks after Service Director Springborn requested $75,000 to complete the remaining work, the City Control board rejected all bids to construct the produce aisles. At issue once again was the price tag. The drawings from Hubbell and Benes called for stone trim that matched what had been used on the market house. C. W. Stage, Director of Public Utilities, called the amount of money that had already gone into building the West Side Market "a public scandal," adding, "I am not in favor of expending several thousands more to get a particular shade of granite." Mayor Baker agreed that it was an unnecessary expense.[34] The dispute was soon resolved and work commenced in mid-July.

When finished the following year, the arcades formed an ell-shape stretching along the north and east sides of the building. Made from materials consistent with those of the Market house exterior, the two roofed concrete walkways were each 20 feet wide, with one "arm" measuring 343 feet long and the other 157 ½ feet. A curved ceiling, echoing the inside space, was supported by brick columns, and between each pair were four feet deep wooden counters. Each stand was allotted seven feet of space.

The open-sided arcades had overhead lights but no running water or heat, and provided minimal protection from the weather. Winter was hard on shoppers but worse for the men, women, and children who spent hours behind the mounds of cabbages and apples, week after frigid week. According to newspaper accounts, members of the West Side Fruit & Vegetable Association, an organization of standholders, were begging the city to do something about it as far back as 1934.[35] But they were still waiting for the aisles to be enclosed in the 1970s when Tony Anselmo was a boy helping out at the family produce stand. "I remember shoveling the snow out of the way so we could drop the awnings to block the wind. The ropes would be covered with ice and wouldn't cooperate. We'd get the kerosene heater going—there were no electrical outlets so that's what we had to use. They gave off so much soot. In the winter, after a day standing next to them if you blew your nose, the handkerchief would be black. We'd roast onions and bake potatoes on top to eat for lunch. They'd get knocked over and fires started all the time. Our parents would tell us kids to get a bucket of snow and put it out."

Although the 1986 master revitalization plan recommended enclosing the produce aisles, there was no money available to do it until 2001, when Mayor White's administration provided the funds. The space behind the stands was extended, garage doors were installed, and central heating was put in.

Clockwise from top: Produce arcade, 1923; Reporter talks with produce vendor Vince DeGrandis, who protested the lack of improvements in the produce arcades, 1970; The produce arcade today
Opposite: A view of the completed Market

A FIRST CLASS INVESTMENT
Repair, Restore, Wrangle, & Revitalize

THE MARKET BUILDING was made to last and it has aged remarkably well. But that doesn't mean it didn't require some loving care along the way. City officials often disagreed about what to do and how to pay for it and tenants had their own ideas. Discussions degenerated into standoffs that could last for years. More than once, things reached critical condition before action was taken.

Beyond daily maintenance, little was done to keep the Market up during its first three decades. In 1946, voters approved funds for some repairs and refurbishing. Although the city owned the physical space, tenants even agreed to spend their own money on new cases and counters—but nothing happened. For years, city officials fought amongst themselves and with the vendors. Rent hikes were proposed, opposed by the merchants because the city had failed to live up to its responsibilities to keep the property in good condition and modernize the facility, and then re-negotiated. In the spring of 1950, Mayor Thomas Burke, questioning whether the city should be in the business of subsidizing private enterprise, hinted that the West Side Market might be for sale. He suggested that the tenants band together and buy it, but they were not able to raise the money.

Reporting on the stalemate in September 22, 1950, the *Cleveland Press* noted the estimated cost of improvements, which included sandblasting and tuck-pointing the exterior, and upgrades to the antiquated electrical, plumbing,

MARKET TAKES 14 YEARS: LET'S FINISH IT NOW

The seven long years of famine in constructing the new West Side market, Lorain avenue and West 25th street are nearly at an end. Inside of three months Mayor Baker, a Moses as well as a Pharoah [*sic*], will lead the children of Cleveland safely into the $750,000 structure, entirely complete.

Seven long years of plenty, plenty of talk, blue prints, and money raising schemes preceded the actual start of work in 1907. Then followed seven years of famine, little or no work, a dab here and there and innumerable delays. However, the dreams of three Pharoahs, Baker, Tom Johnson, and Herman Baehr, will soon be made good.

The new stalls, extending through to West 25 street will be open on all sides. Wares will be sold from stands instead of wagons. Springborn estimates the last bit of work on the building will be done by July 15.

—*Cleveland News*, April 4, 1914

Memories

"I grew up on 41st and Lorain in the 1950s. It was a rough neighborhood. My mom walked me to school until I was ten or eleven. We'd go through the outdoor produce aisles on our way to St. Emerics. When the Market was open there was this guy at the Calabrese fruit stand who'd always throw me an apple, saying 'Here kid, catch.' I wrote about it in my book Hollywood Animal. *In 1993, I came back from California to live in Ohio with my second wife, Naomi. She grew up in Mansfield but had never been to the Market so I took her there. We walked by Calabrese, the same guy was there and he recognized me. 'Hey Joey,' he called out, 'you the guy I been reading about?' And then he threw me an apple."*

—Joe Eszterhas, screenwriter and author

CITY UP IN THE AIR ON MARKET TOWER

The 85-foot [*sic*] tower at the West Side Market became the center of a City Hall rhubarb today on whether it should be razed or remodeled.

Cleveland Press, January 14, 1951

WHY SHOULD CITY SUBSIDIZE MUNICIPAL MARKET STALLS?

Prices in municipal markets are no lower on the whole than elsewhere in the community. The city in effect has been maintaining market places for a privileged few at the expense of all taxpayers.

Cleveland Press, May 11,1951

WEST SIDE MARKET PLAN REJECTED AS INADEQUATE

"Either we ought to spend whatever it takes to make that a market house to be proud of or we ought to save our money, sell it as is, and get out of the market business," said Lee C. Howley, commission member.

Cleveland Press, September 24, 1951

and refrigeration systems, had skyrocketed, jumping from $519,140 in 1949 to $700,000, while the city and tenants "squabbled." However, it seemed the issues had finally been resolved.

> **Although negotiations between tenant and owner were private, it was learned that the city officials finally came to a realization that they had something more than just an investment in a market house. If they let the Market fall apart, the entire neighborhood around Lorain Avenue and W. 25th Street would drop in real property valuation, they decided. So what they started out to do two years ago will now be done.**
> —*Cleveland Press,* September 22, 1950

But the debate raged on and bids for the work continued to rise. Some in City Council argued in favor of partial repairs; members of the City Planning Commission took an all or nothing position.

The tower was especially at risk. During World War II, when raw materials were in short supply, the water tank in the tower was removed and donated to a scrap metal drive. Unfortunately, this severely compromised its structural integrity. In 1951, officials bickered over whether to spend the $14,000 needed for repairs or $12,000 to demolish it. "It's the biggest birdhouse in town," flipped James Lester, City Planning Director, urging a rip it down decision.[36]

Thirteen months of claims, counter claims, and fractious politics followed. The issues were eventually resolved, the motion to delay making funds available for the rehab project was defeated on January 28, 1952, and rehab work began the next year.

Work was finally completed in 1954, with the city and the Tenants' Association together spending $1.1 million. Electric freight elevators replaced the original water powered ones; metal doors and window frames were installed; and new refrigerated glass cases took the place of the old white enamel brick stands. Everybody was happy—but not for long. The next major crisis was parking.

For the Market's first thirty-five years, most customers walked there or came by trolley. Car ownership began to increase after WWII and the trend turned into a boom with the rise of middle-class affluence and the migration from cities to suburbs. Planners and architects could not have foreseen this transportation revolution when the Market was built. By 1961 accommodat-

Memories

John Coyne, whose father Jack owned the Farm Queen Poultry stand, remembers being sent out with bunches of dimes to feed the meters near the Market so people wouldn't get tickets. "Dad's thinking was that people came here to save money. If they had to pay parking fines they might not come back. So it was a good investment and way of keeping customers."

"I joined the Navy and went to war [WWII]. I had a talent for electronics and went into that field, doing research, when I got back. Because of my electrical skills I helped many of the Market tenants. There were problems with the wiring and people were afraid to touch the lights and anything connected to them because they'd get shocked. If something stopped working they'd ask me to fix it. The circuit breakers were in the basement and since there were no codes to speak of when they were originally installed, it was impossible to trace which ones connected where upstairs. So I had to work with everything hot."

—Alvin Stumpf, former employee

Above: Parking lot, May 1954

ing the growing number of automobiles had become a necessity and a point of ongoing contention for vendors who feared they were losing business because there wasn't enough space for patrons' vehicles. The merchants even made a twelve minute film for city council members documenting bumper-to-bumper traffic jams and long waits for a spot on busy Market days.

A large new lot finally opened in 1965, prompting speeches and celebration. It solved the parking problem—temporarily—but there was an unintended and unfortunate consequence. The majority of shoppers were parking at the east end of the market house and entering at the mid-point of the two produce arcades, the elbow of the ell. They typically walked along only one of the aisles, towards W. 25th Street, and went into the building on the north side. This was not what the architects had intended. Instead of grand entrances they had designed multiple doorways and entry points. The idea was that this would be convenient for customers approaching from all directions and give every vendor a position of relatively equal value. This made sense when most shoppers came to the Market on foot or by public transportation. The change in the flow of people in and out of the building and produce arcades resulting from the location of the parking lot, in combination with the fact that most people were driving to the Market, meant that some stands had prime positions and others did not.

Parking—or lack of—has been an ongoing dilemma. Possible solutions have ranged from erecting a multi-level structure to provide the necessary number of spaces to charging for parking. Everyone offers an opinion on the subject, just as they did in 1979 when two modernist murals were installed in the Market. The murals covered the arched windows at the east and west ends of the hall and like so much else about the place, there's a back story that involves disagreement and second-guessing.

A competition was held for mural designs and Nancy Martt was one of the winners. The eighty-five-year-old painter tells the story of how her work, and a piece by friend and fellow painter Robert Takatach, who died in 2003, ended up in the hall and at the center of a spat.

> "Members of the Chagrin Valley Arts Center got letters about the Market mural project. It was winter 1978. We had a record snowfall and a blizzard had left me stranded in the house with the kids. Since I didn't have anything better to do I started sketching. I had three weeks to come up with ideas and submit a design. I did something with livestock and after it was accepted, they asked me to revise and add ducks, fish, cheese, milk, every form of animal protein—you name it. My goal was to get them all in and still have a nice eye-catching composition. This was quite a challenge. Fish, cows, and cheese don't naturally belong together in the same space. It was quite colorful."

Sandy Kucinich, the Mayor's wife, was among those from City Hall who picked the winners, sidestepping a recommendation from the Cleveland Fine Arts Advisory Committee to reject all the submissions. The artists' designs were reproduced on 20 by 40 foot aluminum panels by the Buddy Simon Sign Company. Martt's piece, called "Market Montage" went up first.

Two shoppers had positive comments for *Plain Dealer* writer William Miller, but bakery vendor Mitchell Sielinski's response was, "It stinks."[37] Many of his fellow merchants agreed, speaking their mind in no uncertain terms to *Cleveland Press* reporter Dick Wooten.

> "I think it would look fine in a kindergarten," remarked Christina Sabetta, who sells pizza.
> "It's lousy," said Merle Rini, who has sold fruit at the Market for 50 years. Even more adamant were John and Mary Tricsko, tobacco sellers for 36 years.
> "It's like me putting on a tux with beach sandals," said John. "It clashes with the building." His wife added, "I haven't talked to anyone who likes it."

The cultural dissonance between the Old World setting and Martt's modern work of art, Wooten observed "had an unsettling effect on the merchants and the shoppers...."[38]

Some Market tenants complained that the city should have spent its money on more pressing needs, such as expanding the parking lot or keeping the men's room stocked with soap and paper towels. In fact, the funds used were earmarked for public art and came from a federal grant that also paid for new lights and doors, paint and plaster work, and other rehab projects.

Market Commissioner John Pilch thought Martt's piece was great and had a clever answer for those who questioned some of its unusual details. "When people ask me why the chicken on the painting is blue, I tell them that the market only serves blue ribbon chickens and that seems to satisfy them."[39]

Mayor Kucinich presided over a dedication ceremony on May 30, 1979. "The Mayor said he liked it," Martt recalls, "but I think maybe that was just typical politician talk. When he introduced me I heard a couple of boos from the crowd. An article in the newspaper included a quote from a vendor who said "I think it's awful." I guess it was too modern, too startling and stylized for most people's tastes. They expected something more realistic."

Pilch told the *Cleveland Press* that murals at either end of the concourse were included in the Market's early plan, but he had the facts only partly right. The original proposal was to put in stained glass windows, which never happened because there was no money to pay for them.[40]

Clockwise from top: The fruit and vegetable mural on the east wall, 1980s; Mural by Nancy Martt
Opposite: Market clock tower inside scaffolding during restoration

75,000 CUSTOMERS CAN'T BE WRONG

Back in those so called good old days of 1912 when butter was 32 cents a pound and a man was glad to have a job at $2.50 a day, when Cleveland was trying out its first automobile fire engines and City Council was stirred up over spooners in the parks, the wonderful West Side Market opened for business.

It is doubtful if Newton D. Baker who was then mayor and dedicated the building, or anyone else foresaw its enormous popularity over the years. Now 41 years after its opening on W. 25th Street and Lorain Avenue, the Market attracts more than 75,000 customers weekly.

In those 1912 days of cheap labor and low material prices, the building with its high clock tower was constructed for only $680,000. Almost double that original cost is now being spent to modernize it....

Frank C. Jeroski, who began his market career as an inspector in 1920, and has been city commissioner of markets since 1935 considers the West Side Market a first-class investment....

—*Plain Dealer*, April 26, 1953

The mostly unpopular murals were removed in 2001. Martt says she's proud of her design but admits it could have been better-suited to the space. "I knew about the Market of course but to tell you the truth I had never actually been there. I went for the first time when they were putting up the panels and realized I probably should have gone before I started drawing. I didn't know about all the wonderful architectural details in the building. I would have incorporated some of that. I would definitely have done it differently. I thought it was a good idea when they put the windows back."

The 1950s repairs to the tower had proved to be just a short-term fix. Rescuing the tower—and protecting the pedestrians—became a priority in the '70s. The brickwork and stone trim were deteriorating. A memo between the Director of Public Properties and Market Commissioner Pilch from May 1973, with the header E-M-E-R-G-E-N-C-Y, stated that a large piece of ornamental terra-cotta from the top of the tower had fallen "and just missed a woman before shattering on the sidewalk..." An inspection report the following year warned that even very small pieces of this material dropping from that height could cause fatal injury to a person below. Despite the obvious urgency, it was two years before restoration work began and another two until it was finished. But once again the effort proved to be a band-aid, not a cure.

By the time Paul Volpe, the city's staff architect, got authorization to spend $325,000 to refurbish the tower in 1987, it was seriously compromised. "It was literally coming apart," he explains, "exploding from the inside out with

cracks running vertically through the bricks. This was due primarily to the removal of the water tank. That was a big mistake: the weight of the tank and the steel beams that held it in place had actually helped stabilized the structure. Finding brick to match what was already there kept me awake nights."

Volpe discovered that the cupola was completely rotten and had to be replaced. "We replicated the exact proportions, using a steel frame with a copper skin, and brought in a huge crane to install it. When we removed what was left of the old one it literally fell apart in our hands. The spire, which had been gone for many years, was put back on top as it was originally."

As Commissioner for the city's Division of Architecture, Paul Volpe created a comprehensive four-phase revitalization plan for the Market in 1986. In addition to the tower restoration, it included masonry tuck-pointing, and improvements to the mechanical, plumbing, and electrical systems. The building's red tile roof and exterior brick walls, filthy with decades of soot that had drifted over from steel mills in the Flats—the same mills that had provided jobs to many who bought their food at the Market—was cleaned, along with all the interior tile surfaces, the ceiling, and the floors. The outdoor lighting was redone and all the windows were replaced.

"The building was at a critical juncture," Volpe says. "In my opinion Mayor Voinovich saved the Market. It was teetering on the edge. If the work had not been done at that time the damage might have gotten so bad that it would have been cost prohibitive to repair. He made the decision that gave the place a new lease on life. We fought hard to save it, and we succeeded."

The Millennium Project of 2000, a multi-million dollar investment in infrastructure improvements, brought further upgrades. A capital campaign that kicked off in the final months of 2012 is meant to provide funding from outside sources to ensure the structure's viability for the next hundred years.

> **"The West Side Market has become a great civic monument, an important piece of this city's infrastructure and history. If it had not been built so well, it would likely have been torn down like so many other markets around the country. But the place has an eternal beauty, plus an earned character that people value and the patina of time that cannot be duplicated. The Market should be protected, loved and celebrated."**
> **—Paul Volpe, architect**

Above: Replacing the cupola as part of repairs to the clock tower, 1987

(M)emories

"I was going to make a Christmas card one year. This was sometime in the '90s. My idea was to dress up as Santa and go up to the clock tower. I had to climb the steps with that heavy suit and beard on. I got to a narrow metal platform and opened a big metal door. I stepped out and a huge gust of wind slammed the door shut behind me. There wasn't much room out there on the balcony. I was as tight against the wall as could be and I was one terrified Santa but I'm thinking the whole time, 'What a view!' My friend was on the United Bank Building across from the Market. I could see him staggering across the rooftop there because it was so windy and then he started crawling on his stomach. 'Take the picture, take the picture,' I was yelling. The next year, I wasn't so brave. Tom Kearns had a pork stand. I decided to dress up as Santa and lay in his case for a photo."

—Patrick Delaney, former vendor

Notes

1. Letter to the Editor, *Plain Dealer*, May 31, 1953.

2. *Cleveland Press*, Feb. 15, 1945.

3. *Cleveland Leader*, May 3, 1915.

4. *Plain Dealer*, Dec. 25, 1903.

5. *Cleveland Press*, Nov. 17, 1906.

6. George Condon, *West of the Cuyahoga*, (Kent, OH: Kent State University Press, 2006), 91.

7. "New Market House for West Side," *Ohio Builder* 8 (1906): 29–32.

8. *Plain Dealer*, January 5, 1907.

9. *Plain Dealer*, Mar. 29, 1907.

10. *Plain Dealer*, May 14, 1907.

11. *Plain Dealer*, Nov. 5, 1907.

12. *Cleveland Press*, Oct. 25, 1909.

13. Ibid.

14. *Plain Dealer*, April 3, 1910.

15. Ibid.

16. Charles Kamp, "Municipal Markets in Cleveland," *Annals of the American Academy of Political and Social Science* 50 (1913): 128–30.

17. *Cleveland Press*, Sept. 8, 1911.

18. *Cleveland Leader*, Mar. 1, 1898.

19. *Plain Dealer*, June 19, 1910.

20. *Cleveland Leader*, May 1, 1902.

21. Robert Bremner, "Humanizing Cleveland and Toledo," *American Journal of Economics and Sociology* 13, no. 2 (1954): 182–83.

22. Elroy McKendree Avery, *A History of Cleveland and Its Environs* (Lewis Publishing Company, 1918), 295–96.

23. *Plain Dealer*, Nov. 29, 1981.

24. Annual Report of the Department of Public Service, for Year Ending December 31, 1912, Report of Market Master to Fred C. Alber, Superintendent of Markets. From City Council Archives.

25. *Cleveland Press*, Sept. 8, 1911.

26. *Plain Dealer*, Jan. 13, 1924.

27. *Plain Dealer* July 26, 1908.

28. *Plain Dealer*, Nov. 5, 1907.

29. *Cleveland Press*, Nov. 1937, pgs. 24–25.

30. *Plain Dealer*, April 13, 1910.

31. Cornell, 22–27.

32. Ibid.

33. Ibid.

34. *Plain Dealer*, April 25, 1914.

35. *Cleveland Press*, Feb. 18, 1936.

36. *Cleveland Press*, Jan. 4, 1951.

37. *Plain Dealer*, May 6, 1979.

38. *Cleveland Press*, May 5, 1979.

39. *Plain Dealer*, May 6, 1979.

40. *Plain Dealer*, July 14, 1909.

M emories

"There's no question that the inside folks had it better than those outside. But the market hall isn't mechanically heated and it's not exactly warm and cozy behind the counters either. It was cold at the Market during the winter. I would dress in my 'gotchies,' [long underwear], three sweaters and a heavy jacket. When spring would roll around, I would start shedding my clothes and our customers would say, 'Gee, Ann. Are you losing weight?' I would tell them I was just losing my clothes."

—Ann Churchin, former vendor

"Back in 1976 when Dennis Kucinich was still a councilman in the city, the clock tower was being repaired. One afternoon, Dennis came unannounced with his camera and asked me to take him up. The steps were not in good shape and it wasn't open to the public. Dennis said he would take full responsibility for the visit. We climbed the stairs to the top and he went to the balcony railing and leaned way out to photograph down to the street. My job was to hold on to the back of his pants so he didn't go over."

—Frank Wegling, former Market commissioner

CHAPTER TWO

THE PEOPLE
of the Market

JUST PEACHY!

Barry Neer was the third of four generations of his Jewish family to sell produce at the Market. Between 1948 and 1954, Neer and his father Morris attended every Indians home game—except for those played on a Friday or Saturday, when duties at the Market took priority. As outdoor vendors are, Neer was meticulous about stacking his produce in neat rows and pyramids to catch the eye of the customer, but personally picked and bagged his customer's purchases—always. Once when a customer reached to choose their own fruit, Neer abruptly stopped them. The stunned customer looked at the next in line who said, "You don't have to like his attitude, but you'll love his peaches."

Previous pages, clockwise from top: Keith Stevens, an employee at Wiencek's Poultry; Merchants pose outside the Market during the 65th anniversary celebration, 1977

IMMIGRANTS & ENTREPRENEURS
The Heart of the Market

"I WAS CONCEIVED on a pile of burlap potato bags and born in a banana box," says Barry Neer, in a voice that sounds like miles of gravel road. The one-time produce vendor grew up at the Market in the 1940s and '50s. He probably cut his teeth on fresh fruit, honed his math skills counting change, and developed his coarse and completely memorable personality to interact with all who came to the Market.

Neer knows that the story of his beginnings at the Market would probably make his Jewish mother blush and his father challenge its accuracy, but it's a paradigm to which many of the vendors at Cleveland's West Side Market can relate. It speaks of a time when life was colorful but difficult, families worked together, raised their children at the Market, and worked hard to make a modest living—and produce vendors did indeed put their babies to sleep in banana boxes. Those born to the butchers, bakers, and cheesemongers had it better: they slept under the counters.

> "My dad is 67. He swears he was born under this stand," Mary Cantillon said.
> —*Los Angeles Times*, December 22, 1982

> "I remember when my mother used to bring my sister to the Market when there was no one to babysit her. She would put her in a banana box under the stand. She would put shredded paper in the box that would keep her warm. It was like a manger."
> —Jack Gentille, former vendor

> Charles "Bud" Leu Jr. remembers sleeping on a wooden shelf beneath the glass case that offers bacon skins, smoked shanks, kolbasi, prasky, fresh and smoked liver, and a line up of hot dogs and bratwurst.
> —*Plain Dealer*, May 1, 2004

Part of the story of the people of the West Side Market can be told simply by looking at the names on the stalls and stands. If every family name that

Memories

"The bologna we would sell used to come in a five-foot log, six inches in diameter. In a weekend, we would go through five or six of them. There were six thousand workers in the steel mills who would take four or five sandwiches in their lunch bucket every day. People worked hard down there and liked their bologna."

—Charles "Bud" Leu Jr., former vendor

"My grandfather, Robert Stumpf was one of the original vendors at the Market. He used to make sausage out of his garage and sold it at the Market. Most of his customers were German. Back in the old days a lot of the customers didn't speak English at all or very well. We had a customer who only knew how to say three things in English: 'Ham. One Pound. Slice.'

In the old days we would put the meat on the marble counters and someone would swipe it. We would try and chase them down, but in that crowd everyone looked alike with their babushkas on."

—Becky (Stumpf) Fitch, former employee

appeared over the last hundred years were laid end to end, it might reveal the flow of immigrants to the Cleveland area.

Cleveland offered astonishing examples of the impact of turn of the century immigration on Ohio: in 1900, 75% of the city's population was either foreign-born or first-generation descendants of foreign-born…more than 40 languages could be heard on the streets of Cleveland.[1]

No matter where they came from, in droves or trickles, immigrants did so because their homeland was entangled in war, economic strife, or political conflict and they were looking for freedom, fresh starts, and new opportunities. Cleveland was the perfect destination. Until the 1930s the area's steel, manufacturing, and automotive industries grew rapidly and the demand for unskilled labor was high.

By the time the Market opened in 1912, German immigrants had already put down strong roots in the Cleveland area and it was reflected in names like Ehrnfelt, Badstuber, Fernengel, Weigel, and Stumpf. They were butchers and sausage makers, family trades common in a land blessed with abundant pasture and people skilled in preserving and using every bit of the animal.

The Hungarians were also on their way to building one of the nation's largest ethnic communities in Cleveland. Names like Lovaszy and Farkas, a sausage maker and a baker, appeared.

Clockwise from top: Produce vendors, early 1900s; Robert J. Stumpf sausage stand in the early days of the Market; Charles "Bud" Leu Jr., mid-1940s

emories

"Our weekly trips to the Market began in the early 1960s, a few years after our family immigrated from Europe. We usually began in the fruit and vegetable aisles, where my mother would try and bargain for the best prices. Because of her heavy Romanian accent, some of the vendors could be impatient with her. Even at an early age, I didn't hesitate to step in and become what many of my friends call me now, the best bargain hunter in town!"

—**Kathy Bencze**

"St. Emeric was the butchers' church. We went there on Holy Days and Fridays— especially Good Friday."

—**John Rolston, former vendor**

Over the next thirty years, immigrants continued to arrive from eastern and central Europe and settled in the neighborhoods around the Market. For the Hungarians and Byelorussians that lived in the Tremont neighborhood, the Abbey Avenue Bridge was their footpath to the Market. Finnish immigrants lived down W. 25th Street near Clinton and the Greeks around W. 14th; Croatians lived in the area of St. Clair and the Poles in Slavic Village. Churches were built, serving as anchors in these developing neighborhoods: Our Lady of Mount Carmel and St. Rocco's on Fulton were where the Italians worshiped; St. John Cantius was the Polish church; Annunciation was for the Greeks; and St. Emeric was the Hungarian church and closest to the Market doors.

Whether it was a short walk or a trolley ride from their neighborhood to the West Side Market, this was a place for immigrants to rediscover the "comfort" foods of their homeland; traditional and familiar foods that would grace their daily dinner table and define their holiday celebrations. This was where they could come to find their specialty rye breads, whether German, Lithuanian, Jewish, or Bohemian style, or sausages and smoked meats exactly to their culture's taste—German, Slovenian, Polish, or Hungarian.

Feeling at home in a strange country was difficult in many ways and not being able to communicate easily was a challenge. The West Side Market offered a way to connect not only with familiar food, but also the possibility of finding someone who spoke the same language, both in the person shopping next to them or the merchant on the other side of the counter.

"My family has a multi-generational connection to the West Side Market. My father was a Polish Jewish immigrant and a baker by trade. In the 1960s and 1970s when I was a kid growing up in Cleveland Heights, my dad would take me across town to the West Side Market. He'd wake me and we'd get there very early on Saturday mornings. We bought produce first. Haggling was normal and expected. If he got a couple of extra tomatoes, we felt like we'd hit the jackpot. I didn't realize until many years later what the attraction was for him. He liked being with people from Europe and the interaction with the vendors."
—Jerald Chester

"Michael Zavodnik was from Austria and worked at my stand. He spoke seven languages fluently and at the same time...he could be speaking Hungarian to one woman and then switch and talk German to another."
—John Rolston, former vendor

Counterclockwise from top: The Gottlieb Ehrnfelt stand, circa 1930; C. W. Villwock Stand, circa 1920; Badstuber stand at Market opening, circa 1912
Opposite: Ilia Kazandjieff, circa 1970

"I started working at the Market in January 1971, in the cafeteria bussing dishes. I was only there for four months. Robert Stumpf would come in every Saturday at noon for a bowl of soup. He hired me away. It wasn't really stealing but I spoke German so I could understand his customers.

Stumpf had a lot of German customers. In the early 1970s it was very busy at the Market. The economy was good and customers would come straight from their steel mill shift at five in the morning. So we would have to get to work at 4 AM. I worked for him for thirteen years."
—Mary Pell, employee

Immigrants were people of limited means and the West Side Market was a good place to start a new business and a new life in a new country. Setting up a fruit stall, a vegetable cart on the sidewalk, or a stand inside the Market house, was affordable. No education was necessary, just a willingness to get up before the sun and stay on their feet all day in all kinds of weather and working conditions.

As they still are today, counters and stalls were leased from the City; it was a only matter of purchasing necessary equipment, if any, to conduct business, and selling a product, whether it was produce, meat, or dairy. For budding entrepreneurs and sole proprietors, a stand or a stall, even as small as six feet long, made them part of something prominent—the West Side Market. Yet make no mistake—it was a tough life for many immigrants and the generations of vendors to follow. Working hard was expected and accepted. Many eked out a living that provided schooling for their children, schooling they didn't have themselves, yet quite often their children returned to the business.

Ilia Kazandjieff: Neeeeexxxxtttt!

By the time he arrived in Cleveland at age twenty-two, Ilia Kazandjieff had already served in the Bulgarian army, escaped the communist regime in Bulgaria via the Orient express (where he hid in the toilet compartment), and was detained in a refugee camp in Capua, Italy, for a little over a year. Upon his arrival in Cleveland in 1969, he went to work at a factory. His American sponsor knew of someone at the Market looking for help at a fish stand. "I liked it, I learned fast, and I was selling fish," said Ilia. "I made $125 a week for working three days." In addition to his native language, he picked up more from his multinational friends in the refugee camp: Russian, Italian, Croatian, Serbian, Macedonian, English, Spanish, and a little Greek. "I could talk to five different customers in five different languages at the same time." That certainly had to make the lines move quickly at the stand.

In the melting pot of customers at the Market, any employee who could speak a language besides English was valuable; two languages would have been a bonus; more than three? Jackpot. "The Market was a great place for refugees to come and connect with other countrymen," says Ilia.

He worked thirty-one years at the fish stand, including his eight years of ownership. People remember him for one word, delivered in a loud and distinct tone, which was frequently mimicked by local radio personality, Trapper Jack—"Neeeeexxxxtttt!"

The Schilla Family: The Family Business

Chuck Schilla Jr. was the third and last generation of his family to operate a produce stand at the Market. It's a story sometimes told of how an immigrant came to America in search of a better life and worked hard at building a business that carried the family name and was passed it down to successive generations. The business provided a legacy and the promise of a good future.

Lawrence Schilla and his three older sisters arrived in 1903 at Ellis Island, New York, fresh from Naples, Italy. He was only twelve and his parents stayed behind, never to join them. At some point, he changed the spelling of his name from *Scila* to *Schilla*, perhaps to soften the pronunciation and sound less Italian. It wasn't unusual for immigrants to sometimes face strong prejudice in this country.

By 1917, Lawrence had established himself at the West Side Market and his son, Chuck Sr., was born in 1922. "My father was a kid who grew up at the Market," says his namesake, Chuck Jr., "and left to serve in World War II." When Chuck Sr. returned from the war, he went back to the Market to help his father. At the same time, he also trained as a beautician and got his insurance license, but preferred to be at the Market. "It was in his blood," said Chuck Jr. "He also wanted to stay and help his parents, who were aging and they couldn't run it like a younger person could."

Chuck Jr. ended up doing the same thing. "I had a job offer at IBM in 1968 and turned it down because in my heart, my parents were getting older and I wanted to support them," he says. He knew there would be no one else around to help, so he stayed and expanded the business from two little stands in the corner to three long stands, adding fruit to the mix. "I gave it all to the Market," says Chuck. "I think that you need to be in this business and at the Market for a long time to really understand. You also have to have a deep feeling for family."

Chuck Sr. retired in 1986 and twenty years later, Chuck Jr. closed the business and the Schilla name left the Market forever.

"Working at the Market was hard, not repetitive like on a factory line, and every moment was different," says Chuck Jr. "You might have sold the same type of produce everyday but what made it interesting were the customers, from all walks of life. I never had to listen to the news. I would get it first hand from them. To tell you the truth, I was always happy to help other people enjoy the 'fruits' of my life, if you know what I mean."

emories

"My parents, Augustino and Rose DeCaro, were Sicilian immigrants, both from upper-class families—tough as nails, but that was true of all the immigrants. They opened their produce stand at the West Side Market in 1934, when rent was $34 a quarter."

—Joe DeCaro, vendor, DeCaro Produce

Today (Carmen) Giannone appears as proud of being his own boss—an independent businessman—as he is of the fresh vegetables he sells. "Cost me about $1,500 to set myself up here. Gotta pay the rent, then buy a scale and some bags and pay the parking fees," he said. "It may not be all that expensive, but it's a lot of hard work."

—Crain's Cleveland Business, *September 20, 1982*

The late 1920s was a formative period for the Italian neighborhoods in Cleveland, the largest of which, Big Italy, was located along Woodland and Orange Avenues from E. 9th to E. 40th Streets. Big Italy became the center of the city's fruit and vegetable industry. Many of the immigrants came from Sicily and southern Italy, regions known for their fruit. It was these merchants who introduced Clevelanders to oranges, olive oil, figs, anchovies, bananas, and nuts; common purchases today, but delicacies then.

William Rini was a Sicilian immigrant who started his business in the produce arcade in 1920—he just sold bananas. His grandson, also called William, recalls the stories his own father, Frank Rini, also a produce vendor, used to share with him about the business:

> "My grandfather and my dad, Frank Rini, used to purchase the bananas from J. F. Sanson. They would back their truck up to a railroad boxcar and look over the bananas to make sure they got the best pick—a stalk of green bananas. They would only buy what they could sell in two weeks, loading up the back of the truck and laying the bananas in a nest of shredded paper. They would drive them to my grandfather's house on E. 19th, where the freeway and Jacobs (now called Progressive) Field is and put them into the house through the kitchen window. My grandfather would put banana strings on them and then pass them through a hole in the floor. My dad would take them into the banana room and hang them on hooks. A natural gas heater would help ripen them. Today they use ethylene gas to ripen fruit. Bananas today don't taste like they used to. They were a lot sweeter. Once they had ripened and were firm with no freckles, my grandfather would take them to over the bridge to the West Side Market, hang them on a hook and use a banana knife to cut the bunches off in whatever quantity the customer wanted to buy."

Emery Bacha still runs the family produce business at the West Side Market, one his grandparents started at the Pearl Street Market. He can easily recall

Opposite: Chuck Schilla Jr. and Chuck Schilla Sr. at the family produce stand, 1990s
Above, clockwise from top: Bananas bound for the Market; William Rini, circa 1930

(M)emories

"My two brothers went to college. My dad did not want them to take over the business because it was a hard life. It was a really good business but unusual that three families lived off the income of the stand."

—**Chris Sommer Krisak, former employee**

"John Miller (The Celery King) had a daughter that went to college. It was rare then to have any child go to college in the 1940s and he would insist that she come to work at the Market during her summer break—so she would learn to deal with people and how to be polite."

—**Mario Rini, former vendor**

the names of many of the fruit and vegetable vendors, the "old timers," who a half century ago filled the arcade and lined the sidewalks around the Market while he was growing up.

"There were the Calabreses, Vercurios, Tentalinos, Rinis, Bondis, Albergos (his maternal grandparents), Mercurios, DeGrandis, LoSchiavos, Parmesans, Creamos, Romanos, DeCaros," he recites, pausing to take a breath before adding, "Gentilles, Anselmos, Speranos, Schillas, DiFrancos, Cionciolos, Palmisanos, Guintas" and on. Many of these names appeared on the arcade stalls in the earliest days of the Market. Through them, it's easy to see and hear that Cleveland's Italians dominated the produce trade at the Market, and did so in large numbers, for more than sixty years.

Inside the market house the same was happening. Families who ran businesses for multiple generations took great pride in their longevity as vendors and stood as Market "nobility," earning high regard and respect among their competitors and customers.

The Leu family was once such Market "aristocracy," an empire built on bologna, as Charles "Bud" Leu Jr. would kid. As comical as it may sound, the Leu family lasted four generations at the Market and is still a name that some shoppers recall.

George Leu, a Swiss immigrant and sausage maker, established the family business at the Pearl Street Market and continued as a vendor at the West Side Market from the day it opened. He lasted through times without refrigeration, when the meats were laid out on the cold Carrara glass counters. Leu's son Charles took over behind the counter in the mid-1930s, weathering the meat shortages and rationing of the 1940s and the days when the Municipal Power Plant delivered sketchy electrical service, sporadically leaving the Market in the dark and vendors working by candlelight.

The next generation of Leus had other plans. Charles' son Bob had completed three years of premed studies at Baldwin Wallace College and Charles Jr. "Bud" was accepted into Purdue University's School of Engineering. When their father fell ill, they both returned to help run the business, a lucrative time when customers stood three deep in front of the counter. "I ended up fixing things at the Market anyhow," says Bud, hinting that his aptitude for being technical hardly went to waste. "Leu Brothers" appeared on the stand in 1967 when their father retired.

They continued to run a family business, mostly employing brothers, sisters, aunts, uncles, cousins, and their own children. In 2004, they left the Market for good. The Leu name has not disappeared from the Market, but it helps to know where to look. Around 1992, Bob's son, Terry bought John Rolston's chicken stand, which was across the aisle from the family's lunch meat stand. He has never changed the name of the stand to his own because he knows that throughout the Market there are many noble names built on reputations of good service, good product, and hard-working families. "Besides, people think I'm Rolston," says Terry, "or they just call me 'The Chicken Man.'"

JEWISH VENDORS

The city's Jewish immigrants that arrived before the 1950s experienced a short, yet unique, history at the West Side Market. They came from many different places around the world in search of opportunities that they found throughout the Market.

Sarah Klein was a young Jewish widow with two small children when she left Hungary in 1921. She sold stamped linens for embroidery. Morris Cohodas, born in Lithuania and thirteen when he settled in Geneva, was one of the area's first Jewish farmers and vineyardists to sell his fruits and vegetables at the West Side Market. Albert Davis, a Russian Jew, and his wife Bea operated a produce stand for twenty years. Bessie Ross owned Ross' Bakery, selling what was deliciously described as "hand-formed Kaiser rolls [baked] on hearth bricks so they came out crusty, and bagels, thousands of handmade bagels."[2] The bakery was sold in the 1940s at the start of World War II, but Ross remained at the Market and sourced bakery items from local Hungarian, German, and Russian bakeries.

What was unusual about the Jewish vendors at the West Side Market was that they ran stands both inside the market house, in the produce arcade, and out on the curb, like Yetta and Jack Snitzer, who sold fruits and vegetables from a makeshift stand on the sidewalk for thirty years. Yetta Snitzer recalled that whether Czech, Hungarian, Italian, or German, being at the West Side Market was like family. "We all shivered together in the winter and sweated in the summer."[3] For one ethnicity to cross over into many areas of the Market—where the butchers were primarily German and the Italians were the produce peddlers—was a departure from the norm.

Opposite, from top: Produce vendors unloading crates of fresh asparagus, 1950s; Jimmie Marcellino peddles fruit, circa 1955; Charles "Bud" Leu Jr. reaches into the case, circa 1965

Memories

"In 1936, my uncle Sebastian Paradise had a produce stand at the Market. Like him, most of the vendors were Italian and entire families worked the stands. Our family was there, crying out their produce and the prices. When I was eight years old, I asked if I could help. I still remember how excited I was calling out, 'Buy your cucumbers here!' I suspect people were amused because I was selling more cucumbers than anyone. I got paid with a malted from the grocery store in the Market. Those days were so much simpler."

—Rosemary Paradise Cale

"We had our favorite stands to buy from and became friends with those people. We bought pork chops and bacon at Leu Brothers, only two chops at a time and Bud used to say, 'Should we wrap those pork chops for you or would you rather carry them out under your arm?' Made us laugh each time!"

—Ruth Roden

Counterclockwise from top: The Boutrous Brothers, Joe, Tom, and John; Workers at Badstuber's stand weigh a mound of kielbasa, circa 1960
Opposite: Market Commissioner John Pilch and Cleveland Mayor Carl B. Stokes, circa 1970

In 1973, Mayor Ralph Perk's office issued a report about the West Side Market. It provided a snapshot of the Market, including the nature of what stands sold. It read like a grocery list: "...1 potato, onion, watermelon; 10 bakeries; 14 beef; 1 candy; 6 chicken; 2 fish, fresh clams, oysters, eel, octopi, etc.; 3 lamb; 1 Sauer Kraut (*sic*); 10 smoked meats."[4] It also reported that there were 130 merchants and each could trace their origins to one of twenty ethnicities, a list that included German, Hungarian, Slovenian, Polish, and Romanian—the same ones that defined the first generation of vendors at the Market. "American" was also listed, suggesting that there was a new era of vendors who had no connection with the immigrant movement of the past or that those who took over the family business were creating identities beyond their ethnic heritage.

Even as this report was circulating, change was showing itself in the wave of new vendors at the Market. A decade after the Immigration and Nationality Act of 1965 was enacted and opened the doors of the nation and the city of Cleveland, people from the Middle East, Latin America, and Asia began to establish businesses throughout the market. Like the generations before them, the Market was an affordable way to create opportunity and felt a little like home:

"My parents left Lebanon in 1988. I was four years old, war broke out at that time, and my parents wanted a future for me and my sister. They left family and friends behind so we could grow up in a safer place with better educational opportunities. What made my parents decide to buy a stand at the Market back in 1994 was that it made them feel like they were back home in Lebanon dealing with fresh and exotic fruit. My dad, George Harb and my mom, Samia, have always loved to work for themselves and the Market is a great way for that because you are your own boss down there. They like to bring a smile to people's faces by selling them the best fruit available and

introducing customers to new fruit that they haven't even heard of before. What my parents like best about the Market is that it is outdoors and they are their own boss. They have been here for seventeen years. Most of our customers have become either close friends and others have become a part of our Market family by becoming faces that we see on a week-to-week basis."
—Jessy Harb, employee

Meanwhile inside the market house, families like the Badstubers, Visteins, and Checks were turning over their stands to sons, and people like Ed Meister, Irene Dever, and Vince Bertonaschi were starting their first generation businesses.

Outside, curb vendors were no longer permitted to peddle from the street and some of the Italian produce vendor families were leaving, a few moving their businesses to the suburbs and others closing up shop. Arab American immigrants established businesses in the produce arcade. As with generations of vendors before, the Market was still a wonderful, affordable opportunity to be your own boss.

From his stand on the south side of the produce arcade, a young, handsome, and ambitious Tom Boutrous faces hundreds of collective years of experience and history in his competitors. He was only twenty when he bought his first stand at the Market in 2003, a mere babe among a league of veteran produce vendors. A native-born Lebanese American, he recognized a good opportunity in the West Side Market. "It doesn't matter if you're an immigrant or not," he says. "I started Boutrous Brothers without a lot of money."

As the first generation vendor, Boutrous has the benefit of working with his brothers Joe and John, even if he doesn't have the experience of a father or grandfather to teach him the ropes. His Market family and competitors became his mentors and teachers. "If they've been in business at the Market for a long time, they must be doing something right," he says. "So I just watch."

He notices that Emery Bacha makes his customers feel like he cares about them. Paul Chuppa taught him how to handle employees and Jack Gentille passed along the secrets behind a powerful display of produce, "pile it high and mist it often." Chuck Schilla taught him to extend his business by selling to restaurants. And he knows from watching that people like to see the same face smiling at them from behind the counter and the same hands picking and bagging their produce.

The Market remains an icon of Cleveland's multicultural identity. While some vendors are winding down their time at the Market, others are still building their personal histories and new lives.

ⓜemories

Jesse J. Bradley was a well-liked personality at the Market, a friend of bums and bag ladies, vendors, and customers alike. As a dock foreman, Bradley was responsible for the comings and goings of foods and products as they arrived at the Market loading dock. In 1947, when he first started, Bradley was the only African American employed at the Market. He retired in 1985 after thirty-eight years on the job.

AFRICAN AMERICANS AT THE MARKET

For much of the Market's history, Cleveland's African American community was not a big presence, either as customers or vendors. They were more likely to be found at the Central Market, closer to the neighborhoods where they lived and worked. Two exceptions stand out.

In 1970, Thomas Stallworth, a thirty-five-year-old African American was appointed acting commissioner of the Market by then-Mayor Carl B. Stokes.

In 1973, as the Central Market began to deteriorate physically and the number of vendors there shrank, more African Americans shopped the West Side Market. (The Central Market closed in 1988.)

The West Side Market welcomed its first African American vendor in 1990, when Charles Motley opened a European-style pastry stand. Motley sold Danish, muffins, pies, cakes, and large chocolate chip 'hubcap cookies,' so named because of their size. Unfortunately, the stand didn't last long. Today, while there are many African American customers at the Market, there are still no African American vendors.

Sophie Heng: Another World

Sopheap "Sophie" Heng serves Cambodian food from her stand, KIM SE

In 1999, Sopheap "Sophie" Heng was twenty years old when she arrived in Cleveland from Cambodia. "This was another world," she says. "I had no idea what I would do here. I didn't speak English. All I knew about this place was that the people and food were different."

Heng describes the culture that she grew up in as one that limited opportunities for women. "I lived in a small town," she said. "Girls only went to school and home." Married to a boy from her hometown, the culture followed her, and not knowing the language made it harder.

Her first job was in a factory and she spent a little time in the classroom, but it wasn't until she got to the Market that her life changed. She worked behind the counter at Orlando Bakery. "I could practice my English when I was waiting on customers," she says, and from where she stood on market days, she could observe the American culture as well.

"There was so much more freedom and women could do what they liked to do," she observed, "not what someone else told them to do." A few years later, Sophie divorced and opened a tiny corner stand selling her Cambodian cuisine. "I learned so much, like how to do my own banking and I got my license." Her Cambodian customers loved the food as much her American customers, so the business expanded to two stalls. She named her business KIM SE after her family's construction company back home.

As a Cambodian woman what Sophie is doing is unusual, but as part of the Market, she became family, a modern immigrant with dreams, ambitions, and the desire to succeed. Departing from her culture's norm, Sophie wasn't sure how her family would regard her "American life," but her parents told her that what she was doing made them proud. "I'm so happy to be at the Market," says Sophie. "It changed my life."

Memories

"I remember Rita Graewe. We were treated like her nieces and nephews and were expected to help her like family. We had to move her 500-pound pickle barrel so about ten of us kids would have to roll them up to her stand. It would roll over our toes and break them. The old guys just laughed as they took us to the hospital. It was just how we grew up."

—Dean Santner, former employee

"I'm forty now and I started working with my father, Nate Anselmo, when I was seven. It was truly a family business. If I wasn't at school, I was at the Market. No Boy Scouts for me. No summer vacations. I remember hearing other kids talk about Saturday morning cartoons. I never saw them. I did play football in high school. My dad maybe made it to one or two games because Friday and Saturday were his busiest days."

—Tony Anselmo, former employee

GROWING UP AT THE MARKET
Childhood Memories

IN 1957, Chris Sommer Krisak started working as a counter girl at her grandfather Arnold Sommer's stand at the West Side Market, smiling at customers, making small talk, and neatly wrapping their orders of beef, lamb, and veal in butcher paper. "At first, the customers would say, 'Hey, girl,' to get my attention. Then they started calling me 'miss,' followed by, 'lady.' By the time I left, they were calling me 'ma'm.' That's how long I worked at the Market. I could hear my life moving right in front of me."

There was a time in the history of the West Side Market where everyday was "bring your child to work day." There were no day care centers—families took care of their own. While parents worked the family business, they laid their babies and cranky toddlers in beds fashioned out of boxes or crates, and turned their attention to the customers.

"My whole family has been involved in the Market: my grandfather, Ross Posatiere and all his sons, daughters, cousins and their families. The Calabrese and Cionciolo families were a big part of my life. I grew up at the Market.

My first job at seven years old was to sell lemons and my lunch break was taken right there at the stand. It was cold and my Dad put me by the wood-burning stove to keep warm. There was a big flapping canvas curtain tied down to keep the wind and cold air from freezing the produce...and me. My nap was in a wooden banana box stuffed with shredded newspaper. Some times my dad's helper, Tommy Perez, would take me to the playground at the school behind the Market. My childhood was the best ever and I believe the Market became the very fabric of my life."

—Gayle Posatiere, former employee

Clockwise from top: Chris Sommer Krisak and her sister Janice Sommer Arkangel at their grandfather Arnold Sommer's stand, mid-1960s; Anthony "Banjo" Curiale, a "cooler" boy at ten years old, 1933

Vendors would sometimes gently nudge their adorable children into the aisle near the family stand to offer shoppers samples of their cheese or sausage on frilly toothpicks, and unenthused teens were made to dress in costumes that would surely call attention to the family business.

Many of the children who grew up at the Market are now adults, some are vendors and longtime employees themselves, and the memories of their childhood here are unforgettable ones indeed. Long aisles, plentiful nooks and loads of hiding places around the Market provided the ideal playground for vendors' children. By the time many of the children were old enough to say, "May I help you?" and "Thank you," they became vital components of the family work force—minor labor laws or not. It wasn't about work; it was about working as a family: grandparents; aunts and uncles; cousins; mothers, fathers, and siblings. It was a childhood where many perfected communication and problem-solving skills by taking care of customers and learned to make friends with almost anyone. It was also a time where a kid could miss out on a lot.

In 1913, a year after the West Side Market opened, Robert E. Stumpf Sr. opened a stand and began to sell his homemade German sausages there. His first employee was his five-year-old son, Robert Jr. Over the years, Robert Stumpf Jr. would often tell reporters and journalists about the early days of the Market and Stumpf Meats, now Kitchen Maid Meats. "I used to have to stand on boxes to reach the scales. We started at six in the morning and finished at 11 at night,"[5] or that he and his brother, Wolfram "used to take turns sneaking naps under the counter."[6]

Stumpf's story about working at such a tender age is a unique example about growing up at the West Side Market but also a common scenario: children worked in the business, rarely as young as Stumpf, but more often when they were a little older, stronger, and taller. In 1938, the federal government enacted minor labor laws that set the minimum working age at fourteen, a rule that didn't appear to be highly enforced by the Market or by the vendors who needed young muscle and speed to run product up from the cooler.

Families that worked together at the Market took care of one another. It was also about grooming the next generation, the heir apparent, to take over the stand. "I remember the day I was brought into the Market fold," recalls Larry Vistein. "It was my fourteenth birthday and I was camping out in the woods. My brother ran back and broke the news to me that I was going to work at the Market. It was the summer of 1964 and working was not part of my plan. But what your dad said, you did."

While his dad, Larry "Lad" Vistein would take care of the customers, Larry would run up and down from the cooler all day long to keep the case stocked with fresh meat. "I would clean the stands and at the end of the

Karen Curiale Torreiter: At Work by Nine

Friends since childhood, (L-R) Susan Ehrnfelt, Karen Curiale, and Jack Sabolik

Karen Curiale Torreiter was gainfully employed at the Market by the time she was nine. Her father, Anthony "Banjo" Curiale owned the pork stand where she worked; she had grown tall enough to see over the counter and she would work at a highly discounted rate. To outsiders, putting children to work at such an early age might appear callous, but this was how many children of Market vendors grew up. They questioned it little, complained about it in their teens, yet enjoyed the benefits of working with family and the lifelong friendships that resulted.

"Getting up early was my first job," says Karen, "that and giving up every Saturday from doing things with my friends. It was a way of life for us." It was the same way for her father.

Banjo Curiale worked for other vendors in the Market as a cooler boy and for his mother Anna until he inherited her stand in the 1960s. His primary job was working for Ohio Bell; the pork stand at the Market was a side job. This not only took him away from his young family during the week and on Saturdays, too. So Karen and her brother worked at the Market to spend time with their father. "Family stands were worked by family," says Karen. "You didn't hire out; you kept the business in the family."

In 1971, as Karen approached sixteen, Banjo Curiale closed his stand. It could have been the perfect time for the teen to find another job, one that allowed for pajama parties and hanging out with friends on the weekends. Instead she spent the next five years working at Ken Loucka's pork

stand, thirty-one years behind the counter at the Ehrnfelt family's beef stand, and the last four working for Larry Vistein at his beef stand.

Karen said working for her dad earned her a few bucks but the experience paid off in other ways. "Growing up at the Market, I learned to make friends, especially with older people and met a lot of nice people from all over," she says. "Everyone—the customers and the vendors—raised their families together at the Market. A lot of my customers knew me when I was young and when they were young, too. I went to grade school with Tony Pinzone and Diane Dever and still work with them at the Market."

"Do I ever wish I was doing something else?" Karen questions. "Sometimes I feel like I've missed the boat by not working for a big corporation and retiring with a pension but I would have never had the childhood I did, these friendships, and this kind of rich experience—and my dad was so proud of his family being here."

Memories

"As a teenager, I worked at the Market with my family, didn't get paid, took the bus from Strongsville if I missed my ride, and got fired three or four times before I even got out of bed."

—**Becky (Stumpf) Fitch, former employee**

"I started at the Market in 1938. I was ten years old. How does a ten-year-old get a job at the Market? No one paid attention to work permits."

—**Russ Schwark, former vendor**

"I worked fourteen hours and made $2.25. I gave it all to my mom and she'd give me back 25 cents for myself. That's how it was and nobody questioned it."

—**Alvin Stumpf, former employee**

day I would go down and clean the cooler," says Vistein. "Every Saturday, I would break down the saws and clean them. I had $5 or $6 in my pocket from working all day."

Vistein has forty-seven years of experience under his butcher's coat, twenty-nine of those spent working with his father. Other experienced vendors, including Phil Dreyer, Emil Churchin, Larry Koch and Joe Bistricky also took the young Vistein under their wings, teaching him how to succeed at the Market by being a good vendor and a good person.

Working behind the counter had a way of creating family bonds but it could also put kinks in a young social life. Gary "Fougy" Fougerousse's experience working for his dad Lou at the family's beef stand throughout the 1970s and '80s was in his words both "a problem and a pleasure."

"At twelve, I was tall enough to see over the counter. At thirteen, I knew how to use a knife," he says. "My non-Market friends were spending their free time chasing girls and playing baseball. By the time I was in high school, I could break down a hind or forequarter of beef as good as some of the veteran butchers that were my father's friends and competitors," an education that prepared him for taking over the stand in 1982, where he worked until he closed it in 1994. "The problem was I worked every Saturday so I never had a two-day weekend. I was always the last to show up at weekend weddings and celebrations," he recalls. "The pleasure came later in the lifelong friends I made at the Market—Tony Pinzone, Mark and Janet Penttila—and the time I spent with my father."

Frankie Peters was born in 1955 and by the time he was five years old, he was working in the produce arcade with his uncles Frank, Johnny, and Tony Peters, each of whom had a stand. They would stand him next to pile of watermelons and tell him he couldn't leave until they were all gone. "I used to carry melons to the car for people, earning nickel and dime tips."

Above, from top: Joe Jr., Bill, and Joe Hildebrandt Sr. at the family stand, 1954
Opposite, from top: Becky and Terry Leu at the Leu Brothers stand, circa 1965; Dolores Michaels and Mark Fougerousse at the Market's 60th Anniversary

Memories

"I worked with my dad for my lifetime. I remember when my grandmother Rosie DeCaro was here with my dad. I watched my dad's relationships with the customers and they were a lot like my grandmother's."

—Melissa DeCaro Lau, vendor, DeCaro Produce

"Imagine you're fourteen. You had a great time Friday night at a school football game. Then your dad is standing by your bed at 4 AM telling you to get up and go to work. You go to the Market and the first thing you have to do is go into the cold cooler. Then you had to wait on people who didn't want a kid waiting on them: little old ladies with tiny coin purses who would open them up so slowly and painfully count out the exact change. They would make you write down each and every item they bought on a piece of paper along with the prices. You would have to do the math long hand, then they would check your work—and most of them didn't speak English."

—Bill Hildebrandt, former employee

"They were old school guys and tough with us kids," says Peters. "They wouldn't let you leave to go to the bathroom and made us pee in a brown paper bag, a #4, the cheapest kind. At first I just worked Saturdays, then it was also after school and the summers. I would put in seventy hours with no sitting down, for twenty or twenty-five dollars."

Peggy Penttila grew up at the West Side Market, fell in love and married a boss's son, and still works here behind the counter at the Mediterranean Import Store in the northwest corner. When she was fourteen, Penttila's grandmother, Anna Mae Grady, the original "Pickle Lady" at the Market, helped her get a job with the "Cookie Lady," Dolores Michaels, who had a small stand in the corner. Penttila also worked for Irene Dever and Holger Penttila, her father-in-law. The memories she collected as a child visiting her grandmother's stand describe a classic Market childhood:

> "Everyone at the Market was your mom and dad. If you were hungry, someone would feed you, maybe a slice of bologna or a smokie. If you wanted to read a comic book, you would go to Tricsko's Cigar and Magazine stand. If you wanted a hot dog, you would go to Johnny Hot Dog. If you got tired you would crawl under a counter and go to sleep. We took a lot of naps at the Market.
>
> Everyone knew everyone else. We would play tag up and down the aisles and down the stairs and hide-and-seek under the counters. For fun, we would watch the garbage trucks come and empty the dumpsters in back.
>
> We loved to watch the meat cutters cut up the beef. Del Russ would let us watch as he broke down lamb. We would take the parts to school for show and tell—the tongue, liver, hearts, or eyes. It never bothered any of us. If you wanted to take chicken heads in for show and tell, you would go to Kaufmann Poultry.
>
> There is no other place to grow up like the West Side Market!"

Memories

"We used to collect the old wooden cantaloupe boxes and grape boxes from behind the produce stands and sell them to farmers. Elmer Finger used to give us 25 cents for the big boxes and 5 cents for two grape boxes. We would make about $5 or $6 a day!"

—*Paul Chuppa, former employee*

"I cannot forget the scale! As a child I was weighed on it. I do the same with my children. That was a highlight of going to the West Side Market."

—*Joseph Bradley*

"As the kid of a Market family, it was a badge of honor to walk around wearing a white apron. It made you an 'insider.' We would take the strings and wrap them around our waist and tie them in front. As we got older, we couldn't tie them in front anymore."

—*Ed Badstuber, former employee*

The Carlberg girls, left to right, Erica, Narrin, and Eva

Narrin Carlberg: Bring Your Daughters to Work

Narrin Carlberg raised two daughters at her West Side Market stand, Narrin's Spice and Sauce. Her first daughter, Erica, was born in 1998. "I worked on Saturday, was off on Sunday, and delivered her on Monday," says Carlberg. By Friday she was back at her stand that, in addition to the jars of spices; dried beans and grains; and bottled hot sauces with labels like "Ass in Hell Hot Sauce," now featured a precious newborn tucked in a crib on wheels.

"When she slept I covered the crib with a blanket to block out the bright lights," says Carlberg. "The noise didn't bother her." Erica blended into the Market atmosphere. Until she was ready to go to preschool she was there with her mother every Market Day, except Saturdays, when she would stay home with her father.

"When I was low on merchandise she liked to sit in the product case to play," says Carlberg. Although she didn't take any photos, the visual of a child playing in

their own little world as shoppers walked by is delightfully vivid. "I never thought to take any," she says. "It was just my life, as ordinary as making dinner."

As Erica got a little older, keeping her entertained was more challenging, so Carlberg would bring a tricycle Mondays and Wednesdays when it wasn't so busy. Erica would ride all around the building, up and down the avenues meant for shoppers, but for her, brick roads to wherever her imagination would carry her. "She loved going down that ramp at the end by the delivery doors," Carlberg recalls.

When her second daughter was born in 2004, Carlberg raised her the same way and would often have them both behind the counter at the Market. By then, Erica was a talkative little girl comfortable with greeting the customers and "minding" the stand while her mother went to change her baby sister.

GROWING OLD AT THE MARKET
The Golden Years

LONGTIME EMPLOYEE Tim Jeziorski jokes that in the thirty years he's worked at the West Side Market, few vendors and workers retire in the conventional sense, when they one day simply hang up their aprons and walk out the door never to return. "Some never retire, they just work less hours," he's noticed. That was true of Larry Vistein's father, also named Larry or "Laddy."

"My dad worked forty-four years at the Market before retiring in 1993," says Vistein. "When he wanted to have some fun he would come in, wait on customers and then go home. He did that for about five years."

Other vendors did the same: John Bistricky sold his lamb stand to Michael Turczyk, retired, and then went back to work for the new stand owner. After Fritz Graewe took over his grandmother Rita's stand in the late 1980s, she would make random appearances behind the counter and still reached out into the aisles to offer pickles to children. Irene Dever retired in 2000, but still comes back to the stand that carries her name to work with her daughter, Diane. Although the late Larry Calabrese officially and ceremoniously retired from the family produce business around 2000, a business he and his brother ran since 1946, he still helped his nephew Rick buy produce for the stand on Tuesdays and Thursdays.

There were stand owners, like Sam Santner, Bud Kuhn, Lou Weber, Emil Churchin, Phil Dreyer, Steve Tatalick, and Larry Koch, who, once they retired, didn't feel the need to stay connected to the Market, and as one longtime Market employee who knew them all put it, "they were never to be seen again until their funerals."

Unlike a corporation or business, where once someone reaches a certain age retirement was expected or mandatory, the West Side Market has always been a place where many stand owners and employees are in their sixties, even seventies. One well-known produce vendor who reached his eighties and had no plans to leave.

Above, from top: Vendor Eldon Zerby has fellow vendors sign a birthday card, circa 1955; From left, Lou Weber, unidentified worker, 1962

emories

Joseph Tramer's obituary honored him as "The Dean of Produce." One of the original tenants at the Market, he was only semi-retired from the Market at age eighty-nine when he passed away. He was known for a "ruddy countenance and smile, dealing out words of advice and concern to all."

—**Cleveland Press,** *September 9, 1969*

"I've worked here for forty-two years —there has to be some kind of attraction."

—*Tom Nagel, employee*

Joe DeCaro: Making a Good Living the Hard Way

Joe DeCaro may have grown old behind his produce stand in the short corridor at the West Side Market but he never grew tired of the place. Not when Cleveland's winter would make his hands stiff or when the dog days of summer would sap his stamina. Not from lifting heavy boxes of cabbage or sacks of carrots that only got heavier with each passing year and not from pushing a 4-wheeler stacked high with boxes and crates of produce through thick, wet snow. Most octogenarians would have retired from a career as physically demanding as this long ago.

"Retire? I can't retire," said the affable vendor. "What would I do? I'm going to die at the Market." It's how he wanted his life story to end—among his Market family, the vendors he worked with and the shoppers he served for three generations.

DeCaro was diagnosed with brain cancer in the fall of 2011 and shortly thereafter the familiar face that had greeted generations of customers from stands 65 and 67 in the produce arcade was conspicuously missing. It's not how Joe planned to end his tenure at the Market. Customers expected and counted on seeing him, his blue eyes peering over his bifocals, as much as they expected the asparagus, lettuces, and carrots with the fronds still attached that were staples at the stand.

Before DeCaro left and the memory, wit, and twinkle in his eyes faded, he talked about his life at the West Side Market, one that he considered hard but rewarding; challenging yet a blessing.

"My first job was to work for my mother and father—for free! There were no employees, only family. My dad, Augustino DeCaro, was a small man but he could lift a hundred pounds of potatoes like nothing. He hammered into my head that good food is not cheap; cheap food is not good. I have that on a sign at my stand.

The Depression was on and this little stand, only seven-feet wide supported our family. All six of us kids worked here.

Above: Joe DeCaro; Rosie DeCaro

Memories

"It was painful to see Joe DeCaro walking back and forth to the cooler, all bent over, but I think it would have been more painful for him to stay at home. Joe was part of the inventory at the Market. He made it what it is. We can have different mayors and managers and customers change over time, but guys like Joe? That's what made the Market."

—Miklos Szucs, vendor, Dohar Meats

"I know I'm growing old at the Market because all I can lift is a 25-pound, maybe 50-pound, bag of cabbage."

—Joe DeCaro, vendor, DeCaro Produce

SAYING GOODBYE

Mrs. Spagusa (*sic*) owned the stand next to ours. She asked my dad if I could work for her on Saturdays. My dad said 'no' but I could switch on and off with my brother, Sammy. So we did and got paid one dollar each Saturday. I was bound to make $24 a year! Those were also the days my dad would pay 50 cents for a burlap bag of five dozen Golden Bantam sweet corn.

My mother would wear dresses and skirts to work, never pants—ever, and a hat. She was a real storyteller and loved to talk to her customers. That's like me. I can talk about all kinds of stuff—religion, sports, especially about the Buckeyes, family. I can tell jokes and give out plenty of advice, too.

In 1946, I went into the Army and when I was discharged, I went to Ohio State and graduated with a degree in business. I went to work selling construction equipment in 1964 for about twenty years and I traveled a lot.

My mother and sister ran the stand but the Market was still in my blood, so I came back in 1987. My daughter Melissa started working full time with me and she's as good a buyer as I am. She'll be taking over the business. I'm glad about that because that doesn't happen that much here anymore.

Was this a hard way to make a living? Yes. But was it a good way to make a living? Yes, it was."

Joe DeCaro passed away on May 3, 2012. He didn't live to enjoy the Market's Centennial celebration, where his celebrity as the oldest vendor and one of the most respected and loved would certainly have been recognized, but he was there long enough to be considered a legend.

Some of his fellow vendors and faithful customers call him an icon, others said he was a fixture at the Market. There may never be a consensus on what to call him, but everyone would agree that Joe DeCaro was the Market.

The Capone family opened a produce stand at the Market in 1912 and Mike Capone was the last of five boys in his large Italian family to run it. As his wife Marie tells it, Mike closed the stand in 1940, then enlisted in the United States Air Force, followed by thirty-one years with the Cleveland Transit Authority.

In the late sixties, Mike became quite ill and for a few years struggled with serious health issues. Marie vividly remembers waking on a Saturday morning at 4 AM and realizing Mike was not in the house.

"I couldn't find him anywhere," she said. "I had no idea where he may have gone at that time of morning." About an hour later, still long before the sun came up, the phone rang and it was Mike. "Where the hell are you?" she asked, every bit as relieved as well as concerned. "I came to visit my buddies at the West Side Market," said Mike, who was already on his second cup of coffee.

A week later, Mike passed away, but as Marie remembers, not without saying goodbye to his family at the West Side Market.

Above: Vendor Joe DeCaro takes produce back to the cooler, September 29, 2010

THE GREAT DIVIDE
Working Together Yet Separately

THERE'S A BRICK-PAVED alley about thirty feet wide that runs between the West Side Market house and the produce arcade. It starts at W. 25th and stretches to the back of the building, where it opens into the loading dock area off Lorain Avenue. This alley has always stood between those who make their living inside the building—the butchers, fish purveyors, bakers, and cheesemongers, and those who peddle fruits and vegetables outdoors. Ask anyone of them what has divided them over the past hundred years and most will say it's not just the alley.

Market vendors, past and present, recognize that two very distinct factions make up the whole of the West Side Market—those who worked indoors and those who worked outdoors. They've gone about their business, rarely mixing or mingling socially during business hours or away from the Market. It's not about money or control, a long-held grudge, prejudice, or a slow-simmering feud. When pressed to admit to the reasons, most will say that it's just the way it's always been.

Before the West Side Market was built, the neighborhood shopped the Pearl Street Market, an unsheltered open space where farmers, merchants, and hucksters gathered to sell their product. Rules, regulations, and codes of conduct were either non-existent or difficult to maintain. It didn't matter if the merchant was a skilled sausage maker or peddled root vegetables, the open market space was a great equalizer and everyone endured the same working conditions. No one vendor suffered or benefited more than the next.

In 1868, when a one-story shed was built to provide shelter from the weather, vendors of all types and social classes continued to hawk their wares side by side, subject to the same working conditions and challenges. The construction of the West Side Market changed this—for some. While the building created a better working and shopping environment, it also generated a division between the whole of the Market vendors.

Above, from top: The back of the produce arcade at the end of the day, 1940s; The Market during the first snow of the season, 1972
Opposite, from top: Original merchants pose for photo during 50th anniversary, 1967; Produce vendors pose outside arcade during 50th anniversary celebration

In the early days, status at the West Side Market was greatly influenced by who worked inside and who didn't. The bakers and the butchers, mostly German, and dairy vendors, largely Northern Europeans, were skilled tradesman and enjoyed a higher social standing in this country. As the anchor tenants at the Market, they served customers and provided a steady revenue stream year-round.

The outside vendors were a mix of Italian immigrants, poor and less educated, and regional farmers who brought their harvest to market. Before it became common practice to ship produce from one part of the country to another, the seasonal availability of fruits and vegetables meant that these vendors didn't always have product to bring to market. Eventually, the Italians dominated the outside, acting as the middlemen and buying from local growers and distributors that imported produce from all over the world.

Before he became the supervisor/manager of the West Side Market in 1986, George Bradac owned a meat stand at Cleveland's Central Market for twenty years, where all the vendors conducted business under one roof. Good or bad, everyone shared the same working environment. Little, if any, animosity, jealousy, or hard feelings existed among vendors based on what they sold or where their stand was located. But at the West Side Market, he recognized that things were different.

"There were two merchants associations—one for the produce vendors and one for vendors inside the building and that was unusual," says Bradac. "The city said that they didn't want to deal with two entities and only wanted to hear one voice from the vendors when it came to leases and matters of the Market." As a result, it was probably one of the first times in the history of the Market that both groups worked together.

Bradac commented that even as far back as the 1930s, the outdoor vendors were treated differently. "They were not allowed in the basement where the coolers were while the inside vendors were free to go down there anytime," he recalls. "The produce vendors handed a claim ticket to city workers employed at the Market who would go down and bring up their produce. Back then, the produce vendors kept all their product in a massive room. They didn't have separate lockers like the other vendors did."

Ultimately what most produce vendors felt, said Bradac, was that working outside was a much tougher way to make a living at the Market. Inside there was pageantry to be enjoyed—holiday decorations, live music, and the architecture that reminded all of the grandeur of the building. Outside, the contrast was dramatic.

"There was no electricity, no heat, just canvas awnings to break the wind," says Bradac. Inside the vendors and their products were protected from a harsh winter, hard downpours, strong winds, and blistering heat. Outside, the vendors fired up coal and oil stoves to keep warm and sparks from the stoves often ignited awnings, crates, and boxes, creating chaotic moments in front of the customers. Inside, permanent display cases allowed for meticulous arrangement of meats, cheeses, and breads. Outside vendors scrambled to keep their delicate produce from freezing in the winter.

Bradac also recalls that it was rare to settle fights and disputes among the inside vendors, but outside, disagreements often turned into fights—usually over "stealing" customers or encroaching on a neighboring vendor's space. "Inside, your competitor might be a few stands over," he says, "but outside lots of vendors were selling the same fruit and vegetables next to one another and competition was more aggressive."

Curb vendors added another layer to the gap that already existed between the indoor and outdoor Market vendors. At public markets throughout the world, street hawkers were a vibrant part of atmosphere, but the reality was that they were considered a lower class of merchants—and that was true at the West Side Market, too.

Michael and Roseann DiBlasio at the fruit stand inside the arcade

Memories

"I'm not sure what it was. On the inside we would have price wars but generally we got along very well. There was always animosity between the inside and outside tenants. We never got along. It's just always been that way. We had separate merchants associations, too."

—**John Rolston, former vendor**

"Did you ever get up at 4 AM to push a 2-wheeler full of produce through four inches of snow? These are the nightmares I still have. They didn't have to do that inside the Market."

—**Barry Neer, former vendor**

"Winters outside at the Market were terrible. We had to come and shovel the stands out sometimes. You would always have a salamander [stove] and some kind oil for it. Those fires were very dangerous."

—**Mary Ann Anselmo, former vendor**

When the covered arcade was built in 1914, the Market tried to get the curb vendors off the sidewalks, moving them to the old Pearl Street Market building during the construction. It's not certain how many moved back to the old building, but those who did not continued to set up shop along Lorain Avenue and W. 25th Streets as far as Chatham Avenue and in the alleyways around the Market, usually on Fridays and Saturdays. By 1919, these truck farmers and middlemen were required to buy yearly permits to set up on the sidewalk. While the vendors who had stands in the arcade were putting out awning fires, the curb vendors dealt with bad weather and dangerous street traffic. Heavy rains would create pools and rivers that were obstacles for the customers. It wasn't unusual for an entire makeshift stand to catch fire, threatening sellers ability to continue doing business on the street.

Roseann Anselmo DiBlasio's family has a long history at the Market. Her father John Anselmo and his brothers all had produce businesses that started on the street and eventually moved into the arcade. As a young girl, she worked for the family on the sidewalk and as an adult, Roseann and her husband Mike had their own stand on the curb in the early to mid-sixties. She recalls how difficult it was:

> **"Everyone's trucks were lined up on the sidewalks and they each had designated times to load and unload. We were right up against the curb. There was a yellow line behind us about four feet, not much, but within that boundary you could do what you wanted, but it was right up against the road. You had to be really careful because the back of your stand was the street and there was a lot of traffic.**

Above, from top: Curb vendors along sidewalks around the Market, circa 1965; From left, produce vendors Chuck Schilla Jr., John Anselmo Sr., and Pete Randzaao

Memories

"We always assumed that the guys inside had it much easier. We had canvas, kerosene, and salamanders. On the inside, they would pull up to the dock and walk into the Market. We struggled more. That was our perception that we worked harder. It was one market with two kinds of businesses and we didn't understand what each other did."

—**Dino Gentille, former vendor**

"If I went inside the Market (building) ten times in my life, I would be surprised. My head was outside at my stand."

—**Larry Calabrese, former vendor**

"Yeah, the Italians used to have a lot of fights at the Market. We all fought. 'Here's my stand, and here's your stand.' If your product was even an inch over the line, you could count on a fight."

—**Paul Chuppa, former employee**

Anthony DiFranco: The Way I Heard it…

Anthony DiFranco was the fourth generation of the Schilla and DiFranco families to sell produce at the West Side Market. Around the dining room table at family dinners, the talk was often about the Market and the differences, distance, and disputes between the indoor and outdoor vendors.

"My grandfather would tell me that the outside vendors never felt they had a say in what was going on at the Market while the inside vendors had the commissioner's and the Mayor's ear," recalls DiFranco. "Both my grandfather and uncle served as presidents of the outdoor vendors association so they saw what was happening."

"Maybe it was because the people on the outside were more transient and possibly less educated," says DiFranco. "Inside it seems they all had either a high school or college education and knew more about running a business. But if you're talking about skills, my grandfather could always spot the best fruits and vegetables for his customers."

As a child working at the Market, it appeared to DiFranco that everyone was friends, talked to one another, and still bought from each other. "My father would send me inside to shop for milk and eggs, I would tell them who I was related to and they would treat us very well." What was happening between the vendors, DiFranco sums up, was just the business side of the Market, and not personal.

Former produce vendor Tony DiFranco and his son, Anthony, circa 1975

We were out there all year round. In the winter, it was hell! We would come home and my mother would put Avon cream on our cheeks because our skin was so cold and chapped. When my dad had to keep the tomatoes warm, he would bring them home on the truck. We would unload them, take them into the basement, and cover them with a blanket. The next morning, we would have to take them back to the Market and do the whole thing over again.

On the sidewalk, we had nothing to call our own. When you worked on the sidewalk, you ceased to exist until the next market day."

By 1967, the number of curb vendors had dwindled and soon disappeared. More than thirty years would pass before the outdoor vendors would benefit from the completion of the long-awaited Millennium Project of 2001, which enclosed the arcade with retractable glass doors and delivered electricity and overhead heating, all which greatly improved the working conditions for produce vendors and tightened rent discrepancies among all the stands.

The changes have done little to close the gap between the West Side Market vendors, though. Tradition, ritual, or an unconscious continuation of the way it has been for a hundred years—the two worlds are part of the same Market universe, yet revolve separately.

OPPORTUNITY KNOCKS
Getting Down to Business

THE PROCESS OF becoming a vendor at the West Side Market has remained the same for many years. It starts with an application to occupy a vacant stand, followed by meetings with the West Side Market's tenants association, approval by City Hall, securing all the appropriate licenses, signing the papers, and finally opening for business. It seems a neat, tidy, and a fairly cut-and-dry procedure. It is the details and personal histories, rarely part of the paperwork, that make the stories special.

For John Rolston, "The Chicken King," and former poultry vendor at the West Side Market, the opportunity to become a vendor came around 1970, when his boss Adolph Sebek came in one day and tossed him the keys to the "store." It's a great story that is very telling about how opportunities to become part of Market history arrive.

Rolston spent twenty years working for Sebek, a poultry vendor he describes as a "tough old Bohemian." He started as his cooler boy, worked up to waiting on customers and finally became the stand manager. One morning, Sebek came into the Market, threw his keys on the counter and said to Rolston, "I'm going to Florida," and he didn't mean on vacation. He told Rolston to take care of the stand. For three years, Rolston tended to the details of the business and sent weekly statements to his boss.

At that time, there was a rule that stand owners had to be actively involved with their business. Tom Stallworth, then-commissioner of the Market, enforced the rule and in Sebek's absence, asked Rolston if he would be interested in the opportunity to take over the stand. Rolston said yes and broke the news to the boss. The ruling didn't sit well with Sebek, who came back to Ohio with a lawsuit for the city of Cleveland and Rolston. "It wasn't because he was angry with me," said Rolston. "His stand was taken away without his permission and my name happened to be the one to replace his."

Months of haggling, discussion, and arguments ensued and stretched into the winter months. Finally, Sebek told Rolston it was too cold in Cleveland and he wanted to go back to Florida. "So I asked him to just sell me the business and end this," says Rolston. "Mr. Sebek agreed and asked me to give him a ride to his lawyer to close the deal."

Rolston paid Sebek $1,200 for the business, which was largely a payment for the goodwill Sebek had built with his customers. "You were not allowed to sell the stand," explains Rolston. "You had a lease with the city and renewed every year as long as you didn't do anything wrong. The city owned the stand and the counters. We owned nothing but the scales so it made it difficult to get a loan."

Until the day Sebek died the two remained good friends. Long before all the legal threads became tangled, Sebek loaned Rolston $1,200 for a down payment on a house for his growing family. "Mr. Sebek told me to take it out of the week's receipts and just put a note in the cash drawer saying that I was borrowing the money," says Rolston. At Christmas time, Rolston received a greeting card from Sebek that included the promissory note, torn in half,

Above, from top: The Chicken King, John Rolston gathers parsley to dress up his case; The Sebek stand

forgiving the loan. Coincidentally, a few months later Rolston paid him the same amount to buy the business.

Not all opportunities include a smooth transition to business ownership at the Market. When opportunity knocked for Ed Meister, owner of Meister Dairy, it arrived with a "trial by fire" learning experience:

> "I was selling calculators after graduating from college in the 1970s. It was during a time when Japan began importing calculators that sold for half of what I could. So to make some extra money, I would deliver eggs from my parent's egg farm to Clayton Kuchle at the West Side Market. He had an egg and cheese stand. Kuchle was slowing down and getting ready to retire—he wanted to sell and I wanted to buy. So I took over the stand on Thanksgiving week in 1977. Kuchle agreed to stay on with me for a week to show me the ropes. On that first day, he worked with me for a few hours, said he had to go to the bank and never came back. I guess he was really ready to call it quits. That was my introduction to being a stand owner."

Kuchle may have picked a bad time to retire for Meister's benefit, but Rita Johnston, a longtime employee at the stand, stayed with the new stand owner for his first five years as his mentor in the egg and cheese trade.

There have also been many occasions where vendors ready to retire want to leave the business to a son, daughter, or a loyal employee. The administrative hoops to jump through are basically the same and the transition is typically uncomplicated. Longtime vendors have spent their lifetime building a following of devoted customers, earning their trust and food dollars, and the opportunity to continue doing business under the family name, especially when the new owner is not a blood relation, is of great value and an even greater privilege.

Michael Turczyk bought his stand from his former boss, John Bistricky, who specialized in lamb, sheep, and goat. Turczyk or "Turk" as he's always called by coworkers, started at the Market when he was twelve as a cooler boy for a number of vendors until Bistricky hired him in 2000.

"I never touched lamb before I met him," confesses Turk. "He taught me everything I know about cutting." Bistricky sold the business to the young Turk in 2007, along with his verbal permission to use the family name on the stand for a few additional years. "When you buy a business at the Market, the majority of what you're paying for is the clientele, not the machinery or equipment," says Turczyk. "The Bistricky name was here for fifty-four years and the customers associate that name with good lamb."

The stand at the Market called Edward Badstuber & Sons is actually owned by Matt Minyard, neither a Badstuber or a son, but at one time an employee. "I am a very old-fashioned person," says Minyard. "I was raised to do a good job and if something ain't broke, why fix it." So the Badstuber name, a familiar one to four generations of customers, lives on.

Above, from top: Michael Turczyk; Clayton Kuchle, on the far right, at his egg and cheese stand

Tim Ducu: In the Land of Milk and Honey

Fresh from Yugoslavia, the West Side Market reminded Tim Ducu's family of their homeland. "The noise and the crowds were just like home," he says. "I remember the first time I walked inside the Market. It reminded me of a cathedral. I look up and I remember how it gave me shivers." He recalls a desperate life in Yugoslavia, one that was very poor and where food was scarce. "Then I come here to America, the land of milk and honey, and I end up at the West Side Market surrounded by such abundance," he says. "It was like a dream."

The family used to buy kielbasa from Louie Sliwa, who took one look at the big, strong fourteen-year-old son of a blacksmith and offered him a job. "It was a piece of cake," says Ducu. "I could lift a 100-pound box of meat, no problem."

Ducu worked at the Market for five years alongside Hungarian and Croatian sausage makers who shared their craft with him. "When I was seventeen, I begged my father to sign for me so I could get my own stand," he says. "I had saved enough money, but he wouldn't do it." So Ducu left the Market in 1976.

"You could say I grew up here, not just age wise but in the sense of becoming responsible," says Ducu. "It was kind of like being in the service."

Over the next twenty-five years, he dabbled in professional wrestling, worked building maintenance, and got married. On New Year's Eve 2007, Ducu was shopping at the Market for plantains for his Puerto Rican in-laws and struck up a conversation with one of the stand owners. Her husband was sick, she couldn't manage the stand anymore, and was looking for someone to buy the business. How about Ducu?

He revisited the idea of owning a stand, prayed about it, went to his pastor for counseling, and eight days later signed a contract at the Market. Today there are two Ramos stands, named after his late father-in-law, one for unusual produce with an international selection of hot peppers and Caribbean root vegetables and another for conventional and organic produce.

"I give all my customers a smile and a kind word with their bags," says Ducu, still strong and a bit bigger. "I tell them if you want a good meal, ask a fat man for advice. I sell tomatillos and I explain how to make green salsa. How 'bout that for a kid from Yugoslavia?"

 Memories

"Mr. Sebek was the only man I ever knew who came to work in a suit, white shirt, and a tie," recalls John Rolston. "He would put his apron over them and wait on his customers." Although no spring chicken himself and Adolph Sebek is long gone, Rolston still refers to his former boss as "Mister."

"I had lost my job at forty-six. I prayed to God for some direction. I put my application in for a stand at the Market to make and sell the same Syrian foods I grew up with. Then I prayed to God some more. I went to lunch with my aunt one day and was crying about what I'm going to do. We didn't talk about money. A few weeks later, my aunt Helen, God bless her, gave me $2,000 to start the business. When I opened that envelope, I had a 'gasp' moment!"

—Judy Khoury, vendor, Judy's Oasis

Tony Pinzone: A Gift from Lena

Tony Pinzone has a long list of people to thank for providing him opportunities that helped shape his future at the West Side Market, starting with his mother, Lena. In the summer of 1970, Lena took her thirteen-year-old son down to his Uncle Tony Lupica's fruit stand at the Market to "learn how to work." A year later, Barry Neer hired Tony to work his fruit stand. He worked sixty-five hours that first week and made $35. Every month Tony would give Lena money to cover his tuition at St. Edward High School. He worked at the Market throughout high school, moving indoors to work as a cooler boy at Walter Ehrnfelt's beef stand. By the time he graduated, Tony had paid for his own education.

After high school, Tony worked for Arnold Fernengel, a veteran butcher at the Market. Tony and Fernengel's son, Gordon, became close friends and friendly competitors in the cooler, creating spontaneous contests like who could tie a roast the fastest to make it a showpiece for the meat case or who could break down a 100-pound beef round (from the hind quarter) the quickest.

In 1976, Larry Augustine, a beef vendor, was ready to sell his stand and Tony wanted to buy it. Nineteen was pretty young to own a business, but the Market manager at the time looked the other way and said, "Let's keep that to ourselves."

The selling price of the business was four thousand dollars, which was coincidently exactly how much Lena handed Tony. His mother had put aside the tuition money and gave it back to him. At nineteen, he was the boss.

Tony Pinzone, butcher and owner of Pinzone Meats

"I'm always the last at my stand to get paid," says Pinzone, "but I'm one of the luckiest guys in the Market because of who I worked for." He credits Ehrnfelt for teaching him about production and volume; Fernengel for lessons about presentation and pride in the product; and Fritz Maurath, another employer, for teaching him to keep an eye on the bottom line. "I have a lot of admiration for the people who taught me about running a business at the Market," says Tony. "Each one was so instrumental in my success." But it really all started with Lena, who knew that before success comes opportunity.

Memories

"When I was sixteen, Walter Ehrnfelt let me drive his new van over to the Central Market to pick up something from another vendor. When I was backing into the parking spot, I broke the tail light. The van had two hundred miles on it so I had to fess up. He said, 'So? Go fix it!' Now if I had dropped a steak on the floor—well, that was a different story."

—Tony Pinzone, vendor, Pinzone Meats

"When I was about twelve years old, I had a chance to work at the West Side Market. I worked on Saturday helping unload the truck, washing the produce, and setting up the display so it looked the best. I would receive 25 cents and a thank you to boot! I would go across the street to the RB Baking Company and buy a bag of broken cookies for 10 cents, watch a movie with cartoons for 10 cents, and with 5 cents left over, I would buy an ice cream cone…3 cents for a single scoop, 5 cents for a double!"

—Robert Smith Sr., former employee

The West Side Market was also a lure to kids in the neighborhood, presenting opportunities to make some money, maybe only a quarter or a buck or two, that they would take home to mother or spend on treats and indulgences. One of the easiest jobs to get was in the produce arcade:

> "My parents and nine children lived on the west side from 1930 to 1950, a ten-minute walk from the Market. We were poor, so to help my mom with food and bills, I would get up on Saturday morning at 5 AM and walk to the Market with a friend looking for work. One vendor would give us a job shelling peas and paid us five cents a quart. It wasn't much but we were happy."
> —Margaret Prexta

Grant Lance has been working at the Market ever since his mother shoved him down the right career path when he was twelve. "We lived in the neighborhood and my parents shopped at the Market," says Lance. "We were a big family of eight and the kids took turns going with them to help carry bags." On one visit, George Lombardi, who had a deli counter, asked Lance if he wanted to work for him. Before Lance could say anything, his mother said, "He'll be here Monday." Two years later, Lance went to work at Gordon Fernengel's beef and pork stand and when he turned twenty-two, he purchased his own beef stand.

There are those who can recall their first opportunity to work at the Market, even if it didn't lead to a career:

> "In the summer of 1956, I was twelve years old. I decided to get a job to contribute to our family of seven's income. The only place I could think of getting a job was at the [West Side] Market. My plan was to start at one end of the produce arcade and go to the other end asking, 'Mister, do you need any help?' About half way through I landed my first job with Jack and Merl Rini, who sold a variety of fruit at a two-stand set up. No terms of employment were discussed.
>
> During the summer I worked at the stand full time and earned $30 a week, but the best part of my compensation was that at the end of the week, Jack would fill shopping bags with as much fruit as I could carry home.
>
> One thing I regret not doing back then was keeping a copy of the crate labels on the boxes that the fruit was packaged in. The artwork from such far away places as California and Florida was very interesting and creative to a twelve-year-old."
> —Tom Tindira, former employee

> "I remember 'working' as a twelve-year-old at the West Side Market. My mom had a very small stand in the southwest corner of the Market. We sold cookies like Oreos, Lorna Doones, and chocolate-covered marshmallow coolies, broken pretzels at 10 cents a pound, and bulk potato chips made by the Ross Pretzel and Cone Company on Lorain Avenue."
> —Carol Rader, former employee

Above, from top: A customer stops for a photo with (L to R) vendors Wayne Dido, Fred Weigel, Jay and Val Check, early 1960s; Charles "Bud" Leu Jr. at the Leu Brothers stand

IT'S IN OUR BLOOD
Coming Home

ANYONE WHO WORKS at the West Side Market knows this to be true: It's cold in the winter and hot in the summer. The tiled floors and concrete walks can take a toll on the feet and knees. An eight-hour workday is actually ten or more hours. Saturdays are not a part of the weekend but the work week. There's no shortage of manual labor, as there's always a heavy box to lift, a quarter of beef to wrangle, or carts laden with produce to push or pull. Benefits and bonuses are not always delivered in the form of a check but more often as a genuine "thank yous" when customers are handed their orders.

Despite the hard and less-than-cushy work conditions, there are many vendors and workers who have been at the Market for twenty-five, thirty or even forty years. Some are the second, third, or fourth generations of Market families to inherit the business like Steve Check, Ricky Calabrese, and Larry Vistein. Others like Mary Pell, Tom Nagel, and Orlando Rivera, have worked at the Market either full time or on Saturdays only, as they keep a full-time job outside the Market. Asked what keeps them here, most will use the common and oft repeated catchphrase in the Market: "It's in our blood."

When Joanne Lewis interviewed West Side Market vendors in 1979 and 1980 for her book *To Market, To Market,* she noticed that many of the merchants she spoke with used those exact words: "It's in our blood." "It's a refrain I heard over and over," says Lewis. "Many of the kids are educated professionals but they still come back to take over the family business. People there have a genuine passion for the Market."

> A day at the West Side Market is a very long day indeed, beginning at 4 AM and ending as late as 7 PM, and now after (Nate) Anselmo has finished a day hawking produce at his stall, he goes home only to find the market and its noise invades his sleep. "I can't help it," he says, "This place is in my blood."
> —*Plain Dealer,* July 8, 1974

> "This place was my family's life. It's my life. I think I could do anything I want but I love what I'm doing here. The Market—it just gets in your blood."
> —Terry Leu, vendor, Rolston Poultry

> "This is a lively job. At times, it's frustrating because I work hard and I give up part of my weekend. I've never had a full weekend off. That's my way of life but it's in my blood."
> —Karen Curiale Torreiter, employee

Tim Jeziorski: It's a Wonderful Life

"I was slicing bacon thirty years ago," says Tim Jeziorski, "and here I am today—slicing bacon." Jeziorski was fifteen in 1981 when he started working at the West Side Market as a cooler boy for lunch meat vendor Lou Weber. Young, strong, and eager to please, Jeziorski was hired away over the next seven years by other vendors, including Steve Check, Scott Leu at Hartman's, and Charlie Maurath. Then, at twenty-five, he snagged a 9 to 5 job at Jones Day, Cleveland's prestigious law firm, in support services.

"I had four weeks vacation, ten sick days, paid holidays, steady hours, and a regular office job in a nice, clean, and safe environment," says Jeziorski, "and it was the first time in a long time I had Saturdays off." As good as it sounded, it seemed odd to him to have that kind of time on his hands, so he used his day off to work for D. W. Whitaker Meats, cutting and selling pork and chicken. "I even used my vacation days to work at the Market," he confesses.

After eighteen years at the prestigious firm with all its perks, security, and benefits, Jeziorski had enough of the good life. He quit and returned to the Market. "I gave it all up to work fifty or more hours a week in a place that has leaky faucets, is freezing in the winter, hot in the summer, and I have to work every Saturday," he says. "I've never looked back." Today, he's behind the lunch meat counter at D. W. Whitaker.

Not everyone can last at the Market. "We've had some people here for one day and realize that this is hard work," says Jeziorski, "I had a big kid, a hockey player, working with me a while back. After one day on the job, I heard him complain about how tough this job is. I was surprised and reminded him playing hockey was tough, too, but he said, 'Not like this!'"

The Market preaches hard work but a spirit of community also exists that might not be found in the corporate world, where there are ladders to climb and a hierarchy of colleagues. "When people quit one stand to move to another it might be for money or just a change of scenery," says Jeziorski. Chances are the boss is a friend, too. "There's not a day that goes by where I don't see a stand owner cleaning the stand, cutting meat, or taking out the garbage," says Jeziorski. "You never hear someone say, 'That's not my job.'"

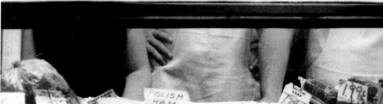

Left to right, Janine Peters, Tim Jeziorski, Lou Weber, Mike Hogan, 1982

Every day, Jeziorski says he feels like he's accomplished something at work and he constantly learns from those on the other side of the counter. It could be about cooking from his regular Saturday customer, a caterer, who shares with Jeziorski how he'll prepare the meats he's buying that day. Or it could be about someone's life, like the elderly German woman who arrives at 7:20 AM on the dot and who has over the years shared snippets of her life history, including living through WWII and riding her motorcycle through Austria. Then again, it could also be about human nature.

"In this place, you can go from a guy who pays for his order with the change in his pocket, his last nickel, and wearing the same coat he has worn since you've worked there to people who always have thick stacks of cash and are dressed to the nines," describes Jeziorski. "It's from one end of the spectrum to the other, but when they stand together on the other side of the counter, they all seem to fit and belong together. They'll start talking with each other about what they are cooking that day. The market is a great equalizer and it's always very interesting."

What's tied Jeziorski to the Market for more than thirty years are the vendors and customers he sees regularly. "We've grown up and grown older together at the Market," he says, "and you know, that kind of stuff makes this place get in your blood."

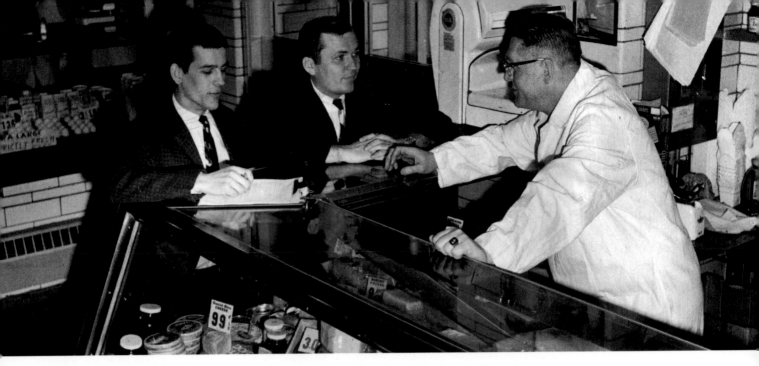

DAIRY SCHOOLED

Walter Simmelink Jr. was a second-generation Market vendor. He earned a bachelor of science degree in dairy technology from Iowa State University, where he scored firsts in butter and cheese making during his sophomore and junior years. After graduating in 1943 and serving in the Army, he returned to the only job he had known since he was a young boy—the dairy stand at the West Side Market that carried the family name.

When his father suffered a stroke in 1964, Walter Jr. took over the business. Like his father, he had dedicated customers, the respect of his fellow vendors—who appointed him president of the West Side Market Merchants Association, and was an excellent businessman. When business at the Market slumped in the late 1940s, he began knocking on doors around Cleveland to capture some pretty impressive corporate accounts: United Airline, Heck's Restaurant, the Theatrical Grill, Ohio Bell, the Cleveland Yacht Club, and a handful of local country clubs.

WEST SIDE MARKET UNIVERSITY
Learning About Life on the Job

LARRY VISTEIN of Vistein Meats holds a bachelor's degree in physical anthropology from Kent State University. He jokes that he's quite adept at cutting a porterhouse from a short loin of beef because his formal education was all about "bones."

Two aisles over, Don Whitaker trims fat from a rolled and stuffed pork roast and nimbly trusses it with butcher's twine. It's a skill he perfected working at the Market during the day, while going to Cleveland State University at night to earn his degree in accounting.

"I would go to class at night smelling like the Market," he says. "After I graduated, I passed up working for an accounting firm to come back to the Market. I bought the pork stand in 1990. Then I hired an accountant. Then I bought a poultry stand and twenty years later a lunch meat stand."

Out in the produce arcade, Emery Bacha's degree in marketing served him a short time in another career, but for more than thirty years in managing his family's business at the West Side Market. "Some people think that I just sell carrots and lettuce," he says, "but there's more to it if I want to run my business well and make a decent living."

Walk down the aisles of the West Side Market and casually poll the men and women behind the counters about the college degrees they hold. The same people who can break down whole chickens in thirty seconds, advise on how to put together a cheese board, and explain how to cook kale or remove the seeds from pomegranates may also have studied literature, nursing, and education—there has even been an attorney or two that have made a career out of the Market.

Most will agree that some of the most valuable lessons and education they received came from WSMU—West Side Market University. The classrooms are behind the counters and stands, in the cooler, and up and down the aisles. The "professors" are grandparents, parents, aunts and uncles, tough bosses, and coworkers who offer a no-frills education about minding one's manners, treating the customer right, being honest and fair, and learning how to communicate with everyone.

Tony Anselmo: Graduate of WSMU

"I like to tell people I went to WSMU," says Tony Anselmo. "I list it under education on my Facebook page! I should get t-shirts made!" The third generation of the Anselmo family to be in the produce business, Tony owns Premier Produce, a wholesale distributor to Cleveland's finest restaurants. He was schooled and groomed for his career at the West Side Market, where his professors were his extended family who started as curb vendors.

Tony's father was Nate. "Nate the Knife, because he cut things up and let people taste it," says Tony. "He'd slice a tomato, put it on a plate with a little salt, and encourage shoppers to try it. Nobody else did that then."

As a kid, Tony watched his father work and noticed that he did things differently than everybody else around them. "He was the first to start selling uncommon things—tomatoes on the vine, mesclun mix, portabella and shiitake mushrooms, and he became known for that," says Tony. "He'd hand out strawberries to the kids. He set up beautiful displays. He had a real eye for color and was one of the first at the Market to deliver to restaurants."

In Tony's eyes, Nate always bought the best produce and let the people touch and pick their own stuff, a practice that many vendors didn't embrace in the produce arcade. "It really annoyed the other vendors," recalls Tony. "He was also honest. If something wasn't going to last, he told the customers to use it right away—and he always responded to complaints."

Nate Anselmo did a brisk business and Tony felt it. "I can't tell you how many trips we had to make up and down from the cooler every market day," recalls Tony. "My feet used to hurt at the end of the day but my dad had a saying—'If you have got time to lean, you got time to clean.'"

Tony credits his father with delivering valuable lessons about hard work and competition in the marketplace and teaching by example. "He was a hawker and a real charmer," recalls Tony. "Whenever the news media came to the Market, he was always the person that got the coverage. He was on stage and he knew how to work the crowd."

The produce arcade was often a cold, drafty, and uncomfortable classroom, hard on a kid. "I spent much of my life there," says Tony. "I didn't always like it but looking back now, I wouldn't change a thing."

Opposite: Walter Simmelink Jr., far right, holds an over the counter meeting
Clockwise from top: Son and father, Tony and Nate Anselmo, 1970s; Irene Dever and Ed Badstuber

CUSTOMER COURTESY 101

While the Market was the perfect classroom for teaching a skill like meat cutting, baking, and more, it was also a classroom for learning about customer service. The "teachers" were never afraid of letting their students know when they were in danger of failing.

Before she owned her own stand in 1971, Irene Dever worked for Ed Badstuber, waiting on customers and slicing lunch meat. One of her most memorable lessons in customer service came directly from Badstuber on a busy Saturday afternoon:

"We used to have this little old man who came to the stand on a weekly basis. He never said a word but just used his hand to point to what he wanted in the case, held up a finger for one pound, a slashing motion that meant it should be cut and would show with his fingers how thick or thin he would want it cut. One Saturday, I just couldn't take his silence anymore, so I impatiently asked, 'Why don't you talk? Can't you just tell me what you want?' Ed heard that and picked me up off my feet and carried me to the back of the stand, sat me on the work table, and told me in no uncertain terms to never, ever speak to a customer like that again."

Neil Tramer: Like Father, Like Son

"I am successful beyond my wildest dreams," says Neil Tramer, "and I attribute the skills I learned to the West Side Market." Accountant and partner in the Beachwood firm Tramer, Shore, and Swick, CPAs, and a graduate of Case Western Reserve University School of Law, Neil's Market pedigree represents the same value, sentiment, and hard work as any venerable degree he frames and hangs in his office.

Neil's grandfather Joseph Tramer was one of the original merchants. A Czechoslovakian immigrant, Joseph and his brother Ben arrived in 1895 as teenagers and made a living peddling produce at the Pearl Street Market.

Joseph spent his lifetime at the Market, passing away in 1970. By then he had earned the title "The Dean of Produce" which appear in the headline for his obituary.[7] "I suspect it was by virtue of his longevity," says Neil, yet Joe's obituary says that "he dealt out words of advice and concern as carefully as he chose perfect peaches and tomatoes for his customers."

Neil's father Sherman grew up behind the Tramer produce stand and went to law school at Case Western Reserve. He graduated in 1939 and left to serve in the European theatre of World War II. Upon his return, he couldn't find a good job as an attorney, so Sherman returned to work with his father. "I think my father was viewed differently than the others at the Market," says Neil. "He was highly educated and most of the people in the produce arcade didn't have that amount of education."

Today, Neil still runs into some of his father's regular customers. "There's one man who will always remind me how much he enjoyed talking with my father because he was versed on so many subjects," says Neil. "He may have sold cucumbers, peppers, and tomatoes but the conversations were meaningful, more than just small talk between a peddler and a customer."

Neil questions why his father never leveraged his education and law degree into doing something more than work at the Market. "On the other hand, he wanted to be there for his father and they shared the struggles of Market life together. It seems he was never able to break away."

Many immigrants like Joseph toughed out a lifetime at the West Side Market to keep food on the table, a roof over their heads, and to provide better opportunities and education for their children. It's interesting how family histories have a unique way of repeating themselves.

As a seven-year-old, Neil would go to Jewish Religious school on Saturdays, then hop the number 32 bus to the Windemere Rapid, which took him to the Market. "I didn't get to do what other kids did," he says. "I worked at the Market."

"In the winter, we used wood and kerosene stoves to keep us warm and awnings to break the wind and some days we would stand there in the cold and just watch our produce freeze," recalls Neil. "When you're a kid that builds character. No matter what else I do in life it pales in comparison to moments like that or when my

Memories

Customer: *"Did you go to college?"*
Retzer: *"Yes, Marquette."*
Customer: *"Really?*
Retzer: *"Yes, the West Side Mar-quette!"*

—Bill Retzer, former employee

"You could talk with a priest and a felon at the same time. Those were the types of skills the Market gives you. And you learn to talk back in broken English!"

—Fritz Graewe, former vendor

"My Uncle Gus helped at the stand. He couldn't read or write but he could do math in his head. A lot of these guys, they didn't have much education, but they were great with numbers and could add up a column of figures fast!"

—Tony Anselmo, former employee

dad would come home having made only $20 on a wintery Monday in the 1970s."

In 1971, Sherman left the Market to work for this brother in the clothing industry and left Neil to run the business. "My dad and I would go to the food terminal once or twice a week to buy produce for the stand," says Neil. "He would always tell me what to buy but sometimes I would buy what I wanted because I was a teenager and I knew everything. He was a conservative buyer and I was the opposite—always buying too much and sometimes, substandard stuff—things he would never do." When Sherman saw the produce that didn't sell, he made Neil work to get rid of it. "I was a quiet kid who had to become a huckster real quick," said Neil.

"Working there helped me develop a high math aptitude," says Neil. "There were no calculators. I learned to do fast math in my head from making change to weighing produce on hanging scales and calculating the cost. I had to deal with a melting pot of people, even those who were trying to steal from us. The West Side Market gave me some life skills I didn't realize I was getting. It helps me communicate with all kinds of people, from an IRS agent to a wealthy client."

On a Saturday afternoon in August 1976, Neil "cut the cord" to the Market and left to go to college. "At the time, if felt good to leave, but I knew even then that the Market had been very good to me," he says.

"One of the proudest moments for my dad was my first year out of law school," recalls Tramer. "He knew I would be making more money my first year in practice than the stand could produce in the same time."

Memories

"You had to be good at handling the crowd and interpreting the sign language of people who didn't speak English. That early exposure to such a diversity of people from all walks of life and so many parts of the world played a big role in my development and my ability to communicate with everybody.

My first job after law school was assistant state attorney for Cook County in Chicago. My background helped me interact with people who couldn't speak English. My dad was a very patient man who treated everyone with respect and he enjoyed the customers. What I learned from him has served me well as a trial lawyer."

—*John Coyne, former employee*

"Everything I learned about the fine art of meat cutting, as well as the finer art of treating people with fairness, honesty, and integrity, I learned from my dad Sam Santner. I worked for him for more than seven years, beginning in the mid-1950s.

I list my graduate school education on my resume but I'm proud to admit that I have an unofficial degree from WSMU's Department of Esoteric Life Learning, 1954–1964"

—*Dean Santner, former employee*

THE LADIES OF THE WEST SIDE MARKET
Women Who Kept House

AT FIRST BLUSH, the Market appears to be a man's world, full of tough jobs, heavy lifting, pushing and pulling carts laden with meats and produce, long hours exposed to winter's cold or summer's heat, and manly banter dotted with colorful language. For a century, media reports characterized the Market as a place where working women could be seen, but men were seen more.

Among the first female stand owners was Marie Stein, a vegetable vendor who was affectionately known as "Grandma" to many of her customers' children and grandchildren.[8] By 1930, she had already weighed and bagged produce for forty-five years for customers at both the Pearl Street Market and the new West Side Market. She raised four children while working as a vendor. In a newspaper account of her longevity at the Market, Mrs. Stein remarked that her work was too important to allow her to stay at home longer than just to eat and sleep. Like any vendor who has ever earned a living at the Market, she knew that missing a day of work impacted the bottom line.

Throughout the history of the West Side Market, the lady vendors were some of the toughest, most resilient, and resourceful characters; hardworking women with business smarts and the ability to juggle personal responsibilities that made success a nonnegotiable goal. If called pioneers, they might laugh and say that their work at the Market is what they did to keep their family fed. As women across the country embraced the women's rights movement, there were more than a handful of women at the Market who worked equally as hard as their husbands and others who owned stands and ran businesses alone, some by choice and others by circumstance.

Today, a walk up and down the aisles of the Market indicates that in this rough-and-tumble place, there are still ladies in the house—businesswomen. Some stands reflect their owner's name, like Kate's Fish, Judy's Oasis, and Annemarie's Dairy, newer businesses in the century-old market. Bakeries, spice shops, and produce stands are not only named after the owners, but the owner is the lady standing behind the counter: Michelle, Theresa, Narrin, and Kristi. Less obvious perhaps are the businesses that keep the family name but have been handed down from parents to daughters—Melissa DeCaro Lau worked with her father Joe for her lifetime and when he passed away after seventy-five years at the Market, she took over; Irene Dever turned over her dairy stand to her daughter Diane, who, like her mother, sees the stand and the Market as her life; and Ilse Sheppard continues to feed the daily line of people at Frank's Bratwurst, the same way her father Franz Ratschki did until he was eighty-six years old.

Above, from top: The Market's infamous and original "Pickle Lady," Rita Graewe; Anna Mae Grady, a vendor known for her sauerkraut

Lena Bova, Rose Consolo, & Mary Gentille: Three Generations of Lady Hucksters

Jack Gentille recalls three generations of women in his family, hucksters all—a blue-collar term that in the early 1900s was synonymous with hard work and modest living. It was also a time when occupations, as well as stands at the Market, were without question handed down to the next generation—because that's what families did.

"My great-grandmother Lena Bova had a produce stand at the Pearl Street Market," says Gentille. "She didn't have a husband so she did it all herself. I heard stories of her going across the Carnegie Bridge from 40th and Woodland in her horse and buggy, with a blanket over her legs and a gun tucked right along side of her."

In 1912, Lena turned the business over to Gentille's grandmother Rose Consolo, who moved it across the street to the new Market. Rose's husband had died after being hit by a streetcar, so she ran the stand with the help of her children. "Back then, you were told what you could sell, so she sold parsley root and kohlrabi and some other things," says Gentille. In 1947, Rose learned to drive a truck—and Gentille recalls, like her mother, she always carried a gun, too.

When Rose developed leg problems, Gentille's mother Mary took over and soon after married Jack's father, a neighboring vendor. "Everyone seemed to marry someone from the Market," he says. "As a wedding gift, my father's family bought them a little corner stand, number 63½. That was rare because this was a time when you couldn't buy a stand, you could only get one if it was passed down."

The family had it open on Saturdays and sold lemons, five for a quarter and a bunch of radishes for ten cents. "My dad carried a full-time job outside the Market," says Gentille. "A lot of Market families needed to have outside jobs."

In 1979, Gentille took over the stand and his daughter Jeanette, the fourth generation, joined him for twenty years before her death. In 2005, the family name Gentille disappeared from the Market, but not without leaving a quiet legacy of women who didn't ask or expect special treatment or favors, but used the opportunity to make a living like any other huckster.

Rita Graewe: The Pickle Lady

Waist-high barrels of sauerkraut weigh about four hundred pounds and Fritz Graewe remembers watching his grandmother Rita Graewe wrestle one or two onto a dolly and wheel it to her stand, called "Rita's." Affectionately known to a few generations of Market shoppers as "The Pickle Lady," Rita was one of the more nurturing figures at the Market. She knew how to run a successful business by taking care of people.

"She came to this country from Westphalia, Germany in 1952, started working for Angie's Bakery, and then for Mrs. Grady, the original Pickle Lady, from whom she bought the stand in 1965," says Graewe. It was supposed to provide a secondary income for the family, but her husband died that same year and she was the sole supporter of three small sons. "All of a sudden she had to learn to drive and how to do business," Fritz recalls. "She told me, 'I knew I wouldn't make a lot of money down here but I would always have food.'"

By most accounts, Rita was one of the best marketers in the place, as well as overly generous. "You would buy $2 worth of stuff and she would give you $3," says Fritz. "She was like that in every way."

"Everybody tells me they remember her because she gave them a pickle—and they all thought they were the only one to visit the Market who got one," he says. "I would never tell them differently but she gave a pickle to everyone! She had a way of making you feel special."

In 1988, Rita turned over the business to Fritz, who kept her name over the stand. He had promised himself and his grandmother that the stand would stay in the family. But in 2007, with her permission, Fritz sold the stand, along with traditions so closely associated with Rita's name.

Nettie Schade: The Chicken Lady

A 1977 *Cleveland Press* profile of Nettie Schade described the then-new owner of Kaufmann Poultry as "handling what has always been considered a man's job with ease and confidence" and at the end of the day, hurrying home to prepare dinner for her family. For Nettie, owning a stand was a matter of opportunity rather than necessity, but she was certainly one of the first in a progression of savvy vendors who just happened to be women.

Nettie was first hired in the 1950s by Carl Kaufmann, who had owned the corner poultry stand since 1932. Her first day on the job, Kaufmann told her to draw (remove the entrails from) a chicken, something she had never done before, but a test she obviously passed. For the next seventeen years, she worked with him, until Kaufmann offered to sell her the stand on the condition that the Kaufmann name remain on the marquee.

Her son Larry, who took over the stand in 1978, and is close to retirement himself, said his mother worked as hard as any man but he never recalls her having a difficult time as a woman in a "man's job." He remembers his mother as a good judge of character, a competent delegator, and a skilled business woman, qualities she may have absorbed from her own mother, who was one of the first female managers at the local Fisher Foods stores in the 1960s. And for a place where behavior and language can at times be rough and crude, he said common courtesy and gentlemanly behavior from the men of the Market prevailed, but then "she seldom ventured down to the coolers," he adds.

"My mom had loyal employees," says Schade, help that lasted, like the kid that came in Saturdays and after school. "When she took over the stand, another poultry stand owner tried to lure him away," says Schade. "He obviously saw the advantage in hiring him, but the kid stuck with my mom."

Vendor Nettie Schade gets an order ready for a customer

emories

"My mother (Nettie Schade) worked as hard as a man but where she had an advantage was that when the customers would ask for cooking advice, she had it all in her head and could easily share a recipe. Most guys don't have that kind of info."

—*Larry Schade, vendor, Kaufmann Poultry*

"Anna Mae Grady was a friend of my mother-in-law's. She opened her business at the West Side Market in the late 1930s with only $800. She was a widow taking care of three children. When I would go to the stand to buy a pound of sauerkraut and it was even a little over, Mrs. Grady would take some off until it was an even pound. That's how she put her children through school."

—*Rose Ulrich*

Antoinette "Lena" Rini

Antoinette Rini: A Hard Life

Mario Rini's grandfather had a produce stand at the original Pearl Street Market and his father Joseph and uncle Marty took over the business once it moved to the West Side Market. In 1939, when Mario was ten, his father died.

"My mom, Antoinette (everyone called her 'Lena') was left with four children, the oldest was fourteen," he says. "She was a fragile person, not big and only had an eighth grade education. Back then, you were supposed to be a housewife and a mother, not a business owner." Rini recalls that the night after they buried his father, his mother cooked the children a supper of soup and cried. The next day, she went to work at the Market.

There was a conflict about who was going to take over the stand—Marty or the widow. "My father's name was on the lease so the Market commissioner, Frank Jeroski, wrote 'Mrs.' in front of his name and she signed the lease to continue use of the stand," says Rini. "It caused hard feelings with my uncle who ended up leaving the Market."

Even though Lena had some experience at the stand, she was now left with buying the produce, setting up the stand, displaying the produce, the bookwork—everything—and having to do it alone. She took her oldest daughter out of school to watch the younger children. Then she learned to drive the truck. Eventually, she hired someone to drive and unload it.

Other vendors like Sherman Tramer, Tony Cionciolo, and Eddie Cook were supportive and sympathetic, but Rini doesn't recall that anyone ever did any of the physical work for her. "My mother did everything a man would do," he says. "I don't know that I ever recognized how hard she worked because she never complained. There were no vacations, no cars, or extras but she sent all of us to Catholic schools. That was important."

Antoinette "Lena" Rini worked her stand at the Market with her son Mario until 1956, when at the age of fifty-four she decided it was time to retire. He was never sure whether she liked her time at the Market but recognized that it was what she knew and that her obligations were to her family.

Memories

"I worked with her [Rita Graewe] since I was ten and she taught me whether it's the customer who spends $100 every six months or the one who spends $3 each week, you take care of them the same way. They pay our rent and keep us here."

—**Fritz Graewe, former vendor**

"Our stand was separated from the guy next to us by a single column. We unintentionally encroached on his stand a bit for a year. When my mother, a widow, who had kept the stand going at the Market and raised four kids, gave up her stand after almost twenty years, he took back the space she had been using. He told me he felt sorry for her because she was a widow and he wouldn't have made her move."

—**Mario Rini, former vendor**

Irene & Diane Dever: Like Mother, Like Daughter

As a young girl, Irene Dever lived close to the Market and would often wander down looking for small jobs, like shelling peas for 3 cents a basket. As she grew older and got married, she began working Saturdays at Ed Badstuber's lunch meat counter. "My brothers and I could hardly wait to go with our dad to pick her up," says daughter Diane. "This was a playground for us. Everyone knew us and that my mom worked here and we would get free slices of bologna." It was a big part of their life; Diane remembers the day that her mom came home and told the family Irene Keller asked her if she wanted to buy her dairy stand. "My dad told her to go for it," recalls Diane.

In 1971, Irene Dever, now forty years old, was a stand owner at the West Side Market, and whether by design or accident, she worked on getting Diane to fall in love with the place, too. So she "hired" her—at nine years old. "Diane would come with me to the Market about 4 AM on Saturdays," says Irene. "She would crawl under the counter and finish her sleep until I woke her at 8 AM. I told her to go wash her face and get ready—we had customers." Irene's sons and husband would often be at the stand, too, waiting on customers, slicing cheese to order, cutting chunks of butter, and dishing up salads, but Diane and Irene made the Market their lives.

In the mid-1990s, Irene retired and Diane took over as keeper of some of the long-standing traditions, like selling cups of buttermilk, whole milk with the flakes of butter, for only 25 cents. "We've never raised the price and when they finish, they say it's just how they remember it,"says Diane.

Mother and daughter also think differently. "I try to buy products from the little guy, like our eggs and maple syrup," she says. "People today want local and home-

Mother and daughter vendors, Irene and Diane Dever

grown products. When my mom was here, she would buy from larger distributors. My mom never took a vacation and she still tells me what to do," says Diane. The daughter takes vacations and runs her new ideas for the business by her mom, who will inevitably ask, "Are you sure you want to do that?"

"There are sometimes when I'm laughing out loud at work and I say to myself, 'Oh, my God. It's her!'" says Diane. "I hear myself saying the same things she did, like when customers come in with their kids who are growing up, I'll say, 'Oh, he can't be that old,' or 'Where did the time go?'"

"Even the customers say, 'You're turning into your mother,'" says Diane. "Well, if I have to turn into somebody, it's okay that it's her." The name above the stand still says "Irene Dever" and Diane has no plans to replace her mother's name. "She worked too hard at this stand," she says. "Besides half the customers think I'm Irene anyhow."

Memories

"When I got my stand at the Market, some of the guys started a rumor that I wouldn't last six months. I lasted forty years and never got any special treatment or favors. I was lucky that I had Walter Simmelink Jr. and 'Hogie' Penttila, both dairy stands owners, and my competitors. Along with Lou Fougerousse, a beef vendor, they helped teach me how to run my business. You couldn't have better friends than that."

—*Irene Dever, former vendor*

"There were a lot of strong, powerful, independent women at the Market. It was a place where women could thrive in business, a way for them to take care of themselves and their families. Husbands would die and with the help of their kids, these tough ladies took over and kept things running.

I think the Market was unique in that way, especially back in the day when women didn't have the kind of equality in society that they do now. But the female vendors at the Market work hard and are treated the same as the guys."

—*Patrick Delaney, former vendor*

A GENEROUS NATURE
Charity, Niceties, & Random Acts of Kindness

CHARITY MAY BEGIN at home, but it has often and frequently spilled over into the West Side Market. From behind the counter, vendors see everyone who shops the Market, from the privileged to the underserved.

Many a needy customers has found more than they paid for when they unpack their bags at home and others are charged less than what the sign announces. Credit is granted on a handshake and debt forgiveness has been extended to customers who have fallen on hard times. There are plenty of accounts and memories of times when a merchant has helped a customer. But to find those stories, it takes some searching because while many are happy to help, few are willing to brag about it.

Cleveland's Little Sisters of the Poor's mission is to provide for the needs of Cleveland's aged poor who are in their care and they do that through the tradition of begging. For as long as anyone at the West Side Market can remember, the order has had a quiet but regular presence here and many generations of vendors have donated meat and produce without the need for thanks or accolades.

More than a century ago, the original home of the order and their residents was at E. 22nd Street and Woodland Avenue and the collecting Sisters, those who beg for food or gather donations, used to walk to the Market. Today, the order and the Saint Mary and Joseph residents home is located further away, so the tradition continues from the "begging van." Friday morning is the day one might catch a glimpse of the Sisters at the Market.

For thirty years, Sister Mary Catherine was the collecting Sister, going stand-to-stand and stall-to-stall collecting food donations. Produce vendor Jack Gentille recalls her steady presence at the Market.

"I remember Sister coming down with her driver, Sam," says Gentille. "My mother Mary would give to her all the time, whatever she had on the stand. Not just my mother, but I would say half the vendors in that Market would give to the Little Sisters and to this day a lot of the wholesalers at the Northern Ohio Food Terminal donate to them."

Even as her health began to fail, Sister Mary Catherine would still make her weekly trips to West Side Market using a wheelchair or walker. "Her face was

CHICKEN & CHARITY

Father Bernard Scarborough was the founder of a nearby halfway house, called the Matt Talbot Inn, that provided treatment for men with drug and alcohol addictions. Dressed in the long robes of the Franciscan order, Father Bernard would come into the Market seeking food for his residents.

"Father would have a long black change purse," recalls former poultry vendor John Rolston. "He would come to the stand and open the purse, show me it was empty, and say, "I have twenty-one men this week, John. Do you think I have enough to feed them?" Rolston said it was a standing joke and it always got the priest enough chicken to feed his flock.

Above: Little Sisters of the Poor

Memories

"The second or third year she had the stand, my mother invested in a bread slicer. It made a lot of crumbs and she gave them to a little old lady who said she liked to feed the pigeons in Lincoln Park. My mom thought maybe she was poor and hungry and was eating them herself, so for a few years whenever the woman came in for the crumbs she'd give her a loaf of bread, too, and not charge her for it. Then there was a story in the paper about this lady. Turns out she really was feeding the birds."

—Beverly Tabacco, former employee

"Nicky Roberto sold spaghetti and beans. He was a bachelor, good-looking and a snappy dresser. I once had a customer that was homeless and used to sleep under the bridge on W. 14th. His shoes were so worn that the soles would slap against the concrete. So Nicky thought he would be nice and brought this guy a pair of his shoes—$150 alligator shoes. This guy takes one look at the shoes and says, 'What are you trying to do? Ruin my feet!?'"

—Irene Dever, former vendor

Above, from top: NEOCH vendors sell *The Homeless Grapevine* outside the produce arcade; Rocco Meyo, captain at the Hildebrandt Meat stand

recognized by many vendors," said Sister Jean, who often accompanied her. "We would go to many different stalls and they would give us eggs, bread, cheese, meats, fruits, and vegetables…and it was always fresh!"

When West Side Market shoppers walk to the produce arcade from the parking lot, they're likely to see a homeless man or woman peddling newspapers from W. 24th Street, a narrow stretch closed to street traffic but busy with shopper foot traffic. To pass by the displaced and poor while entering this food lovers' paradise presents an uncomfortable contrast, but these homeless people are earning a living—not begging.

The Homeless Grapevine is a newspaper written by clients of the Northeast Ohio Coalition for the Homeless (NEOCH), an advocacy and public education program for the area's itinerant. Those who peddle the papers buy and resell them for a profit at many locations around the city, but the Market location is a coveted one.

From this spot, Angelo Anderson, once homeless, sold issues of the paper and the generosity of West Side Market shoppers, in part, helped him get off the streets fifteen years ago. Today, Angelo works at a men's shelter downtown and is a regular shopper at the West Side Market. "The merchants treat me like I've been a lifelong customers and have taken up other collections for the homeless, like coats and hygiene products," says Anderson. "They also ask what's going on at the shelter and what they can do to help."

When the homeless first started selling the paper at the Market twenty years ago, fights would break out over the prized spot and panhandling at the door had gotten out of control. Market cop Jimmy Traynor met with Brian Davis, community organizer for NEOCH, and the two struck an unwritten agreement that puts one person selling the paper in one spot—and it has kept the peace.

"This is a good place for our sellers to earn a living and to meet a lot of different people from all parts of the city," says Davis. "It also helps people embrace the idea of people helping themselves by selling the newspaper as a way to get off and stay off the streets." Traynor agrees. "Just because you're poor doesn't mean you're trouble," he says. "I know, I see these people all the time." In 2010, the *Homeless Grapevine* changed its name to the *Street Chronicle* and it remains the only street newspaper in Cleveland.

Ⓜ emories

"My mom, Mary Gentille, was a giving lady and her customers depended on her. Some customers (immigrants) who were new to the Market would come and pay in foreign money. She would take it, not knowing if it was enough, but at least the customer would have food for their family. Some would owe her and come back the next day to pay for the food she gave them."

—**Maryann Gentille, former employee**

"The Little Sisters of Poor would come by the Market on Fridays and stand in the background behind customers that stood in rows two to three people deep. My dad would notice them and immediately wrap meat for them and hand it to them over the crowds. I would like to think that was his insurance that he made it to heaven."

—**Ed Badstuber, former employee**

FED BY ROSIE

We never knew her last name or her Market pedigree when we bought our cabbages and carrots. To my husband and I, she was just Rosie, a small, talkative, and generous lady who made sure we didn't go hungry.

It was 1971 and we were a new couple—young, on our own, poor and, like many of our friends, freshly-minted vegetarians. Giving up meat was motivated by the need to economize as well as ethical concerns and the era's emerging health consciousness.

Neither of us knew much of anything about food or cooking. Swiss chard, celery root, and escarole were uncharted territory. We'd never seen fresh beets or okra in our mothers' kitchens. Thanks to Rosie, we learned to love and prepare all these and many other vegetables.

We'd show up at her stand weekly, chat for a while, and then make our choices. She'd tell us what we owed and while we counted out the dollars and cents, she filled another bag with stuff, big bunches of leafy greens always sticking out of the top. "You'ze guyz just take this," she'd say every time with a big smile, handing us the extra produce and waving off our offers to give her some more money. She made it seem like a gift we had to accept rather than charity.

I don't know how she knew we were living on the edge or what prompted her to care but Rosie's kindness kept our plates filled and lifted our spirits at a time when it mattered and we've never forgotten.

I didn't realize that she was a DeCaro, the owner of the produce stand, and one of the vendors who had been

Rosie DeCaro

at the Market for decades until working on this book. When I did, it was too late to tell Joe what his mother had meant to us—the tumor in his brain had begun to do its damage—but I was able to share my story with his daughter Melissa, who now runs the business. She wasn't surprised to hear about her grandmother's generosity but it made her happy and for me that was a way to repay some of what I owe this wonderful woman.

—Laura Taxel

Ⓜemories

"The Little Sisters of the Poor would come down to our stand (Hildebrandt's) in the 1950s. Rocco Meyo would get a bunch of meats together, fill up a shopping bag, sometimes two, and give it to the Sisters—plus a dollar out of his own pocket."

—**Bill Retzer, former employee**

"My dad Sam Santner had his own meat stand at the Market until the early 1970s. I can attest that he truly liked people. One day he was waiting on an elderly, rather impoverished-looking lady, who seemed to be struggling with buying his cheapest soup bones. He said, 'Well, Mom, we're having a problem with our inventory management today and I'm hopeful you can help us out.' He then proceeded to fill her bag with meat pieces from different cuts in the counter. Her thanks were a few cents from a well-worn change purse, her joyful exclamation in some foreign language, and a beaming, toothless smile. My dad could not have been happier with the transaction."

—**Dean Santner, former employee**

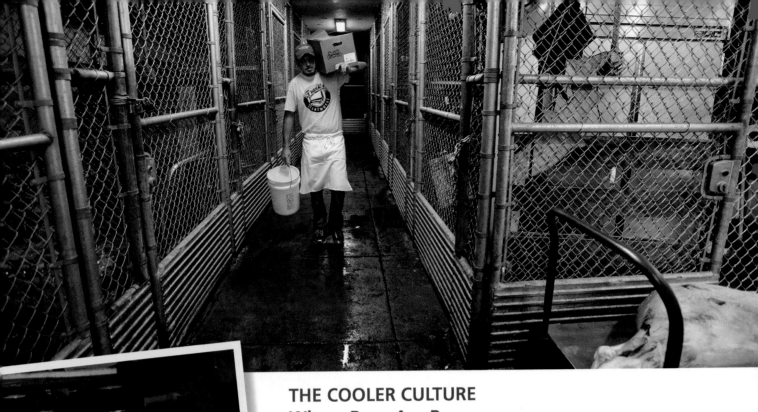

THE COOLER CULTURE
Where Boys Are Boys

BENEATH THE RED-TILED FLOORS of the West Side Market building is the basement or what Market workers call "the coolers." It's a part of the Market completely off-limits to the public, although more than once an errant visitor has found their way down, by accident or design, only to be escorted out by Market vendors or security.

> "John Sommer and I were cooler boys at the Market in the 1950s and '60s, each of us working for our dads. I moved on to a career in furniture design and John to a career in law enforcement with the FBI and the HIDTA—High Intensity Drug Task Area. We got together around 2007 and went back to the Market on a nostalgic tour. We wandered down into the coolers the way we had thousands of times when we were cooler boys and got caught by a guard who was pretty officious and told us in no uncertain terms to leave. I'm trying to tell him the story about how we had worked down here, these were our father's coolers... but he wasn't interested. I'm trying to get John to show him his badge and his weapon so this guy will know we're okay, but John played by the rules. There we were, two guys in our early sixties, still causing trouble in the cooler."
> —Dean Santner, former employee

From the top: The cooler below the Market floor; Tom Conway and Chuck Maurath, former cooler boys

It's rare to see published photos of the coolers. This utilitarian space lacks the visual appeal and architectural beauty that the rest of the Market enjoys—and down there, it's always cold, in the mid-thirties. Not knowing or laying eyes on what's in the basement has often led to wild speculation, too. On occasion there were erroneous reports and wide-spread rumors that there was a slaughterhouse in the basement, which was never true.

The cooler is actually two cavernous corridors that stretch from one end of the Market to the other. Off to the sides, a series of heavy insulated doors open to clusters of galvanized fenced lockers. Each Market vendor has their own locker for keeping products like cheese, eggs, milk, and butter cold.

Jim Petras: Becoming a Cooler Boy

For legions of young men, working as a cooler boy was their first job, and more often their favorite job. Some started as young as twelve, but they were typically teenagers—young, strong, and willing to work hard for the meat and poultry vendors, because those were the jobs where the muscle was needed. Beginning in the late 1960s, Jim Petras worked as a cooler boy for Walter Ehrnfelt all throughout high school and college. "It was a badge of honor to work at the Market," he says, "and lots of my friends at St. Ed's [St. Edward's High School] did." He provides the perfect job description:

"At that time, many of the vendors used boys, cooler boys, as runners to carry stuff up from the basement and then back down again at the end of the day. The Ehrnfelts only sold beef and they hired me because I weighed 220 pounds and was a tackle on the football team. Whole sides of beef hung from hooks in the cooler. I'd have to wrap my arms around them in a kind of bear hug, lift, and then carry them to the table for cutting. It took a lot of brute force.

I arrived at 5 AM on Saturdays. The building was dark and empty upstairs, but it was a beehive of activity in the basement and I spent most of my time down there. I was a meat 'schlepper.' It's always really cold so the first thing I'd do is put on a long heavy coat that the boss supplied—it was none too clean and you just hoped there'd be one that was sort of your size. Over that I wore a white coat and a fresh white apron. By the end of the day these would be all bloody.

If I was the first one in, I unlocked our cage and began getting stuff ready for the counter. I started as a 'go-fer.' Once I'd moved up a notch in the pecking order, my job was to make the ground beef and the Ehrnfelts taught me how to do some cutting.

Down in the cooler, Walter Ehrnfelt prepares to break down a forequarter of beef

By 6:30 AM, I had to have the dolly loaded with the two containers (of ground beef) plus a mix of roasts, steaks, soup meat, and other parts. I wheeled it to the elevators, and then to the stand for set-up. It took two or three trips to fully stock the counter. Depending on how busy we were, I'd be shuttling back and forth all day to keep the counter full and then I had to help clean up after we closed. Once you had some seniority and if you had any kind of presence or personality, you'd get to work behind the counter serving customers. That was a plum job."

A plum job perhaps, but one that was largely reserved for the "counter girls," teenagers who were the "faces" behind the counter, hardworking also, but not prone or permitted to go down to the coolers. "The coolers were a guy's world," says Gordon Fernengel, vendor and former cooler boy. "You never saw girls coming up or down from the cooler."

Memories

"I used to work as a cooler boy at Pinzone Meats in the 1980s. When five o'clock would roll around we would crank up 'Cleveland Rocks' throughout the Market, so you knew it was quitting time. We would break down and clean up all the equipment in the coolers. Sometimes beers would come out. Then we would head upstairs to clean up the cases and the floors. By the time I would get home, I would have a layer of fat all over me—because sometimes we would have meat fights, too. When I would step into the hot shower, I would smell like a hot dog cooking."

—**Bill Retzer Jr., former employee**

"Like a lot of my friends from St. Edwards, I worked for a butcher at the West Side Market when I was in high school in the late '60s. When nobody was watching, we boys would take gobs of thick white beef fat and fling them up to the ceiling. If they hit, they stuck up there and wouldn't fall down until days later, with any luck hitting somebody on the head. We'd bet on what day and time they'd come down and the kind of person they'd come down on. It was a kind of tradition, passed on from one group of kids to the next."

—**Jim Petras, former employee**

A COOL JOB FOR A GIRL

"When I was about fifteen, I asked to become a 'cooler girl.' It was sort of a new concept to my dad (Don Miller), but he said okay.

I loved it on so many levels! First of all, it got me out of the stand and gave me an activity besides standing and waiting on customers.

Second, I was a teenage girl and there were all those teenage boys headed down to the cooler. Ahhh! The opportunity to flirt—not to mention these were boys with great work ethics.

Third, I got strong. Sometimes when you went to the cooler, you took the 2-wheeler to bring up the boxes of meat; other times you would carry the box upstairs instead. I loved carrying boxes up on my shoulder. Remember, these were the 1960s and 1970s and girls weren't really supposed to be strong. I didn't know it then, but in some ways, I was breaking some 'glass ceilings' at the Market by being a 'cooler girl.'"

—Susan "Sam" Miller,
former employee

Meat vendors used their lockers as a butcher shop, where skilled cutters with electric meat and bone saws and hand blades broke down quarters of beef, whole hogs, lamb, and goat into cuts the customers recognize when laid out in the cases.

Essentially, the cooler is a drab and chilly place—with the exception of the decades of stories hatched by the cooler culture—generations of boys and young men known as "cooler boys" who did the grunt work and heavy lifting for their bosses, primarily butchers and poultry vendors. The cooler boys ran between the basement and stands to keep the cases filled with product throughout busy market days and cleaned up at the end of the day. In between there was always time for goofing off and playing tricks, jokes, and pranks on each other—and sometimes on the boss.

Like photos of the cooler, most of these stories have never been published. Many of the accounts and memories are youthful and amusing. Others are coarse and inappropriate, plenty are unprintable, and more remain private property—not to be shared. The ones that can be told prove that being an industrious cooler boy was anything but all work—there was a lot of play.

"My dad sheltered us (girls). We weren't supposed to be in the coolers," says Janet Penttila, who grew up at the Market working at her father's dairy stand. "It was rough and colorful…and a place for the guys. At the Market there were gender specific jobs. The cooler guys would shuttle the meat up and down and the counter girls made it look pretty and waited on customers. Cooler boys did not wait on customers."

Memories

"The useful life of a cooler boy is short. They peak between fifteen and seventeen when they are the spry and worldly."

—**Michael Turczyk, vendor, Turczyk's**

"The coolers dictated who you knew and who you hung around with. It depended on who was in the same corridor you were."

—**Chuck Maurath, former vendor**

"The cooler kept the beer cold."

—**Tom Nagel, employee**

COOLER GAMES

Cooler boys were hired for youth, muscle, and stamina, but with those qualities came raging hormones and immaturity. They had to keep up a vigorous pace, especially on Saturdays in the 1960s and '70s when shoppers flooded the Market, but were never too busy to cook up a game, a scheme, or a scenario that had potential for a reprimand or a firing. The games former cooler boys played are legendary.

"When you went into the coolers, you never knew what you were going to see. It could be an improvised rock concert or a wrestling match. It was all good as long as the meat kept coming up and no one was going to the hospital."
—**Gordon Fernengel, vendor, Fernengel's**

"I laid face down on a 4-wheeler and some of the guys put a thick cutting board up the back of my cooler coat, stuck a butcher's knife in it and smeared liver blood all around it. Then they took me upstairs, wheeled me through the Market and left me for 'dead' at my boss's stand. It was just another time Arnold Fernengel almost fired me."
—**Tony Pinzone, vendor, Pinzone Meats**

"When I was a kid, there was a guy who worked there that gave me and everyone else a hard time—a real clock watcher. Every Friday, at few minutes before quitting time, he would tear down to the cooler to get his 4-wheeler so he could start moving his stuff back down to the cooler. You could set your watch by this guy. It was important for him to be the first out of the building on Friday. Once someone nailed his cooler door shut. He couldn't budge it one inch. I could hear him screaming from upstairs."
—**Gordon Fernengel, vendor, Fernengel's**

"The guys in the cooler used to play 'bone' hockey with brooms. We would slap puck-shaped bones across the floor between goals we would set up between bone barrels. The games were pretty intense. We would come up all sweaty even though the cooler was 30°F."
—**Gary Fougerousse, former vendor**

"One time I went through all the coolers gathering up the 'bone dust.' We would make sculptures out of them. Some were kind of perverted."
—**Michael Turczyk, vendor, Turczyk's**

"By the end of the day, the floor in the basement was pretty slick. We used to sit in these large meat pots on wheels used for moving around ground meat. Someone would push you down the hall and that pot would bounce off the walls like in a pinball game. You had to be pretty crazy to get in it."
—**Tim Rini, former employee**

"There undoubtedly was a lot of questionable behavior in the coolers and while many shared stories with me about games, tricks, and general foolish behavior, most people were shy about acknowledging that there was the occasional tryst or quickie in the chill of the coolers. The rumors persist but details are rarely offered. Whenever I brought up the subject, I would get looks, from shy to sly, and comments that feigned ignorance. 'Sex in the cooler?,' says longtime Market employee, Tim Jeziorski. 'Wait a minute! Why didn't I know about this? I would have liked to have sex in the cooler!'"
—**Marilou Suszko**

"Some of the guys would set up 'dirty' movies in one of the coolers on Saturday afternoons. We all knew they were there and would come down to watch and then we would get in trouble from our bosses for watching and not working. They weren't happy about it so one of the bosses called the police who planned to show up and break it up. One of the guys running the movies caught wind of this. So when the police showed up and said, 'You're in trouble,' we said, 'For what!?' Someone had changed the dirty movies to home movies of someone's vacation."
—**Tim Rini, former employee**

Opposite: The ladies of the Robert Stumpf Jr. family: granddaughter, Robin Fitch; daughter, Rebecca Stumpf Fitch; and wife, Martha Stumpf

Tim Rini: Make 'em Laugh

Tim Rini is the grandson of Lena Rini and the son of Mario Rini, both one-time produce vendors. But his connection to the Market came long after the Rinis left the produce arcade in the 1950s. He was a "cooler boy" for Walter Ehrnfelt in the early 1970s and in addition to muscle and a good work ethic, he demonstrated a good understanding of sales and marketing:

"It was my job to be at the Market after school and on weekends and bring up everything the stand needed. Cooler boys were allowed to grind meat but nothing more than that. We would use a two-way radio to hear what was needed or the butcher would make a list and you would bring up meat in baskets, a cart, even your apron. We would stack our wheeled carts high with meat and make it look decorative. We would make a lot of noise and chatter, 'Our stand is F4, follow us!' It worked. The bigger the show, the more people you would have following you. The guys used to make me carry beef tongue in my apron. It was pretty inappropriate but people would laugh as you passed them in the aisles. As a kid at the Market, you did whatever was necessary to make people laugh.

I must have walked up and down that aisle hundreds of times in the two years I was there. It was such a friendly walk. Everyone would holler 'Hi!' to you. Here's what I learned working as a cooler boy at the Market: You have to get to work early, you have to work until you're done, and you have to enjoy what you're doing."

WELCOME TO THE CLUB

Being a cooler boy was like being part of a brotherhood or a fraternity. It involved some degree of secrecy, some code of behavior, a hierarchy, and some form of initiation or ceremony that marked acceptance. The ritual wasn't always the same but there were a few favorites.

Gordon Fernengel, a beef and pork vendor who grew up at the Market working for his father Arnold, describes how in a pay-it-forward gesture, he and a group of former cooler boys who own stands or still work at the Market, engaged in hazing the new hires:

"When a new cooler boy was hired at one of our stands, we would initiate them by telling them to go find the 'counter stretcher.' I would tell them Tony Pinzone had it; Tony would tell them he didn't have it; go to Joe Bistricky; he would send him to Tom Nagel who would send him to Tim Jeziorski, and so on. This kid would travel all over the Market for something that didn't exist," recounts Fernengel. "We would also tell them to go get a bucket of steam or a left-handed screwdriver, but the counter stretcher was the number one initiation."

"I was a high school wrestler, heading to Purdue on a scholarship. I was the guy who tossed the newbies in the bone barrel. It had all the fat, bones, and trimming waiting to be collected by a rendering company that used them for dog food or soap."
—Ed Badstuber, former employee

"The older guys would get you by the collar of your shirts and back of your apron and hang you on a meat hook far enough off the ground so you couldn't get down easily. You would 'earn' getting hung up by teasing someone or giving the older cooler guys just enough lip. I was on the hook more than once."
—Tim Rini, former employee

"I started working at the Market in 1981. I was thirteen and Steve "Jay" Check hired me as a cooler boy. My first day on the job, this kid comes up to me in a white cooler coat and he's screaming holding his arm. His hand looks like it's missing and it's all bloody. I'm thinking he cut his hand off! He had a pork hock up his sleeve. My heart was really pounding. Cooler boys today are a little more mature and the pranks are not the same. My most valuable lesson in the cooler was learning the hierarchy of cooler boys. You didn't cut in line at the cleaning sinks and the older ones fetched the beers."
—Don Whitaker, vendor, D. W. Whitaker Meats

AFTER HOURS
Letting Your Hair Down

THROUGHOUT THE ENTIRE history of the Market, there always seemed to be a need for watering holes, after-hour gathering places, or more family-friendly events like fishing trips, dances, or picnics where merchants and workers met to forget about or recount the day. Friendships made and nurtured during Market hours were sealed over lunches, a beer, or many beers. Joanne Lewis, author of *To Market, To Market*, remarked that there were activities in the neighborhood for shoppers, too.

> **"Some of the older merchants that I talked to remembered when the Market was open late on Saturday nights. There were a few bars and a bordello in the neighborhood and the guys would go there while their women shopped."**

The bordello is long gone, as well as all the favorite haunts of Market vendors and workers, casualties of wrecking balls, neighborhood development, and small strip malls. The people of the Market have changed, too. "It's different now," observes longtime Market employee, Tom Nagel. "There used to be a lot of guys working here that were World War II vets, shot and beer guys. It was a different demographic then."

Mary Rose Oakar said that when she was councilperson in this neighborhood in the 1970s, there were fifty-two bars up and down Lorain Avenue and around W. 25th Street. This provides an idea of the range of choices for socializing over drinks after a hard day at the Market, but only a few places stood out as the official "unofficial" after-hours spot and "break rooms" for some Market workers.

Bender's, Torian's, and Felice's were three simple beer joints that stood in a row facing W. 25th Street. They were virtually a hop, skip, and a jump across Lorain Avenue from the east entrances of the Market. This made it easy for workers to sneak away for a shot and a beer during business hours and get back behind the counter before their bosses, employees, or customers even knew they were gone.

Although each bar catered to the neighborhood, Market shoppers and the workforce at the Market kept them alive. "Bender's had to be there since

Opposite: Gordon Fernengel and Tony Pinzone, mid-1970s
Above: Bender's Bar was just steps away from the West Side Market on W. 25th

emories

"My dad (Fritz Maurath) would go in the back door at Bender's to use the bathroom, say hello and have a double-header—a beer with a chaser. My brother would kid about it and say that he would do it so fast, he could get back to the Market before the light on the corner of Lorain and 25th changed."

—Chuck Maurath, *former vendor*

"I spent the first eleven years of my life in Cleveland. Every Saturday my parents, sister, and I would walk to the West Side Market. I loved when it was just my Dad and me because there was a bar near the Market. I believe it was named Bender's. We would go there first. They had the best hot roast beef with mashed potatoes and gravy. I would eat that while my dad enjoyed a 'liquid' lunch. We would then walk around the Market listening to the vendors yell out their specials. I can remember being scared to death of being separated from my folks because it was wall-to-wall people."

—Debi Bartow

MARY'S TAVERN

"My grandparents bought a tavern on W. 29th (where St. Ignatius' practice field is now) in 1948 and called it 'Mary's Tavern.' Every Saturday my grandmother Mary Berg would go to the West Side Market to buy food for the tavern. She would take me with her to carry her bags.

The Leu Brothers were her favorite vendors, always so nice and polite to her. The people she bought from were the same ones who would come to the tavern after work, but most of her customers were Market shoppers and local tradesmen.

Lots of guys from the steel mills worked a half-day on Saturday and would stop at her place after work to get the 'Market report.' They would ask her what looked good at the Market that day. 'How did the smokies look? How about the prasky? Who had good salami?'

My dad used to bartend there on Saturday nights and I would go with him because every Saturday I knew grandma would be making kielbasa and beans for dinner at the tavern."

—Jim McDermott

the 1950s and it was the 'cutters' (butchers) bar," said former vendor Chuck Maurath. "It wasn't unusual during the day to see shoppers having a beer. Their full shopping bags would be lined up against the wall."

Torian's, owned by the Peters' family, who were also produce vendors at the West Side Market, was another regular stop and Maurath says that this is where produce vendors would gather. But for more than thirty years, Felice's was the bar of choice for many vendors.

Tom Nagel has worked at the Market for more than forty-five years and he says that Felice's had a monopoly on attracting Market workers. "The employee parking lot was just beyond Felice's back door," he says. "Everyone who worked at the Market had to walk past Felice's back door."

Frank and Sadie Felice opened the bar and restaurant in the 1960s and fed and "watered" at least two generations of Market workers. Although the bar was actually named Mainstreet, Market workers always knew it as Felice's. There was nothing fancy about it by any account and it seems that the hours, menus, and codes of conduct were often tweaked to accommodate the vendors' odd schedules and specific tastes—and often just because these steady customers were regarded as friends as well as extended family.

In the late 1980s, the three bars and parking lot gave way to a strip mall and Felice's moved north to a location on 25th Street. Following Frank Felice's death in 1996, his grandson David Petras attempted to reinvent the neighborhood bar, which by then had moved north of the Market. He kept the red and white awning that spelled out Felice's and conducted business as usual during the day—shots and beers. At night, it turned into a trendy nightclub called Venom. "When we're Felice's, they talk about the old days," said Petras. "When we're Venom, they talk about what they are going to do next."[9] Both Venom and Felice's closed in 2000.

Today, if vendors and employees gather after work, it's typically for one or two beers and at the Market Café located inside the West Side Market. Nagel points out that thirty years ago, vendors had five or six people working behind the stand on a busy Saturday. "That meant at least 600 people worked the Market on a Saturday." Today, Nagel says maybe half that many work on a Saturday, the older guys are gone, and the rest? "The rest of us are just getting older," he says. "I think everyone just goes home now."

Memories

"There was also Grillie's on 26th and Lorain. You would go there if you didn't want anyone to see you. It wasn't unusual to see a policeman in there with a gun, cause a lot of people used to cash their checks there."

—Chuck Maurath, former vendor

"If you worked the Market as a teen, Felice's is where you had your first beer, whether you were of drinking age or not. It wasn't unusual either to stay at the Market until 11 PM on a Saturday night and have a few beers behind the stand or in the cooler. We would send the cooler boys to buy it for us. The laws were a lot looser then."

—Tim Jeziorski, employee

"Felice's was pretty much built around the West Side Market. Vendors and workers could come and go all day long."

—Frank Felice, nephew of Frank and Sadie Felice

The West Side Market Fruit & Vegetable Dealers Association Annual Picnic, 1961

Outside the Market, vendors and workers created more opportunities for fun and celebration and just being together. "There were a bunch of us who would get together on occasion at The Columbia Ball Room in Columbia Station [southwest of Cleveland] for the Christmas Dance or Harvest Dance organized by the merchants," says Irene Dever, a former vendor. "We would eat, dance, and drink. Nettie Schade, Leonard Sommer, Dave Hamm, Larry Schade—boy, did we have a good time! And when Bob Stumpf bought the Rhinelander out in North Olmsted [a Cleveland suburb], we would go there in the evenings, too."

After-hours softball games came together on Wednesday nights during the summer in St. Emeric's parking lot behind the Market. "It was the inside vendors versus the outside vendors," recalls Diane Dever. "It was one of the rare times where both sets of vendors got together socially and it was pretty competitive."

Chuck Maurath remembers going to graduation parties for the kids of vendors, clambakes, and once to Del Russ's farm to celebrate his fiftieth wedding anniversary. "Nothing could happen in your personal life that the rest of the Market wasn't invited to," says Maurath.

THE MARKET TAVERN

It's possible that in 1934, the Market Tavern on W. 28th was drawing a beer for its most notable customer, Elliott Ness, while workers from the West Side Market wandered in for their lunch break. The tavern was a known haunt of Ness, as well as the place merchants went for good hot roast beef sandwiches.

The tavern purposely mingled its patrons at big round tables, reserved for no one in particular. As a teen working at his father's butcher's counter, Chuck Maurath would head there to eat. "My dad would give us some money to get lunch and you would never know who you would be sitting with," says Maurath. "Chances are it would be a Market person, but lots of times it was a judge, a cop or a lawyer."

When Mary Rose Oakar became a councilperson in the 1970s, this was where she met with vendors and members of the Market's merchants association to talk over problems.

The Market Tavern space is now occupied by the Great Lakes Brewing Company and customers belly up to the same wooden bar where a few generations of hungry and thirsty Market workers did.

Memories

"Everyone did the same days work no matter how old you were so hanging out after work with the older gang at the Market was special. They always took you under their wing."

—**Mary Pell, employee**

"My dad Holgar Penttila loved to fish. He and Johnny Tricsko, who owned the cigar stand, owned a boat together and there were many organized fishing trips with other vendors like Don Miller."

—**Janet Penttila, former vendor**

"The Market is a lot of people working together. We compete but we help each other too. It's definitely more than just a bunch of tenants sharing space. It's a kind of neighborhood. At the end of the day, we stand around, gossip about the customers and each other."

—**Gary Thomas, vendor, Ohio City Pasta**

THE GYPSIES

At the turn of the twentieth century, about a thousand gypsies lived in Ohio City, most of Romanian or Hungarian descent. Tight, tribal families, they functioned as their own communities. By the 1980s, the neighborhood gypsy population had dwindled. There was never a shortage of pickpockets and con artists at the Market but vendors often tell stories about the gypsies and their fast moving scams, like the one that played out in front of Larry Schade in the 1970s.

"The gypsies used to be regulars at the Market, always trying to bargain and often playing the money-changing game. I watched my nephew learn about this the hard way. This gypsy family came in and brought a beautiful young woman who acted as a distraction for the young counter guys. They asked my nephew to break a large bill and then they started quickly switching money back and forth. Before he knew it, they had scammed him for some money. I suppose I could have stopped it, but a few years later when he went to college, I reminded him that what he learned from the gypsies was something he wouldn't learn at business school."

LAW, ORDER, & BEHAVING BADLY
Good Guys, Bad Guys at the Market

THERE IS NO sensational crime at the West Side Market, little that makes it into the weekly police blotter, and even less that commands a newspaper headline, but the "Market" beat, one that also includes the businesses near W. 25th Street and Lorain Avenue, is one of the best beats in town.

Throughout the history of the Market, vendors typically watched out for one another and their customers. At times the West Side Market's Merchants Association hired off-duty policemen to patrol the Market and the parking lot, but only two Cleveland patrolmen were known to have been assigned to the official, full-time "Market" beat by the Cleveland Police Department. There to enforce the law and safeguard the public, the officers were embraced as part of the larger Market family.

Relationships between the people who worked at the West Side Market were not always a "love fest." The West Side Market Tenants Association files are filled with memos and letters describing shouting matches and incidents involving pushing, shoving, and fighting, all followed by disciplinary action, like having to close a stand for a day or two.

In 2009, Larry Schade, a model tenant for more than thirty years was made to shutter his stand, Kaufmann Poultry on a Friday, one of the busiest market days.

> "There used to be a rule that you were not supposed to push a 2-wheeler [a hand cart] through the arcade. One of my employees, E. J. Plylpiv was caught doing that. Someone reported it to the Market manager, who had to write me up and shut down my stand for the day.
>
> So I got a bunch of helium balloons and bright signs that said 'Thanks, E. J.' and 'Closed for company picnic.' That's exactly what we did. We had a picnic at Edgewater Marina with all the employees, their families, and some of our customers, about fifty people. We had the time of our life... kind of like making lemonade out of a lemon."

The most egregious offenders were forced to close their stands and leave the Market permanently. Melissa DeCaro Lau's family produce stand is in the shorter corridor of the arcade off Lorain Avenue. She remembers her father telling a story about a vendor who had his stand taken away from him—and his revenge.

Memories

"There most definitely was a 'gypsy' presence at the Market. Whenever they would come in, the word was out to watch your wallet. The women would come in in these long overcoats and the rumor was they would steal the kids."

—*Bill Retzer, former employee*

"When a vendor would call out 'Code 39,' it meant someone shady or a regular troublemaker was in the Market. Everyone would keep a better eye on their counters and customers."

—*Charles "Bud" Leu Jr., former vendor*

"Some of the older butchers used to tell me that when the lights would go out way back in the day, when meats were laid out on the counter and not protected by a glass case, everyone would come out from behind their counters and lock hands around the meats so people wouldn't run off with their product."

—*Tony Pinzone, vendor, Pinzone Meats*

Bill Busse: Keeping the Peace

Between 1982 and 1994, Bill Busse spent twelve years in front of the counter as the beat patrolman for the Market and surrounding neighborhood and fourteen more behind the counter, working as a meat cutter for Ehrnfelts, as counter help for Penttila's Dairy and in the Mediterranean Import Foods in the corner of the Market.

A typical day for Busse was to watch for panhandlers and the pickpockets who would sandwich older people between them as they got on the busses around the Market. Food stamps traded for fast cash was another problem. In between keeping the peace, Busse often played good cop to the locals. "There was a lady that used to come down to the Market with a pull-behind shopping cart lined with garbage bags," he recounts. "One day, someone stole her cart and she told me she had hundreds of dollars stashed between the bags. She didn't look like someone who would have that kind of money." Busse patrolled the neighborhood and found the cart by a dumpster near St. Ignatius. In between the bags there was indeed $800 in cash.

Skirmishes between vendors and with customers were not uncommon and the Market cop was frequently the intermediary. Busse remembers one vendor telling a customer he would cut his fingers off if he kept pushing on the watermelons to find the perfect one. The customer was outraged, and as a surgeon who obviously made a living with all ten fingers, took the "threat" to the Busse, who smoothed things out.

The homeless and hungry found the Market dumpsters a good source of discarded food and Busse would constantly chase them out of the containers, but not for lack

Former Patrolman Bill Busse

of compassion. "They would always get mad at me," he says, "but I had to wonder if they would get sick."

After twelve years on the Market beat, countless lunches at Frank's Bratwurst, Johnny Hot Dog, and Felice's, Busse retired, proud to admit that he hardly ever took a day off work, saying, "It was such a great job that I was afraid I would miss something."

Memories

"When there was a known thief in the Market, the butchers would clang their cleavers against the metal counters as a warning to others, maybe a threat. The thieves knew what it meant and left quickly."

—*Ed Badstuber, former employee*

"The Poor Clare Nuns would come in once a week to get food for their mission, and most people gave generously to them. We always donated bread to them and all the other nuns who came around.

Once a group of three 'nuns' were going from stand to stand asking for handouts and begging for money. They were getting both until a vendor noticed a pant leg suddenly peeking out from one of the habits. He shouted at the bogus sisters and the men took off, jettisoning packages of food as they ran. About half a dozen workers chased after them."

—*Beverly Tabacco, former employee*

SIGNAL 99!

That's the code at the Market when someone needs a bank escort. Some vendors recall years ago, when the world and the Market were a different place, they would send their kids to the banks multiple times on a busy day, with a sack of cash or even cradling coins and bills in their aprons, to make a deposit. Being a bank escort at the West Side Market is not part of the patrolman's job description, but Market patrolman Jimmy Traynor remarks, "these are mom and pop operations. When they can't leave their stand, they trust me to do it for them."

"Carl Monday (a Cleveland investigative television reporter for more than forty years) used to make an issue of this," recalls Bill Busse. "I used to run to the bank if the merchants needed change on a busy Saturday," he recalls. "As far as I was concerned this was part of my job, to make sure the merchants didn't get robbed or mugged. Signal 99 was a service."

Above: Johnny Tricsko at his cigar and newsstand

"In the late 1950s there was an egg vendor who had a stand close to the Lorain Road entrance. The eggs weren't refrigerated so I think the city health inspector cited him and the Market booted him out. He was really angry and he put some kind of Bohemian curse on the stand. I guess it worked because since then, there have been a half a dozen vendors who have tried to start a business at that stand and they never lasted."

Frank Wegling was the Market's Supervisor of Weights and Measures in the early 1980s. By virtue of having an office near the Market manager, he was also involved in the daily supervision of the Market, which included settling arguments between vendors. He recalls one of the more colorful disputes:

"I was in the office on a Saturday near closing time. A mother and her small child came up to the office and the child was screaming. There was blood in his ear and on his shoulder and I was just about to call the squad. The mother said it wasn't blood. Turns out two of the vendors in the produce arcade got into a fight and were throwing tomatoes back and forth. By the time I got down there, it was broken up, but the two tenants were disciplined."

Memories

"Some of the guys used to play the numbers at the Market in the 1950s. There was a bookie that would go around collecting money from the vendors and writing betting slips. One day, the cops got wise to what he was doing and started chasing him through the Market. The bookie outran the cop, eating the betting slips as he ran."

—Bill Retzer, former employee

"Johnny Tricsko owned the cigar stand next to my mom's stand, Johnny Hot Dog. She would let him know when she was going across the street to the bank to make a deposit. He'd pull a pistol out of a drawer and walk her there. I'd say, 60 percent of the vendors were armed. This was a cash business and a rough world.

When I was a kid, there were pickpockets. The vendors would keep an eye out for them, and if they spotted one, they'd come out from behind the counter, drag them into the alley and beat 'em up. The cops looked the other way. Once a guy stole the cash box from a little old lady. He got chased, didn't get very far. Enough said."

—Tony Anselmo, former employee

Jimmy Traynor: The Beat Goes On

Former Patrolman Jimmy Traynor

Jimmy Traynor, a stocky, blue-eyed "Irish Catholic boy" had been assigned to the Market beat for eighteen years and retired from his post and the Cleveland Police force as the Market turned one hundred. His beat is always maintained on foot, one of the only walking beats left in town. "I know the pattern of this place," says Traynor. "The job of a beat cop is to know who is supposed to be where and when, all up and down the street and in the Market."

Traynor has run down his share of purse snatchers and pickpockets up and down the sidewalks in front of the Market, told panhandlers and drunks to keep moving, and recalls Frank Miller, Cleveland's king of the gypsies— a skilled scammer and counterfeiter known and carefully watched by the vendors. He's seen heart attacks, deaths, and saved people in trouble, too. Yet his most unique role, one that just evolved with the job, is that of guidance counselor and customer service representative.

"I got to talk with people about their everyday activities and problems," says Traynor. Market patrons and vendors alike came to him over the years when they had problems with business or family, like how to discipline their kids. "Nine out of ten conflicts were about customers who didn't get what they thought they paid for," says Traynor. Overly-ripe produce and underweight purchases topped the list of complaints and it usually happened in the produce arcade, where customers and vendors were more likely to engage in bargaining and deal-making.

Even though Traynor wore a badge, his Market family had his back. He remembers a particular domestic dispute that played out on the Lorain Road sidewalk outside the Market. "Some guy and his wife were really going at it. When I got outside, I saw that the guy was really big. I thought, 'uh-oh.' When I got to him, he let me cuff him easily, without resistance," says Traynor. When he turned around, Traynor saw a bunch of the butchers standing there in their bloody aprons with their knives, and realized that the perpetrator had some motivation to cooperate. "The entertainment here is unbelievable," says Traynor. "Most people pay for this type of entertainment."

Traynor remains a part of the Market family following his retirement. He helps his wife, Regina, work the P-Nut Gallery tucked in a corner of the Market; and with Gus Mougianis from the Mediterranean Import Store, they manage the Market Café. "I'm a Market person," he says, "and this is family."

Ⓜ emories

"We had this lady who used to come down and stand in front of the counter, like she was window shopping but she never bought anything. Then we started getting these calls from customers that they didn't get their complete order. We started to notice that this was happening a lot when this lady was here and figured out that she was lifting customers' orders. So this is what we did. We scooped up sawdust, chicken skins, and cigarette butts and wrapped it in a nice package. Then I put a label on it that read 'Baby Lamb Chops—$67.' I put it on the counter in plain sight where she could see it. She scooped it off the counter and into her bag and said, 'See you guys next week.' We never saw her again. We may have lost a 'customer' but it was worth it. I would have loved to have been a fly on the wall when she opened it."

—Larry Schade, vendor, Kaufmann Poultry

THE NEXT HUNDRED YEARS
History in the Making

EVERY PERSON who walks into the West Side Market, including the newest vendor to set up shop and the young couple discovering the place for the first time, instantly becomes part of its story. The future of the Market starts every day in many different ways.

Predicting how the Market will change in the next hundred years is much trickier than recording the history. The effort is a combination of speculation and educated guessing, hope, and some wishing. What's known for sure is that nothing will stay the same, especially when it comes to the people.

"When I came to the Market in 1973, there were a bunch of us," says career butcher, Gordon Fernengel. "My dad's stand was Arnold D. Fernengel and when I came in he put up 'and Son.' There was Don Miller and Son; Steve Check and Son; Edward Badstuber and Sons; John Rolston and Sons. We were the next generation ready to step in. It's not like that anymore."

In the first hundred years of the Market, almost every stand heralded the family name: Wendt, Weigel, and Pawlowski, Schwark, Dreyer, and Churchin. The tradition today is carried on by vendors like Czuchraj, Vistein, Pinzone, and Foster, but some stands are named after the product, like Urban Herbs and The Cheese Shop; Ohio City Pasta; Oooooooh…Fudge; Old Country Sausage and P-Nut Gallery.

The sons, like Fernengel, Larry Vistein, and Jerry Czuchraj, and the daughters, like Diane Dever and Tina Spanos, that took over their parents businesses are still too young to retire. But it's uncertain who will take over when they are ready to move on.

"I don't have any sons to take over the business," explains Jerry Chucray of J & J Czuchraj Meats. (The family changed the spelling of their name to make it easier to pronounce.) "My girls are on different career paths and some of this work requires a man's strength," he says. His wife Jill, who works the stand

Counterclockwise from top: Edward J. Weigel's beef, pork, and veal stand, circa 1920; John Anselmo, 1976

with him, agrees. "It would be wonderful if one of our daughters decides to carry this on, but it's their decision."

The couple's daughter, Amanda Chucray, twenty-three, recently graduated from college with a math degree and she's torn. "I'm working at my parents stand while I look for a job or until I go back for my Masters degree," she says. "I'd hate to see our family lose the stand when my parents retire. If I leave, will I ever be able to come back?"

While times have changed and the ritual of handing a business down to family today may not be as common, it hasn't vanished either. Irene Dever passed the business she built for thirty years to her daughter Diane and the DeCaro legacy continues with Melissa DeCaro Lau, but when there's no blood relative to turn to, vendors like Larry Schade turn to Market family.

His mother Nettie Schade bought the poultry stand in the early 1970s, agreeing with the owner Carl Kaufmann that the name would remain. Larry obliged when he assumed the business in 1978. It does not carry the Schade name, but it's still a family business and will continue as one while he moves toward retirement.

"It's been in our family for over forty years," says Schade. He plans to hand it over to Vern Zielinski, not blood, but a loyal employee at the stand for twenty years. "Hey, when you work with someone that long," says Schade, "they become family."

What was true a hundred years ago at the Market is still true today. Those who run their small businesses here are part of something big and prestigious. Every day the owners and their employees look into the eyes of their customers, shake their hands, share, and listen to stories of their personal lives.

"We're not like Walmart or any big box store," says Jeff Campbell of Campbell's Popcorn Shop. "There are some things about the Market you do not want to change. No one wants crafts or candles and big corporations do not belong here."

"A market like this that has sustained itself for a hundred years means that you'll see something new and an evolution of the vendors in the next hundred years," predicts Campbell. "More than anything, I hope it always stays family-oriented."

Above, from top: Left to right, Larry Schade, John Tricsko, and Dave Hamm celebrate the Market's 60th Anniversary; Butcher Vince Bertonaschi, first generation stand owner, reviews his order list

Memories

"*The customers have changed a lot. In 1965 there were still a lot of first generation Germans, Hungarians, Russian, Greeks, Romanians, and Yugoslavians; in 1985 more Arab Americans. Our customers change with world politics. Now they come in from the same neighborhoods, Tremont and Ohio City, within walking distance, but they are 'yuppies,' not Hungarians or Russians. The crowd at the West Side still reflects a blend of cultures from all around the city."*

—**Maria Mougianis, vendor, Mediterranean Imported Foods**

In his will, Matt Minyard, owner of Edward Badstuber & Sons, has stipulated that if anything happens to him, one of his employees, a young man who started working for him at thirteen and hasn't missed a day in the past six years, will inherit the business. Minyard says that giving it to him, "keeps things inside the Market family."

The Campbells:
Still About Family

Campbell's Popcorn stand stretches along the south wall of the Market, close to the giant antique freight scale. It seems like a cruel joke or poor planning at best, as customers munch on endless samples of sweet and savory popcorn and ogle chocolate-dipped treats like pretzels, cookies, and marshmallows and caramel apples.

Jeff Campbell has always loved popcorn and family, not necessarily in that order, but bringing them together at the West Side Market felt like the perfect combination. Jeff, his wife Lynn, daughters Laura, 26, Bethany, 24, and Holly, 22, and their son, Clark, 28, all work the family businesses at the Market: the Popcorn Shop, The Juice Garden, and Grandma Frieda's Fresh Bake, a cupcake stand and the only stand at the Market to bake on-site. The sweet aroma of baking cake wafts a few aisles over to the popcorn stand, reminding Jeff that he may be the only vendor competing against himself.

Frosted cupcakes, popcorn, and super-healthy juices and smoothies are a contrast to the thick-cut steaks, smoked sausage, and poultry stands surrounding Campbell, but he says that those stands will always define the Market. "This is first and foremost a meat market and it will always stay that way," he says. While what he sells reflects a new way of thinking at the Market, the way he works remains in a traditional vein—it's family working together.

"Sometimes we get into each others business maybe a bit too much," says Campbell, but as a family they gather often, sometimes around the Sunday dinner table, to talk shop and bounce around new product and marketing ideas. The Campbells don't see themselves creating new history at the Market as much as they see themselves carrying on the tradition of a family-owned business. Back in 2003, Campbell started his business with that end in mind. He doesn't wonder what might happen to the stands when he's ready, if ever, to retire—he can see it.

emories

"I would love to see a more sustainable Market, one that uses solar panels and windmills for power, but I wouldn't change the building or the architecture. I would also like to see more local product and local vendors—but no national chains!"

—**Tom Dunderman, vendor, The Basketeria**

"The stand owners that have been here for years...I respect them. They've been through the good times and bad. They are hardworking people and make the Market work. Vince (Vince's Meats) works six days a week! This is earning a buck the honest way."

—**Matt Minyard, vendor, Edward Badstuber & Sons**

Christine Zuniga-Eadie: The Next Generation

She's petite, chic, and her high heels click on the hard-tiled floors as she makes her rounds as the newest manager of the hundred-year-old West Side Market. Christine Zuniga-Eadie, thirty years old and a native of Texas, resembles no other manager before her. Unlike many of them, she had never worked at the Market. Her predecessor George Bradac was a brawny meat cutter and stand owner at the Central Market and Parma Meats before becoming super-visor at the West Side Market in 1986; Frank Wegling, the son of Hungarian immigrants, lived in the neighborhood and worked for Walter Simmelink Jr. at his dairy stand before becoming Supervisor of Weights and Measures in 1975, a title which encompassed the daily operations of the Market; and John Pilch was also a neighborhood kid who worked in the produce arcade trimming vegetables, became a councilman, and was later appointed as the Market commissioner.

Although she hasn't been in the proverbial trenches, never used a meat blade, bagged produce, or pushed a 4-wheeler, Zuniga-Eadie arrived on the job in 2010 with fresh energy, enthusiasm, an education in urban planning, an identity as an emerging leader in the Cleveland com-munity, and an honest admission that she doesn't know everything. As she moves about the Market she always picks up on comments from shoppers and visitors about how exciting the Market is.

"By nature, I'm a good listener," says Zuniga-Eadie, who is the first woman in the history of the Market to serve as manager. "I've been learning from what the vendors have shared with me over the past two years," she says. "I know for sure that there is no shortage of opinion here."

A visual survey of vendors behind the stands confirms that Zuniga-Eadie is of another generation, half the age of many. She is surrounded by two camps: vendors who like things the way they are and others who want to tweak tradition and shake up the Market experience for a new generation of shoppers.

"I'm not trapped into thinking this is how it's always been done so we should keep doing it this way," she says. "I dig deeper and question why." Yet as she becomes a "Cleve-lander," she can already put her finger on what makes the Market so special—its past.

Zuniga-Eadie knows that vendors consider themselves a family, with a history to share and stories to back it up. "Lis-tening to them draws me into this family and it helps me understand a lot about how the Market works," she says.

Memories

Mark Penttila, son of former dairy vendor Holger Penttila, worked at the family stand as a young man throughout the 1970s and eventually left to pursue an engineering career. But Saturdays were still reserved for working at the Market. In the late 1990s, he returned to the Market and today works full time at the Mediterra-nean Import store. "This place," says Penttila, "It just gets in the blood."

"The Market is beautiful and architecturally significant, but what ultimately makes it special are the vendors. Take them out, turn over the stands to chain business or people who don't take personal pride in the products they sell and it's nothing. Buying things from those you know, much of it made by hand by them, that's something that sets this place apart."

—*Sam McNulty, Market patron and Ohio City restaurateur*

The Ehrnfelt Family: The Last Generation

Three years shy of hitting the hundredth anniversary milestone for both the West Side Market and their business, the Ehrnfelt family closed their beef stand, one of the longest-operating at the Market. Walter Ehrnfelt III (Wally) was the fourth and last generation in his family to work the family business. With his father, Walter Ehrnfelt Jr., the popular Market figure and former Mayor of Strongsville, gone and no one in the family willing to step in and take over, Wally bowed to instinct and sold the business. "It was just time," he said and like a hit television show, it's always better to go out when you're on top.

The steer head that sits at the corner of E4, staring southwest, is an Ehrnfelt family heirloom, older than the Market, and possibly older than his great-grandfather Gottlieb Ehrnfelt who started the business at the Market. It's hard to imagine how many families met back under the steer head after going their separate ways through the aisles.

"The Market connected generations of our family as it has connected generations of the families who shop here," says Wally. "People found comfort knowing that they shopped the same way their parents did and walked the same floor. We would see this progression of many family histories."

"The most compelling aspect of the Market was not the compensation package, it was the relationships with the people," said Wally. "My dad was a terrible meat cutter and everyone knew it. But what a great salesman."

Wally talks of his grandmother, the legendary Eleanore, a regular behind the Ehrnfelt stand, who had an explosive temper and a fierce loyalty to her family. "It's hard to

Wally Ehrnfelt and his father Walter Ehrnfelt Jr. at the family beef stand, 1972

admit that she wouldn't hesitate to cuss at a customer who rubbed her the wrong way." In her later years at the Market, the "flavor" of Eleanore was best experienced from afar.

"We got the little stand in the corner opposite Frank's Bratwurst, called it 'Wally's' and put her in her own little world to sell our meat," recalls Wally. "She chased a careless customer who dripped mustard on her stand down the Market aisles. Didn't matter where you put her—she was still Eleanore."

Memories

"Often buying a bit of meat was an afterthought. What some people really came for was the conversation. It was a real social scene. They'd chat with Eleanore or Walter [Ehrnfelt] about their families, what had happened the past week, even share their problems. Despite how tough she could be, Eleanore would sometimes spend twenty minutes talking to somebody. It was a kind of over-the-counter therapy."

—**Jim Petras, former employee**

"Everyone has someone in their life that when you come to that fork in the road they shove you down the right way. That was Walter Ehrnfelt. If you worked hard for him, there wasn't enough he could do for you."

—**Tony Pinzone, vendor, Pinzone Meats**

Candace Berthold's stand, The Olive and Grape, is tucked in the corner of the Market next to a busy entrance. It's one of the first stands shoppers encounter as they enter from the southeast door. Selling her products, imported olive oils, infused vinegars, and seasoning blends, is her main priority, but welcoming people to the Market with a "hello" is a close second. She serves as an ambassador of sorts, but in her four short years at the Market, Berthold has been a keen observer of the comings and goings of not only the shoppers but of her fellow vendors:

"During the first fifty years, this place was a life for a family—twenty-four hours a day, seven days a week. Now people pursue other options, so you don't see as many family members working the stands. And maybe the newer vendors that come into the Market don't have the mind-set that the Market has been a great place for family business. If they are coming from another career to the Market, how they work here is not even close to how they worked before. Now they might not have the time to foster those relationships that vendors in the past did.

There will always be friendships in the Market and although the Market will change with time, it will still remain unique. Vendors will still build their business around their relationships with the customers. The shopping experience you can get here will never be found anywhere else. If you open a brand new building, you won't be able to recreate the loyalties and traditions at the West Side Market. Even shoppers change when they come through the doors. I see it every market day. They are mingling with the vendors and each other. They're talking, but not on their cell phones. Once they go out they walk back into another world.

Time marches on. For sure, the next hundred years will be nothing like the first hundred years!"

Walter Ehrnfelt Jr. cutting beef at his stand, 1976

Notes

1. George W. Knepper, *Ohio and Its People* (Kent, OH: The Kent State University Press, 1989).

2. *Cleveland Jewish News,* Jan. 15, 1994.

3. *Cleveland Jewish News,* Feb. 22, 1994.

4. City of Cleveland, The West Side Market, 1973. A copy is available in the office at the West Side Market.

5. *Plain Dealer*, Nov. 15, 1981.

6. *Plain Dealer*, Aug. 25, 1972.

7. *Cleveland Press*, Sept. 9, 1969.

8. *Cleveland Press*, July 19, 1930.

9. *Plain Dealer*, Nov. 8, 2002.

CHAPTER THREE

THE FOOD
from the Market

CHANGING TASTES
Bringing Food to the Table

FOR ONE HUNDRED years, people have come to the West Side Market for food. A look at what fills their carts and sacks might tell what's for dinner tonight as much as it provides insight into family life, culinary customs, and trends. It offers snapshots of the many ethnic groups that have called Cleveland home and the merchants who've served them.

Like her mother and grandmother before her, one woman is choosing ingredients for dinner, moving purposely up and down the aisles, rarely stopping to "window" shop. But in 2012 the items on her list reflect very different eating habits than her mother and grandmother before her: fresh Chilean Sea Bass filets; a round of crusty rustic Italian bread; a bunch of bright green arugula; an artisan goat cheese from Ohio and a French Brie; and two champagne mangos, perfectly ripe.

> "Every Saturday throughout the 1960s, we went 'marketing' at the West Side Market. We carried our oilcloth shopping bags up and down the tiled aisles, smelling the odors of foods. We stopped here for poultry, there for lunch meat, and yet at another stand for pork. The highlight was always the pickle and sauerkraut lady who would let us reach into the barrels…for our treat."
> —Marge Vamasey

A man purchases a pair of porterhouse steaks neatly wrapped in white butcher paper. The "tails" are still attached, two extra and wonderfully flavorful bites typically not found on steaks in the grocery store. Each is cut, just as he asked, 1½ inches thick, ideal for grilling, and a testament to the skills of his butcher.

> "I have a picture of a T-bone steak on my phone. It was one that I cut and it was just beautifully marbled, everything was just right. I knew it would be perfect and that it would cut with a fork. I guess I really like being a butcher."
> —Vince Bertonaschi, vendor, Vince's Meats

One astute vendor sees his regular customer, a little white-haired "baba," slowly making her way up the aisle, so he reaches into his case to get her order ready. He knows that she wants just a few slices of a cold cut long unavailable at deli counters elsewhere but that lives on at this one stand at the Market. Her happiness is important to him. It's how business is done here.

> "I may not sell as much headcheese as I used to but when an eighty-five-year-old woman comes every other week for her quarter pound of headcheese, how can you stop making it?"
> —Miklos Szucs, vendor, Dohar Meats

Previous pages, clockwise from top: A butcher hones his knife at the chopping block; The crew at the Hildebrandt lunch meat stand, circa 1950

Another buyer has been coming to the Market since he was a child. Now, he brings his grandson along to gather the essentials for the family's holiday celebration. The extra hands, small but willing, help carry the Easter breads and smoked Polish kielbasas that are part of the meal. Vendors carry these traditional things because they understand what they mean to their customers.

> "At Easter we would sell butter lambs. They were about three-ounces but some of our customers would have to look at every single one, very closely, before choosing. We would also sell dyed eggs and there were some that wanted a certain color mix as part of their tradition. We also sold goose eggs. Some liked the taste but mostly the *pysanky* (Ukrainian Easter eggs) makers would buy them because they were so big and the shells were so thick."
> —Janet Penttila, former vendor

Simple acts of commerce define the Market day. But shopping in a place that radiates the feel of an old-world marketplace while stocking the products today's consumers crave and finding merchants who cater to personal tastes brings a special kind of pleasure. First and foremost a trip to the Market is about food—but it has always come with something extra—far more than what fits into a basket or a bag.

> "My parents had their favorite stands but the butter and cheese stand always fascinated me as a child. The lady could cut exactly a pound of butter or however much you wanted each time. There had to be a trick to this feat.
>
> My dad relished herring and would buy a small wooden keg, about two pounds, of the salted fish whenever he could afford it. My Polish mother was particular where she bought pigs' feet. She would cook them for hours with spices, remove the meat from the bones, place it all in a loaf pan, and chill until it gelled. It was called *studzienina*. The lady who ground horseradish on 25th Street was there in all kinds of weather and when I grind horseradish at Easter, I really appreciate her endurance. We would bring empty jars for her to fill."
> —Lillian "Patsy" Mills

Opposite, from top: Shoppers crowd the aisles in July 1946; Working at the Hildebrandt stand (L to R), Bill Retzer, Rocco Meyo, and an unidentified lady, 1950s
Above, from top: Butcher Steve Selezanu hands a happy customer his order, date unknown; A Market shopper shares her shopping list

"When we went to the West Side Market beginning in the 1970s, I always sought out that perfect cup of buttermilk that had flakes of butter floating on top, served in a waxy paper cup. Then it was off to get lemon fingers…and pizza bagels! My mom and Aunt always liked this egg concoction with raisins that was only available during Easter. I think it's called *sirets*. I always loved the hustle of people with their white uniforms pulling wooden carts with meat piled on them."
—Kim Leighton

"Our first stop was Lovaszy Hungarian meat stand. Mom would buy their cottage ham, rice sausage, blood sausage (my dad's favorite), and also fresh Hungarian sausage. To this day I still purchase the rice sausage and it continues to be my favorite.

We would buy fresh goose liver lunch meat and would fry it and put it on Vera's rye bread with mustard. My mouth waters just thinking about the taste. We would then head to the cheese stand to get our butter and baker's cheese to fill our pierogis. It was difficult to find a supplier for baker's cheese except at this Market. We couldn't forget the fresh poppy seed that mom used to bake her famous poppy seed rolls for the holidays.

Another favorite was the pork knuckles and pork hocks. My dad would boil them forever and mix them with a jellied substance, which he would eat chilled with vinegar, salt, and pepper. He called it *kalte füsse* which means, 'cold feet.' Yuk!!

We would buy dad Limburger cheese and he would put the cheese with a slice of fresh onion on that rye bread and he was in heaven! I remember the smell being so pungent I would have to leave the room."
—Elaine Trizzino

"In the late thirties and forties, my mother would buy dried mushrooms imported from Poland and make a wonderful soup from them. A few days before Easter, she bought the best kielbasa, real butter, and dried cottage cheese. We stopped at the bakery for pumpernickel bread and poppy seed and nut rolls. There was a chicken man who had live chickens. You would pick the one you wanted and he would get it ready for you to take home—cleaned and plucked.

We bought the vegetables for the soup my mother would use with the chicken…parsley, celery, carrots, and onions. If I was good, I would get a pomegranate, which we called a 'Chinese apple.'

I'm eighty-six and a half years old and my daughter takes me there once every six months and I still love going to the Market!"
—Wanda Hovanec

Above, from top: Chilled buttermilk has been a favorite on-the-go treat for generations of shoppers; Charles Farone (L) worked for his nephew, John Anselmo (R) for a bushel of produce and gas money

"During the 1940s, my grandmother, mother, and I would purchase fresh ground horseradish from a little stand outside the Market by the 25th Street entrance. That poor lady's face was always red and she had teary eyes from grinding the horseradish. Before we would head home, we would stop at a dairy stand for a treat of fresh buttermilk. It always tasted delicious."
—Norma Ruttkay

"I remember the Ehrnfelt stand, which was there from the time the Market opened in 1912. We shopped at Leu's stand where we bought smoked hams, bacon, cold cuts, and wieners—they weren't called hot dogs then! Our next stop was at a cheese stand for sharp New York State Cheddar. Chickens were five or six pounds for roasting or stewing and small fryers were not available as they are today. Our never-forgotten purchase was peanut butter."
—Elizabeth "Mitzi" McWeeny

For Germans, Poles, Slovaks, Italians, Hungarians, Croatians, and other nationality groups that settled here, the look and feel of the Market was comforting. They relied on the emporium to help recreate the food cultures they left behind. It was a way to exert control over their circumstances, maintain their identities, and bring some familiarity into their American lives.

It continues to serve Cleveland's immigrant communities, both emerging and established, by selling the foods familiar to their taste buds and ingredients used in their traditional cuisines. The Market, in a small but important way, extends a welcome to those trying to make their home here.

"We had an Asian family that asked if we could get a cow's udder. For as much as you can find at the Market, that's not something we sold so we called around to the packinghouses and found one. When it came in we helped get it to the customer's car, milk dripping all over. They were so excited! It was an important ingredient for a soup they made in their homeland—udder soup!"
—Wally Ehrnfelt, former vendor

"I came to Cleveland in 1946 from Plymouth, England, as a war bride. On Saturdays, my husband, his brothers, and their wives and I would meet at the Bridge Inn, where the boys would have a pint of beer, shoot pool and the women and children would go to the Market to shop. At the fish stand, I discovered they carried what we called in England 'winkles,' a sea snail in a little black shell, picked out with a pin and eaten. So much meat, bread, and cheese—I had not seen such abundance for many years. Cheese cut off the wheel, butter cut off a block! At the end of our adventure we had to get a wiener and a bun from the back of the Market."
—Catherine Chald

WEST SIDE MARKET
by Alex Gildzen

pierogis
Hungarian sausage
dark cherry strudel

sometimes
memory lives
on the tongue

Above, from top: Sausage vendor Charles "Bud" Leu Jr. of the Leu Brothers stand tempts customers with franks

Above: Rita Graewe looks out from her stand "Rita's," famous for sauerkraut and pickled products

Rita Graewe was indeed The Pickle Lady, doling out pickles to young visitors at the Market for almost twenty-five years, but she also sold four hundred pounds of sauerkraut a week, and up to two thousand pounds between Christmas and New Year, for Eastern European customers' traditional pork and sauerkraut dinners.

"We would put a bag over our hand, reach in, and grab the kraut out of a barrel," recalls her grandson and successor, Fritz Graewe. Sweet, friendly, and hard-working, Rita knew that her ethnic customers wanted apricot and prune *lekvars* for their baking and pierogi making, pickled vegetables, and freshly-ground horseradish mixed with red beets during Easter. She hung a sign that read: *Savanyitott Leveles Kaposzta*, Hungarian for "soured cabbage leaf," a specialty product that might not have appealed to the masses, but a must for her ladies rolling stuffed cabbage or *szarma*.

"She would core and salt cabbage heads and let them ferment," describes Fritz. "It would stink up the whole house. She would haul the buckets to the Market and her Eastern European customers loved her for it."

Rita turned the business, but not the soured cabbage recipe, over to Fritz. Determined to carry on the tradition, he enlisted the help of a Romanian and a Hungarian customer. "I converted all of their broken English 'handfuls of this' and 'pinches of that' into a recipe I could use," he said. Today the sign remains and makes sense (or a difference) only to those who know what they are looking for.

The dishes that reflected the ethnicities and traditions of the cooks spoke volumes about the immigrant need to remain connected to their heritage and the pleasures of sharing it with family.

"There was one special traditional Lithuanian dish my father made every winter called *koseliena* (chopped meat in aspic). He'd go to the Market butchers, carefully checking what they had in the cases and choosing the different parts that he wanted; pigs' feet, pork hocks,

turkey neck bones, chicken—whatever looked good. At home, he'd wash everything, put it in a big pot to boil with peppercorns, onions, and carrots, drain, rinse, and boil it all again. He gave music lessons in the house, and if he was with a student, our job was to watch the pot and add water if necessary. When it was done he'd strain and save the liquid and pull the meat off the bones. Nothing went to waste. He'd fry up the chicken skin in butter, add eggs, and we'd eat that for lunch. He put the shredded meat in glass dishes, poured the broth on top and left the pans to cool overnight by the back door in the mudroom. We'd have it cut in squares with a mixture of mayonnaise and horseradish. I considered it a treat. Every batch was discussed and analyzed and decisions made about whether to do something differently next time."
—Kristina Kuprevicius

"My best memory was the holidays. That meant we were having a sweet pickled ham that could only be purchased at the West Side Market. My grandmother would get up at 5 AM to start cooking it—boil and drain, boil and drain—for hours. The finished product was like nothing you have ever tasted—sweet and juicy. It made the best ham sandwiches. Later in the week, my grandmother would make bean soup and after that, split pea soup. Since we always got a whole ham, there was plenty of bone to go around. After we were done, it was my dog Chipper's turn. She got the bone in the end. Today's hams are good, some better than others, but nothing like a sweet pickled ham."
—Pat Dorbanski

"My brothers and I did not look forward to some of the dinners our father would prepare from his bag of Market goodies like pigs' feet, blood sausage, liver, and stuff we had no idea what it was. When we would sit down for dinner and weren't sure what was on the plate, we would ask our father what it was. He would answer, 'Chicken.'"
—Paul Jira

Over time, the types of food displayed in the cases, stacked on the shelves, or mounded on the stands changed. The selection broadened as new ethnic groups took root in the neighborhood. The first generation of immigrants gave way to the second generation, who enjoyed both American foods, as well as some from their own heritage. Fewer families had six, seven, or more hungry mouths to feed. Dinner traditions were in flux. The first to notice these changes were the vendors.

"We used to cater to generational customers, but they are fading. They were the ones buying *Zungenwurst* (blood tongue) and headcheese but when those sales dropped off, we had to discontinue those items. The only place in the Market to get headcheese now is at Dohar. Still, 40

LONG CUT PIG FEET $1.89 LB

"PROIZVODI IZ DOMOVINE"

That's what a sign that hung above Tina Martini's dairy stand read. Translated it means, "Products from the Homeland," specifically Yugoslavia. A reporter noticed it, too:

"It's so my people can find me... Vegetable flavored bouillon powder and fruit syrups imported from Yugoslavia are big sellers.

You can make a hundred drinks with just water, or if you're rich, with 7-Up. And with this Vegeta, you can flavor pork chops or chicken in a hurry ...and these Vafel Leafy, these cookie sheets, you just fill them with chocolate or strawberry filling and in ten minutes, you have dessert. You want my recipe?"

—*Plain Dealer*, May 13, 1981

percent of my customers are immigrants and they shop differently than my American customers. They eat! They order five pounds of this and eight of that. Americans buy half pounds or a pound of something."
—Mark Neiden, vendor, Old Country Sausage

"Households where the woman was the stay-at-home housewife, I don't see that anymore. I don't see a lot of dinners prepared the way they used to be…a meat, potato, and vegetable. People are buying quick-cooking cuts and ground meats. My older customers are the ones buying soup meat, but the younger ones don't cook comfort foods, big pot roasts and stews, like they used to because it takes time. It doesn't take talent and you don't have to be a chef, you just have to have the time to cook."
—Vince Bertonaschi, vendor, Vince's Meats

"We still get people from the neighborhood who shop here regularly, but the highways made it easier to go elsewhere and some people have moved to the suburbs. But what's interesting is that the children and grandchildren of people who used to shop here, the ones who knew how to cook, come here to shop with the same vendors and get the ingredients to create the same dishes."
—Tony Pinzone, vendor, Pinzone Meats

Vendors adapted to what they saw and what their customers began to ask for—or no longer asked for. Dairy vendor Annemarie Geffert can't be all things to all customers, but attempts to keep a balance between those who still embrace old world cooking and what a new generation of Market shoppers might be surprised and happy to find at her stand.

"My little old lady customers, the ones with babushkas and accents, need their dry cottage cheese," says Geffert. "There is still a whole generation doing a lot of baking around the holidays, like strudel and cheesecake for Christmas and *babka*, a sweet cake for Easter. They can't

Above: Roasts, chops, and ribs fill the case at Kaufmann's meat stand in the 1950s

bake without it but I do see the need fading." Items like butter lambs, molded from sweet creamery butter, adorned with little red ribbons and peppercorns for eyes, are only available during Easter for those who carry on the Eastern European tradition of the blessed Easter Basket held in many Cleveland churches. It's a ceremony that also includes butter-rich breads, sausages, hams, eggs, and horseradish. Geffert still sells some of the foods unique to this tradition but wonders if people know or remember the symbolism or rituals that accompany them.

> "Even over the past ten years, I've noticed a different crowd coming to the Market. There are people with more money. Still, at Easter the little old ladies come in and they have to have slab bacon for their Easter baskets."
> —Matt Minyard, vendor, Edward Badstuber & Sons

> "It's a struggle to get but I still carry mincemeat for my British and French customers who use it in their baking. So many people anymore really don't understand what it is: a blend of apples, oranges, raisins, brandy, and warm spices. It smells so good!"
> —Annemarie Geffert, vendor, Annemarie's Dairy

> "I was once interviewed for an article about the Market. It was around Easter. The place was very busy. The reporter wanted to know why so many of the women were carrying baskets. So I explained that they'd fill them with food and take them to their church to be blessed by the priest. It's an ethnic tradition."
> —Alvin Stumpf, former employee

While Geffert sees one customer's need for a specific food or ingredient fading, she also notices that another shopper arrives with an entirely new shopping list that doesn't reflect an ethnicity but rather a lifestyle that Geffert herself practices and provides for others at her stand.

Tofu, Brewer's yeast, seitan, local eggs from the Cuyahoga Valley, honey from Ashland, non-homogenized milk—the kind where the cream still rises to the top—in glass bottles from Hartz-

Above, from top: Butchers Brian Foster and Jack Sabolik trim legs of locally-raised lamb; Although he owned a beef stand, Walter Ehrnfelt steps in for a fellow vendor to wait on customers

SALSA
HABANERO PEPPER,
PAPAYA, PINEAPPLE,
MANGO, CILANTRO,
RED ONION
HOT
$4.75 LARGE
$3.25 SMALL

Sides and salsas on display at Orale!

ler's Dairy in Wooster, and local artisan goat cheeses fill her dairy case. Signs that read "local" and "natural" attract customers the same way ones written in a Spanish or Arabic would attract people of those ethnicities.

Brian Foster has spent twenty-five years behind a butcher block cutting beef into pot roasts, stew meat, and brisket—for the budget-minded traditional cook—and lamb and goat into shanks, necks, ribs, heads, and offal for his Albanian, Greek, and Arab customers. He's also learned the language of "locavores," people who seek out foods grown or produced close to home. A few years ago, Foster posted signs on his stand announcing the availability of both Ohio grass-fed beef and pastured lamb. "The customers who want these meats know that they are usually available only once a month," says Foster, "and they don't argue about the higher price."

Tom and Anita Dunderman stumbled into organic produce during their first year of business in the produce arcade as the Basketeria. "We started selling organic carrots and celery," says Tom. "The flavor was great and it was at a time when people were beginning to recognize the health benefits of organics and they were asking for more."

While the couple was excited to fill a niche for organics, they challenged the perception of the Market as a place where food was inexpensive. Organic or not, a carrot looks like a carrot. "We would get yelled at daily about the price of organics, which can be twice as much as conventionally-grown carrots," he says. "To keep the peace, we had to start carrying both kinds."

Sauerkraut, rye bread, and bologna still connect some customers to the past, but foods like falafel sandwiches and Cambodian spring rolls invite them to expand their palate with flavors from other parts of the globe. The presence of prepared foods at the Market, ready-to-eats like soups, sweet and savory crepes made on the spot, and fresh fruit smoothies may not be new or revolutionary in the grand scheme of foods, but the variety indicates that at the Market people can experience the best of both worlds.

Ⓜemories

"There are two schools of food at the Market: the traditionalists and the progressives. We don't want to give up tradition, we just think that adding good prepared food does it one better."

—Judy Khoury, vendor, Judy's Oasis

"'Nudge Mama' was my Hungarian grandmother and she always served her traditional ethnic food: stuffed cabbage; chicken paprikash; Easter cheese; kielbasa and hurka; and a wonderful creamed squash dish with dill and peppers. Prepared far from her familiar home, it was always fresh from the Market. When I shop there, I have a connection to her world.

I stroll down the aisles looking for Hungarian hot peppers, green peppers, and cubanells and select them with the same great care as Nudge would. I still make this wonderful journey almost every week. My wife Becky now joins me. We will select a vegetable, fruit, cheese, poultry, fish, or meat that we have never tasted before, research some recipes, and introduce ourselves to some amazing new tastes."

—Tom Sawyer

FROM SCRATCH TO FAST:
TWEAKING TRADITION

When Judy Khoury and Roberto Rodriguez opened their stands at the Market, hers serving Syrian and Lebanese foods and his contemporary Mexican fare, visitors "ate up" the addition of these cultural cuisines but for some of their fellow vendors, it was an idea they couldn't quite warm up to.

"They called us 'fast food,'" said Khoury. In a place full of fresh cuts of meat and poultry, fish and produce—foods that required a cook's touch—some saw the addition of ready-to-eat foods from Judy's Oasis, like baba ghanouj, *fatiyar*, and *sfeeha* (Middle Eastern pies), and homemade chiles rellenos and microwave-ready enchiladas from Orale! as convenience foods that didn't quite fit the traditions of the Market. Khoury and Rodriguez saw their stands as adding even more variety to a place that thrives on diversity—in the foods sold and the cultures served.

"We are the vendors starting out the next hundred years," says Khoury. "The next generation is eating differently. You can see the evolution of this place not only in our stands, but even at the chicken stands. Chicken sausage! Who ever heard of that fifty years ago, but that's what people want these days."

Both entrepreneurs opened on the same day, September 1, 1999, filling a growing niche among a generation that didn't know the Market like their parents or grandparents—a generation that didn't have the time or desire to cook, but had adventuresome taste buds. While some fellow vendors saw prepared foods as a threat to the way things had been done at the Market, Rodriguez saw it as a complimentary.

"You won't find anyone doing what vendors like us are doing at a supermarket, so when someone comes here to buy our food, they're probably discovering other vendors, too," says Rodriguez. "We might be tweaking tradition, but we're probably starting new ones, too."

"Some of my customers started coming here when I first opened," says Khoury. "They were kids then, adults now, and they bring their own kids. These are the same things some of the longtime vendors have seen in their customers for years."

Judy Khoury and Roberto Rodriquez, a new age of Market vendors

"I've been here thirteen years and I'm still the new kid on the block," says Rodriguez. "But like the other vendors I'm every bit as devoted to my business, my customers, and the Market."

"People that come to me don't just buy what I sell, they ask for suggestions about where to buy other things, like a rib steak or chicken, so I send them where I buy from in the Market," he says. "Where can they get a poblano? I don't send them to the supermarket, I send them out in the arcade or down the aisle to where I shop."

"I think that stands like mine, Judy's, KIM SE Cambodian Food, Ohio City Pasta, and Pierogi Palace add to what's already here," says Rodriguez. "We certainly call attention to it."

WILL WORK FOR FOOD
A Smorgasbord of Talent

THE RHYTHMIC SOUND of a butcher's knife being drawn across a sharpening steel in the West Side Market is a lot like that of a musician warming up for a concert at Cleveland's Severance Hall. While some of the Market performances might not always draw an audience or earn a round of applause, they are no less a show of talent and artistry. There's the poultry vendor who can gracefully reduce a whole chicken to pieces in a minute with a few well-placed cuts of his knife; the fish monger who efficiently scales and fillets a whole grouper; the butcher that knows how to roll cut a center-cut pork loin with gentle swipes of a boning blade and give a new and nervous cook instruction on how to stuff, tie, and roast it; and the sausage maker that proudly arranges the links he's brought from his own smokehouse.

Skill is on display every day at the Market. The crepe maker prepares each paper-thin pancake right before his customers' eyes, handing it to them over the counter, still warm, in a paper cone. A pastry decorator pipes hundreds of swirling crowns on the cupcakes she displays in orderly rows in her case. The bread baker's talents are implied as she arrives with her loaves in the morning, trailed by the aroma of bread pulled fresh from the ovens at her baking facility.

Above: A butcher takes a minute to pose in his cooler amid hanging meat ready to hit the butcher's block, 1970s

Ⓜemories

"Nothing has really come along to revolutionize the way I break down halves or forequarters of beef. I'm still using a saw that's seventy-five years old and it runs like a top."

—Steve Check, vendor, Steven Check Jr.

"I would cut meat in the cooler wearing insulated moon boots, a military type boot that had a valve, and a down jacket. The temperature was always in the thirties, a dry cold. The chicken coolers were a bit damper. In the 1960s, meat was delivered a couple of times a week and broken down daily. As you sold it upstairs, you would call downstairs to get it replenished. It went on all day long. On Tuesday and Thursday, there was no screwing around. You cut meat. For contests of strength, we would take 125-pound hindquarters and have races to see who could get it up the stairs the fastest."

—Joe Bistricky, former vendor

Some skills are not as obvious. The cheesemonger's talent lies in selecting and sourcing the finest products from around the world and knowing the origin and taste of each wheel or chunk. Another vendor keeps local honey and maple syrup on the shelves by searching out the best producers in the region. And then there's the knowledge of the specific flavor a spice will add to a recipe that a worker shares with each ounce she sells. Things waits to be sliced to order, weighed, put in a box, or neatly wrapped as soon as the customer points and says, "I want that one!" It requires a certain kind of know-how to stir someone's appetite at the mere sight of food, an ability demonstrated at the Market daily.

There was a time in America, as well as Cleveland, when neighborhood butcher shops were common and the butchers were highly skilled at selecting, handling, boning and filleting, displaying, marketing, and selling their product. With the advent of mass refrigeration and quicker distribution, supermarkets began selling meats precut and packaged in plastic-wrapped foam trays. Variety was limited. But not at the West Side Market: butchers, along with fishmongers and poultry vendors, are still doing what they've always done, preparing products themselves to satisfy their customers' demands.

"I could say that butchers are the hardest working in the Market but I would probably have a lot of people angry with me," says career butcher Vince Bertonaschi, "but we certainly are the most skilled—us and the sausage makers."

Both trades have been part of the Market's foodscape for a century and important players in keeping the Market anchored as a genuine food market and not a tourist attraction.

Butchering is a physically demanding job. Today a fraction of the meat vendors bring in "boxed meat," hogs and cattle already broken down into primal cuts, which they will take a few steps further to yield a variety of products. But the "old days" of personally selecting cattle and breaking down fore- and hind-quarters in the coolers, while not practiced exclusively any longer, are not entirely gone—a number of butchers here still work the same way. Lambs, pigs, and goats are small enough to arrive as whole carcasses and beef comes in hefty halves and quarters. Using band saws, hand saws, and muscle, these traditionalists produce the T-bones, hanger steaks, chops, tenderloins, legs, and specialty cuts they display in their cases. It's something the Market is known for.

Gordon Fernengel, a third-generation butcher, made numerous trips to the hectic stockyard with his father Arnold throughout the 1970s as he was developing his own expertise, a process that for him began before the meat was placed on the butcher block. Eventually, Fernengel was able to look at sides of beef hanging "on the rail" and decide if they were good enough for his customers and worthy of his skills.

"If you were good at what you did, you didn't walk into the packing house and say, 'I'll take five,'" says Fernengel. "We would have to get there early to get the best pick—a particular size, color, and quality."

"When you're learning, all the 'swinging beef' (whole-dressed cattle that hang from rails), looks the same, but after a while, you could see the ones with more meat on them," he says. "You had to look at how fat it was and where

ELEMENT OF SURPRISE

Mark Penttila has worked behind the counter at Mediterranean Imported Foods in the corner of the Market for fifteen years and knows that the only way to turn someone on to a new cheese is with a little sliver or a chunk served on a piece of parchment paper. "Sometimes you realize they are just having lunch when they've eaten their eighth piece," he's observed.

Knowing just what's likely to appeal to a particular customer comes from tasting a lot of cheese, here and at his father Holger Penttila's dairy stand in the 1960s and '70s. "If a customer is unsure of what they want and asks to be surprised, I might ask a few questions," says Mark. "Some people will be easy to please, you know who they are. They're probably that way in life, too."

Looking at a young couple shopping with a toddler, he offers a personal recommendation. "I tell them I think they would like 'Baby-sitter' cheese," he says. The cheese is actually a Cambozola, a combination of a French soft-ripened, triple-cream cheese and Italian Gorgonzola. "It goes well with a bottle of wine and a baby-sitter," he adds.

Margaret and Steve Selezanu at their meat stand, 1960s

IN HIS PRIME

For thirty years, until the 1980s, Steve Selezanu was the only butcher at the Market to sell prime aged beef. His daughter Linda recalls that he would buy quarters of beef and hang them in his cooler for weeks on end.

"You couldn't do this with just any meat. It had to be prime, with a lot of fat on it," she recalls. As the meat aged, it began to sprout "hair." "It looked horrible, all moldy and fuzzy," she says. "What was happening is that the tough tissue was breaking down naturally and the meat was getting really tender and flavorful." The customers who could afford it would order specific cuts. "He would trim off the bad stuff and underneath the meat was as pink and tender as it could be, like you could cut it with a fork," says Linda, who met her husband Joe Bistricky, from another family of butchers, while working at the Market. "The day he married into my family was the day he said he started eating a lot of steak," she laughs.

the fat built up. Choosing by just color was tricky but you always looked for an orangey-red."

Fernengel can remember walking with his dad through the packinghouse, watching as he ran his finger across the meat. "He taught me to look for a 'sweet feel,' kind of like how water and sugar feel mixed together," the younger Fernengel explains. "Not sticky, but moist. You didn't want the one that was too dry and my dad could tell what it ate. Grass eaters had little moisture and the color wouldn't hold up well in the case." They would tag the ones they wanted and within hours, the two-hundred-pound quarters would arrive at the Market loading dock and then into the cooler downstairs. Over the next few days, forequarters were turned into chuck roasts, brisket, short ribs, and shanks; and the hindquarters into flank and porterhouse steaks, and boneless rump roasts.

Many years ago, butchers sold large, economical cuts that would feed a big family and it was not unusual for cooks on a very tight budget to do some of the work themselves. "Customers used to ask the butchers for larger, primal cuts like a peeled knuckle (also known as a sirloin tip) and break it down themselves at home into stew meat, roulade, braciola, and a roast," remembers Bertonaschi. "Today, we do all that for them, but the next generation of butchers will do even more than we're doing."

The Market's butchers stand out when it comes to specialty cuts, those never found in a grocery store. Whether it's one important to cultural cuisine, an ethnic celebration, or something an adventurous cook hotly pursues, this is the place to start. From offal to organ meats, and just plain oddball requests, nothing is out of the realm or beyond the skill level of the butchers. They know the animal from nose to tail and most are familiar with what their customers are eating.

"I know the Italians love tripe and they cook it in a tomato sauce and the Latinos put it in *menudo*, a traditional chile-based Mexican soup," says Bertonaschi. "I was the first guy in the place to cut a thin layer of meat off the forequarter for my customers from Argentina. They wanted that to stuff and roll up. Mexicans and Puerto Ricans like the hearts. They marinate them and put them on the grill. Lots of people come here looking for something they remember from their country."

Butchers know that just about every part of the animal can be useful and profitable. Today's generation doesn't consistently buy some of the lesser cuts, but vendors need to supply the few that do. "Lots of us still have beef tongue in our cases," says Bertonaschi. "The customers who like these were raised on farms where they would use everything but the 'moo.'"

Michael Turczyk prepares lamb for his Eastern European and Middle Eastern customers and goat for his East Indian and Latino customers. "My Arab customers love lamb heads," he says. "They pack it with spices and bake it in the oven. The Egyptians use it to make a cream-based soup and the oldest member of the household gets to eat the eyeballs, it's some kind of tradition and done for good luck." Raw lamb for kibbee that will feed his Lebanese customers must come from the leg and be as lean as possible and the spleen is a delicacy cooked up just like beef or veal liver.

Sausage is often made from the lesser parts of the animal, yet the profession of sausage maker is one that's highly respected in many countries and at the Market. The ability to translate the taste of a culture through sausage is a remarkable talent. Market vendors sell sausage, a broad term for the flavorful and fatty encased meats that encompass a variety of shapes, from slender smokies, plump brats, and fat rice rings to Polish or Hungarian sausages in which the addition or omission of one simple ingredient, like paprika or garlic, makes all the difference.

When the Market first opened and before refrigeration was dependable for keeping meats fresh, sausage makers cranked out their product every few days in off-site shops, smokehouses, even garages. Before the 1950s, Hildebrandt Provision Company would pack their sausages in wooden barrels and haul them to the Market on the back of a truck. "This was before cardboard boxes," says Bill Hildebrandt. "Because our plant was so close to the Market, we would just cover it with paper and canvas."

Steve Selezanu, who made fresh bulk sausage on-site, had a following for his Old Kentucky pork sausage with sage, but the majority of sausage makers made varieties that suited specific ethnic groups. Germans went to Robert Stumpf for bratwurst; Badstuber's for Slovenian sausage; Ukrainian and Polish customers wanted kielbasa and smokies from J & J Czuchrajs; and Hungarians went to Joseph Pinter's for blood sausage and Dohar/Lovaszy for garlicky paprika sausage.

"My father-in-law Steve Dohar came to Cleveland from Hungary in 1951," explains Miklos Szucs, his son-in-law and one-time apprentice. "His second day here he walked into the Market and got a job working for Emery Lovaszy. It was the first stand he came upon. At that time, Lovaszy only carried fresh pork. Steve spent five years in an Austrian refugee camp, where he learned to butcher hogs and make sausage. He asked Lovaszy if he could make sausage for the stand and started with fresh Hungarian garlic sausage. After that, he added hurka (rice ring), headcheese, and smoked bacon."

RACK of LAMB
1399

A worker at the Hildebrandt Provision Company readies salami sticks for hanging and aging

Memories

"The guys who used to work in the steel mills had big families and they would eat big suppers. The beef guys at Hartman's used to have standing customers every week for their special pot roasts. They were fifteen-inches long and eight-inches wide. This was their Sunday dinner."

—*Charles "Bud" Leu Jr., former vendor*

"Walking around the Market is like an anatomy lesson in animal parts."

—*Jerald Chester*

"Rocky Mountain Oysters, or bull testicles... lots of people want to try them, but my regulars swear that it gives them a boost of testosterone. Hey, if they think it does, it does!"

—*Vince Bertonaschi, vendor, Vince's Meats*

Dohar bought the business in 1972 and changed the name on the stand from Lovaszy to Dohar. Szucs and Angela, his wife and Dohar's daughter, have carried on the tradition of making Hungarian sausage for the past twenty-five years, using the same old-world recipes and methods Dohar passed on.

"I make sure not to change the recipes or the ratio of spices to meat. I wouldn't say the recipe is a secret but I still wouldn't give it to anyone. When people ask what's in the sausage, I tell them 85 percent lean meat, paprika, lots of garlic, and salt…the only thing missing are ingredients you can't pronounce (no additives). That's why when I sell out and customers get mad, I tell them we don't make sausage that has a long shelf life."

Jerry Chucray's father was also an immigrant from the Ukraine, arriving in the 1950s. "He had friends who knew how to make sausages and one had a stand at the Market," says Chucray. "It was very busy then. They rented a place together on Fulton where they made sausages." Chucray still cranks out sausage in the same place, a hundred-year-old building with no heat, and he fires the smokehouse with real wood.

"Originally we concentrated on traditional European styles because that's what our immigrant customers wanted to eat," he says. "Their children eat differently and we've had to adjust and expand. Thirty years ago we had fifteen varieties of handmade sausage. Now we have forty. We still do the traditional stuff but also many made with chicken, chorizo. We've got more unusual and sophisticated combinations."

Above, from top: Billy Badstuber offers up fresh sausage at the family stand; From left, Joseph and Hugo Hildebrandt and one of the driver salesmen sit on the running board of the company delivery truck, 1922

Memories

"I have a personal take on which is the 'best' sausage. It's only the best for whoever likes it. If you don't like garlic, you won't like our Hungarian sausage. It's a personal decision. That's why the Market is so good; you can find such a wide variety. If you cannot find one you like here, you are never going to find one that you like."

—Miklos Szucs, vendor, Dohar Meats

"Candy, fresh rye bread, chocolate coconut cake, headcheese, and smokies seemed to be what we would always get…and a gray sausage looking thing at Dohar that they called hurka but my mother called quicheca (sic), a rice sausage that breaks open when cooked."

—Natalie Shipula

"Shortly before she passed away, I went to visit Rita Graewe (aka The Pickle Lady) in the nursing home. She was happy to see me but happier to see the mettwurst I brought her from the Market."

—Mark Neiden, vendor, Old Country Sausage

The Würst of Times: Mark Neiden

Mark Neiden knew nothing about producing German sausage—other than he wanted to make it in the old-world style and he wanted to make it for West Side Market customers. He put an ad in a German trade magazine advertising for a *Würstchenmacher* (sausage maker) to teach him the trade in six months.

Ernst Hermle, a master sausage maker from Gosheim, arrived in Ohio, tweaked a few recipes, and started sharing the intricacies of the craft with Neiden.

"In Germany, this is a lofty and respected profession and six months is not a lot of time to learn a centuries-old trade," says Neiden, so Hermle stayed a year, guiding Neiden and his family through the history, process, and use of the proper equipment. "One of our bowl cutters or choppers was made in 1941 during World War II," he says. "Even during metal shortages people still wanted their sausage and the makers still wanted good equipment."

In 1982, the family opened the Old Country Sausage Kitchen in Maple Heights, where they make and smoke all the sausage Neiden has sold at the Market for the past thirteen years. Forty percent of his customers are immigrants and his American customers are children of immigrants. "You don't start eating *leberwurst* (or the more Americanized term, liverwurst) at thirty-five," he says. "You have to eat it as a baby or a toddler."

The Kitchen also cranks out *landjaeger*, a flat, smoked, and dried sausage, a German smokie, that hunters would carry in medieval times; bratwurst, a sausage for frying that in Germany varies widely by region, city, and family; and *weisswurst*, a veal sausage that should be boiled in water, "like a German hot dog," says Neiden. For Easter and Christmas, customers want their kielbasa and *rummettwurst*, fat casings filled with smoked pork spread. "Germans used to hang these on their Christmas tree," he says.

"The Market has adapted to changing tastes like turkey, chicken, and tofu sausage, but authentic kielbasa and sausages will always stay the same," says Neiden. "That's not just a Market tradition; it is who we are as Cleveland."

Memories

"Aufschnitt. *When I hear a customer say that, it means they want a mixture of everything I've got in the case. It also means they're German. Germans eat sausage and cold cuts for breakfast.*"

—**Mark Neiden, vendor, Old Country Sausage**

"*Some people have different names for the same sausage depending on where they came from.* Kishka *could be a rice ring or a barley ring.*"

—**Becky (Stumpf) Fitch,
former employee**

"*Cleveland, like Milwaukee, had a lot of European immigrants. The Italians and Germans were known for blending meat products into sausage and they had meat at every meal.*"

—**Bill Hildebrandt, former employee**

Chicken at the Market was and still is a whole different animal—literally and figuratively. Squawking birds were sold on the sidewalks and at the live poultry building adjacent to the Market. Until the early 1960s, freshly-killed and plucked birds packed in ice arrived in large wooden barrels weighing up to 600 pounds—some came from local farmers but more were supplied by brokers.

A poultry vendor's skill was demonstrated in speed, strength, and endurance—maneuvering heavy containers; cleaning the birds in cold surroundings; and dividing the whole birds into smaller pieces as market goers' preferences changed. "We would take the barrels back every week to the stockyard to have them filled up with more chicken," remembers Bill Pawlowski, whose family owned Henry's Poultry from the early 1940s until 2001. "Cleaning the birds was the worst job ever," recalls Pawlowski. "They were plucked, but we had to clean the entrails and remove the heads and feet; my dad's hands were as soft as a baby's bottom from all the chickens he cleaned. We used to save all the feet and we would just give them away. Soup makers always swore by the flavor the bones and skins would give."

John Rolston, a poultry vendor for more than fifty years, recalls a time when more chicken at the Market was sold with the heads and feet intact. "The customers preferred to finish the jobs themselves," he said. "In those days, no one had discovered cut-up chicken."

In the early 1970s, Rolston's poultry stand was the first location in the Cleveland area to sell Perdue chicken. "At the time, most of the Perdue farmers were in Maine and Frank Perdue didn't want to come this far from the east coast," says Rolston, "but I got him to agree, promoted them as natural chicken, and started a trend. As an extra incentive for customers to buy them, we put dollar bills inside the cavities of some."

In 1992, Terry Leu bought Rolston's business. "Just like cutting beef, you had to have a good teacher," says Leu. "I did with Rolston. I wanted to be as good or better than him, so my goal was to beat the teacher."

Above, from top: Workers at Carl Kaufmann's poultry stand wait on customers; Jack and Peggy Coyne smile from their poultry stand

Memories

"You would work cleaning chicken in the cooler for the better part of a day, starting at 5 AM. We used to keep pans of hot water in there to warm up. In the summer, the hot light bulbs would throw off a lot of heat. It was a challenge to keep everything fresh."

—John Rolston, former vendor

"When I first started working at the Market, the chickens used to come in defeathered and nothing else. When we would clean them, we used to collect a couple dozen eggs from inside every week. Sometimes the undeveloped yolks looked like a little cluster of grapes, which my grandmother used to make her noodles."

—Bill Pawlowski, former vendor

"I have a group of kids come in every year for a field trip. This one little girl questioned what all the chicken parts were so I held up a whole chicken to show her that this is what a chicken looked like before it's cuts up into parts. She said, 'You're kidding?' For her, a chicken was supposed to look like a McNugget™."

—Terry Leu, vendor, Rolston Poultry

"My customers will tell me how good I am at cutting up chicken. I tell them the first million I practiced on were hard, but now I could do this with my eyes closed," he jokes. "My best skill is my hand-eye coordination and the fact that I've swung this cleaver over a million chickens and still haven't lost a finger which is pretty impressive."

When Rolston first took Leu under his wing to teach him the business, people were still buying whole chickens and as a courtesy, vendors would cut them into pieces. "There was a time when the grocery store butcher would charge his customers to do this," says Leu, "but it's always been part of the service at the Market."

In the 1970s, a chicken dinner was still a special meal for a family but at the same time, poultry vendors noticed their customers were not only eating more chicken but preferred specific pieces. "Wings used to get thrown out in the 1970s, but as chicken became more affordable and people saw it as healthier, wings became popular bar food and we began selling a ton," says Leu.

Although poultry vendors don't appear to perform the same scope of cuts as beef vendors, there are still times when customers make specific requests. "My East Indian customers want the skin for their curry and the pieces chopped into smaller pieces," says Leu. Customers will ask for "spatchcocking," or removing the backbone so the bird lays flat to cook evenly and quickly; or "airline" chicken, a boneless breast with the wing attached. He recalls a long-time customer who always asked for the whole bird to be split in half, not from neck to tail, but around the middle. "In his mind, it was the best of both worlds and it's how he grew up. To tell you the truth, I don't know what most of the cuts people want these days are called, but if they tell me what they want, I'm sure I could do it for them."

Market vendors are all cooking experts, albeit in very narrow fields. Terry Leu can tell his customers how to roast a whole chicken to perfection and why backs, necks, and feet make the richest flavored chicken stock; butcher Tony Pinzone can deliver the short course in grilling a steak to medium-rare as well as explain why ground chuck makes the best burger; Kate McIntyre of Kate's Fish can explain how to poach a whole salmon, as well as the nuances of buying fish.

Other sellers gladly help customers reconstruct a dish they remember their grandmother, who kept the recipe to herself, served often. The Market is the

Memories

"My first job was to pull the fat off the chicken backs because we sold it separately. Then I learned how to cut up whole chickens into parts. Eventually I graduated to dealing with customers. We had all kinds from many different ethnic backgrounds and they liked to tell me how they cooked chicken. Then there were the chicken feet…people used them to cook and eat, but some just wanted to see them or get them as a joke. If anybody asked me what to do with chicken feet I'd say, 'You can boil them, bake them, fry them, roast them, or hang 'em from your rearview mirror.'"

—*John Coyne, former employee*

"What's kind of grown for us in recent years is Turducken. We have a guy who will come in during the holidays and bone-out twenty chickens, stuff them in twenty boned-out ducks, and stuff that into twenty boned-out turkeys."

—*Larry Schade, vendor, Kaufmann Poultry*

original "food network," connecting customers and vendors who routinely exchange information about cooking and recipes.

Long before celebrity chefs made it trendy to get back to the stove, the West Side Market vendors were giving over-the-counter lessons and tips to their customers, from new brides with no kitchen experience and those looking to shake up a boring routine, to the more adventurous eater and ambitious cook looking for the latest and greatest foods.

Myron Iwaskewych of M. J. Meats claimed fame for his liverwurst. An old European recipe, it makes a delicious Sloppy Joe, European style. "All you do," according to Iwaskewych, "is crumble it into a pan, heat it through and spread on bread…special spices and Hungarian paprika give it a wonderful taste."
—*Plain Dealer*, May 13, 1981

"Way back, people didn't need a cookbook or a recipe to make a meal because it would slow them down," observed Bertonaschi. "Today a lot of cooks follow the 'Michael Symon Says' rule. When Michael says to cook beef cheeks, I better have beef cheeks to sell."

Customers come in and share with vendors their great successes and near failures in the kitchen. "I have a Saturday customer who does a lot of catering and he always tells me what he's doing, what he's cooking," says longtime Market employee, Tim Jeziorski. "You can't leave here any day and say that you

Above, from top: A family inspects a Thanksgiving turkey before purchase; A shopper checks out the produce

Ⓜ emories

"I like to eat and I like to cook so I can help customers by telling them what to do with a roast." I get a lot of younger people who need tips. I can always tell if a specific cut of beef, like flank steak, was featured on the Food Network…people will come in asking for it for weeks afterwards. I notice older folks shop more thriftily. They're still the ones buying soup meat, short ribs, and pot roast. The younger ones want steaks and our pre-made shish kebabs."

—*Jeremiah Wiencek, vendor, Wiencek's Meats*

"I'll admit that I can be kind of sarcastic, but I get impatient with certain thinking—customers who come in and think that they can have any kind of fish they want, anytime they want it. When someone asks me on Wednesday if I'll have any striped bass or monkfish by Saturday, I have to explain that first the fisherman has to catch it, then I have to know about it, and then they have to sell it to us. Buying fish is not like buying chicken or pork chops. The customer who 'gets it' will know that if they want Copper River salmon, they have to wait until the end of May before looking for it."

—*Kate McIntyre, vendor, Kate's Fish*

Mary Pell: The Sense of Smell

The smells of the Market have the ability to stir the appetite and memories of shoppers. Aromas of fresh peaches, ripe strawberries, and sharp garlic blend together and travel across the aisles of the produce arcade on warm, breezy days and have a subtle way of suggesting what would taste good. Inside the distinct smell of fatty smoked sausages, freshly-baked breads, and sharp, pungent cheeses combine into one beautiful scent, a special recipe everyone wants but that cannot be duplicated.

Mary Pell works at Urban Herbs, a stand that carries seasonings, spices, flavorings, and dried herbs, defining ingredients in ethnic cooking. She says the most interesting questions come from people trying to recreate a fragrance they remember.

"I always find customers trying to connect with the recipes and foods their mother or grandmother prepared by trying to identify the spices they smelled as it was cooking," says Pell. "They will often bring their purchase, maybe meat or chicken, from another stand and ask a lot of questions about what they could use to recreate that memorable dish."

Pell calls on her thirty years of experience working for various vendors, including those that sold beef, smoked sausage, and dairy products, and a lifetime as a cook to help people find their way back to a taste. She knows that paprika, the brick-red ground pepper, is a classic for Hungarian dishes like chicken paprikash and that garlic and oregano are defining flavors in Greek dishes like lamb kebabs. "The Middle Eastern cooks use sumac and *zatar*, a spice blend for dipping oils for breads," she says, "and the Polish add a lot of dill and caraway in their cooking that uses sauerkraut." Germans season pork with fennel and mace, the English like curries for chicken and lentil dishes, and the Irish, "they are still trying to learn to cook with spices," she kids, "but they're coming around."

M emories

"One Christmas holiday, the demand for carp was high and the stand ran short, so the crew made a run to Huron and filled up the back of the pick-up truck with fish. When we got back to the Market, it was late, we were tired, and figured it would be okay until the next morning because it was cold enough. The temperature dropped to four degrees and the next morning, we had a solid block of fish in the truck bed. As it thawed out, some started moving."

—Jim Moroney, former employee

didn't learn something, whether it's about cooking or human nature. While we teach them, we learn from them, too. They tell us what they use these meats and cuts for. I find myself saying, 'How about that?' just like baseball's great sportscaster Mel Allen used to say."

The fishmonger's skill lies in choosing, displaying, and processing fresh fish in minutes, as much as it does in the theatrics and hawking needed to attract attention. Really fresh fish, still moving, were always an effective prop. "Live carp were great to hold up and show the kids," said Jim Moroney, who, beginning in the 1960s, worked at his uncle George Moroney's fish stand for twenty years. "We would holler, 'look how fresh our fish are!'"

Ilia Kazandjieff, who also scaled, filleted, and weighed fish at Moroney's for twenty years, was a Bulgarian showman who could draw a crowd with fresh fish "puppetry" and spontaneous displays of calisthenics on a makeshift chin-up bar in front of the stand. When he bought the stand in 1992, delivery by air freight was improving and he was able to cast a wider net to bring fish in from all over the world: African perch from Lake Victoria, Chilean Sea Bass, and tilapia. "It used to be called St. Peter's fish because it came from Israel and Palestine," says Ilia. Fresh orange roughy arrived from New Zealand and goatfish, named for the "goatee" it sported, came from Spain.

He continued to identify and cater to the tastes of the Market's ethnic customers. "The British, Scottish, and Irish liked periwinkles, flounder, salt cod, turbot, and halibut," he observed. "The Germans liked whole cod and herring. I could sell three to four hundred pounds a week. My Chinese customers wanted snapping turtles for a special stew. The Hungarians wanted carp, Russians wanted sturgeon, and Scandinavians loved smoked eels and rainbow trout. The Italians would come at Easter for salt cod and eels for Good Friday," he recalls. "The eels were still moving and we would have to skin them alive using special gloves."

Above: George Moroney and the catch of the day, fresh carp

Fish monger Ilia Kazandjieff offers customers a closer look at the fresh catch

In planning the Market, no detail was left to chance. The first fresh fish market was built off to the side, where the aroma of the trout, grouper, squid, and clams wouldn't overpower the more appealing perfume of other foods.

Before the 1980s, the contents of the case reflected Lake Erie's commercial fishing heyday. Perch, small mouth bass, smelt, and walleye were delivered throughout the season. "Clevelanders loved their perch," says Jim Moroney, who worked in the fish market in the 1960s and '70s. Whether it was mullet, sea bass, porgies trucked in from the eastern seaboard, or fish pulled from Lake Erie, most arrived whole to be cleaned, gutted, and filleted as customers bought them.

"The fish we sold said a lot about the people from the neighborhood," says Jim. Italians, Spanish, and Greeks had the same taste, buying squid and octopus for calamari or to stuff before cooking. African American customers liked catfish, skinned with the heads left on. "Europeans and Jews loved carp," he says. "They would have us scale it and either leave it whole or cut it into segments, but not all the way through. Then they would poach it and set it in a gelatin to make an aspic."

"We would cook up different fish and let them taste it," says Ilia. "Sea squab, blowfish, and puffers from around the New Jersey coast," he says. "We would call them chicken of the sea, 'cause they looked like a piece of chicken."

When the Rolling Stones came to Cleveland for a concert in the late 1990s, they sent their chef to Ilia for $500 worth of swordfish. Not to be upstaged, Pink Floyd sent their chef to the stand later that same year for halibut.

It's only since 1989 that fresh fish vendors were welcome into the main hall. "We were allowed to set up a stand along the outside wall," says Sharon Brown, who owned S & S Seafood, the first fish stand to operate under the new rules. "The management felt it kept the smells off to the side. But I always thought that the smell of good fresh fish and seafood was a plus and just part of all the food smells you expect here, like when you walk by Czuchraj's and smell smokies or pizza bagels when you pass Friccacio's."

When Kate McIntyre brought Kate's Fish to the Market floor a dozen years ago, she was still selling to the ethnic crowd. "Then our customers were older, Eastern European, and Asian, overall an ethnic, earthier, blue-collar customer that knew how to handle fish," she says. Today, Kate makes regular trips to the airport to pick up fishermen's fresh catch flown in from Alaska, Hawaii, Florida, and the West Coast. While transportation and technology can put fish in the case soon after it's snagged, Kate still sees some customers who can't wrap their heads around the idea of whole fish. "White-bread Americans are looking for square pieces of fish, what they recognize in the grocery store. Few of them want to bother with the heads and tails themselves."

PERSONAL TASTE: ORIGINAL RECIPES

The Market has been home to a handful of innovators, inventors, and entrepreneurs who built businesses, reputations, and legacies through proprietary recipes, secret ingredients, and patented processes that reflected not only family heritage but demonstrated a spirit of culinary creativity. Some of these foods had big followings and customers were willing to stand in line for them.

Robert Stumpf Jr. was dedicated to tradition, still using "a tattered German sausage makers recipe book which dated back to the early 1800s."[1] Ahead of his time as well, he was labeled "an inveterate experimenter,"[2] producing and selling long-smoked hams and bacon that were low in nitrates "because people are just so damn worried about additives."[3]

As Stumpf prepared to carry on his father's sausage making business, the first task was to recreate the recipes. "[My father] had all the recipes in his head," said Alvin Stumpf, Robert's brother. "I was a scientific-minded kid so when my father would grab a handful of spices to show me the right amount to use, I'd make him pour it onto a paper plate so I could weigh it on a gram scale first and write the quantity down. Good thing I did because my dad died on December 24, just before midnight that year.

I was the one who saved the recipes and gave them to my brother. He found a place for a new sausage making factory not far from the Market."

"My dad had a friend, a doctor, who came into the Market and said to him, I can't eat your meats anymore," says Stumpf's daughter, Becky (Stumpf) Fitch. "He was worried about diabetes and most meats are cured with a lot of sugar and salt." Stumpf watched his friend deliver the news while munching on an apple and thought maybe apple juice, sweet and sugary, but not like the sugar he was using, would solve the problem. After a year of tests and trials using the juice, lowering sodium levels to get just the right taste, and judging customer's reactions to the new product, Stumpf applied for a patent in the early 1980s and Kitchen Maid Apple Cured Meats became a staple at the Market.

Bill Hildebrandt remembers that his family-named lunch meat and hot dogs were so popular that they had two stands at the Market from 1912 until 1971. "The aisles were only so wide. Customers would stand three deep," he recalls. "We would sell lunch meat and smoked sausage and we made the hot dogs for Cedar Point, but we were famous for our spiced ham and salami."

The original recipes are written out on loose-leaf paper and locked up in a vault. They remain as much a closely-guarded family secret as a challenge. "The recipe for the spiced ham is scaled for four hundred pounds," says Hildebrandt. "I don't know that anyone is willing to break it down."

In the 1960s, Edward Badstuber & Sons was the single largest outlet for Bob Evans sausage in Northern Ohio—and Ed Badstuber Jr. recalls a visit by the real Bob Evans, complete with the signature white hat. But he also recalls a story his father told him about passing up an opportunity.

"In 1957, my dad was approached by a company looking for investors," says Badstuber. "For $5,000 he was offered the rights to a new ham slicing process called 'spiral slicing.' He didn't like the hams or the messy coating, so he said 'no thanks.' Someone else jumped at the offer and today it's known as the HoneyBaked Ham Company."

SHOPPING FOR THE MARKET
The Major Food Groups

AS EARLY AS 1858, farmers were gathering to sell their produce on the parcel at Pearl (now W. 25th Street) and Lorain Avenue. When a wooden shelter went up ten years later, the Pearl Street Market was in business. Area farmers brought in their harvest and butchers brought in Texas beef, a popular seller. Porterhouse steaks sold for twelve cents a pound. Pork roasts were five cents a pound, beef a penny more, and fish was so plentiful that merchants were only getting a dime for two pounds.[4]

City leaders were moving forward with the planning and development of the West Side Market and envisioned a place where northeast Ohio farmers could sell what they grew, a "place for suburban trolley freight cars to bring in country produce and unload it within the building."[5] Tracks were never laid to the Market; instead many of the vendors relied on the steady resources of the region to buy the meats, poultry, produce, and more to stock their stands and supply their customers.

In the early days, produce vendors bought fresh fruits and vegetables from the wholesale food district market and commission houses scattered along Broadway, Woodland, and Central Avenues, from E. Sixth to E. Ninth Street. Local farmers would bring their seasonal harvest into the wholesaler market and rail delivered foods from all around the country.

The Gentilles, a family of produce vendors that got their start at the Pearl Street Market and conducted business at the West Side Market until 2000, experienced first-hand the changes in how vendors brought their products to their stands. Jack Gentille, the fourth generation to run the business, recalls how his family and other vendors got the fruits and vegetables that were sold both on the street and under the arcade.

"There were at least forty commission houses in that area," he says. "In the early days, many would specialize in a certain product: there was one for celery, another for avocados, maybe one would sell carrots." That narrow specialization was also a reflection of the Market at the time: market management limited produce vendors in the variety and scope of what they could sell.

Myrtle Chappell, the famous Horseradish Lady, was known for her singular pungent product; Charles Guinta dealt exclusively in garlic; and Gen-

Above, from top: Vendors selling fruit and vegetables from the sidewalks around the Market
Opposite: Robert Stumpf in his sausage factory

THE FOOD FROM THE MARKET ❖ 131

Above, from top: Jim Calabrese hands a customer his purchase; Produce vendors from all over the area load produce onto their trucks at the Northern Ohio Food Terminal, 1940s; Rail cars full of produce line up behind the food terminal

tille recalls that when the holidays rolled around only two outside vendors were permitted to sell chestnuts, pecans, walnuts, and filberts.

"At one time, we had a small corner stand where we could only sell lemons," says Gentille. "You really can't make a lot of money selling lemons so I asked to sell Ohio sweet corn, Iowa Chief, when it was available. The two products went together: people ate sweet corn and drank lemonade in the summer." In a time when a lot of people were trying to make a modest living peddling produce, this type of reasoning was insightful and fair-minded.

"There was a wholesale market on 19th and Woodland and farmers would come in from all over the area with homegrown produce when it was in season," says Gentille. "They would come in on Tuesdays and Thursdays around midnight. Vendors had to get there early, like 1 AM to get the best and get the quantity because farmers could only fit so much in their trucks. My grandmother sold the oddball stuff like homegrown spinach, kohlrabi, parsley root, endive, and escarole. If we weren't there early, we lost out." Produce vendors would haul their buys back to the Market in horse-drawn wagons or small pickup trucks.

The wholesale market and small commission houses were eventually replaced in the 1930s by a modernized terminal which included four reinforced-concrete buildings, an auction building, and a Growers' Market. Gentille said that area farmers continued to bring their seasonal crops there up until the 1960s when he noticed a turning point. "A lot of farmers just stopped growing because it was hard work, there was no one to take over the farm and there definitely was not a lot of money in this business," he says, so vendors started relying more on produce brought in by rail.

There were a few area farmers who still grew and sold directly at the Market. In the 1960s and '70s, a farmer named Walter Shank was known for the apples and ciders he would bring from his Avon orchard and sell through the Calabrese family. But a farmer named Norman Dill, a second-generation produce vendor, appeared to be years ahead of the trend for locally-grown,

Ⓜemories

"My dad would haul produce in his Model T truck from the Northern Ohio Food Terminal when it opened in the late 1920s. At least a dozen railroads came in there."

—Joe DeCaro, vendor, DeCaro Produce

"When the Market was in its heyday, before there were any big supermarkets, it was very busy at the food terminal. There was always a fight over parking. I would stay in the truck and lock the doors while my big brothers went out."

—Nate Anselmo, former vendor

"I can remember at one time where there were hundreds of acres of greenhouses in Brooklyn Heights. They would grow two tomato crops a year that we would buy and sell at the Market."

—Joe DeCaro, vendor, DeCaro Produce

THE DUNDERMANS: GETTING THEIR HANDS DIRTY

When Tom and Anita Dunderman first opened the Baske-teria a dozen years ago, they would come to work May through October with dirt under their fingernails and on their shoes, straight from the fields where they picked the produce themselves—super fresh, peak of ripeness, homegrown. When the harvest wasn't on, they could be found among other produce vendors at the Northern Ohio Food Terminal, pouring over peppers from California and onions from Oregon; lettuce from Arizona, and just before Ohio's tomato crop ripened, varieties from Arkansas, "Kind of like a pre-taste of what's to come," says Tom.

"When we decided to open a stand, our goal was to bring organics as well as local products into the Market," he says. "We have a great state with lots of farms and felt they needed a presence at the Market. It was the right thing to do, not the trendy thing."

The Dundermans work with six local farmers, four of whom are certified organic, to grow produce for the stand. "We rely on them more and the terminal less every year," says Tom. Over the winter, the couple will meet with the farmers to discuss the growing seasons, the one past and one to come. "We look through seed catalogs and talk about what they can grow and what we can sell."

When Ohio's growing season is in full tilt, the Basketeria can put seventy to eighty homegrown, seasonal vegetables on the stand. "In November, we can still have ten local products like hard shell squash, kale, Swiss chard, broccoli, cauliflower, and cabbage until a hard freeze stops the harvest."

But the West Side Market is not a farmers market. "People who shop here expect avocados, pineapples, and bananas and we just can't rely on seasonal, homegrown foods," says Tom. "I'll buy Ohio-grown asparagus in May and June, but people still want it at Christmastime and in February, so I have to find other sources to offer it year-round."

seasonal food. Between the 1950s and '80s, Dill, a former greenhouse grower, organized a group of small family farmers throughout northeast Ohio to supply produce for his stand. He would often travel a hundred miles to collect his inventory: apricots, cherries, peaches, and apples from area orchards; tomatoes, lettuces, eggplant, onions, potatoes, and corn from dirt farmers, as well as onion sets and vegetable plants for his customers who preferred to grow their own.

An 1985 article in *Gourmet Magazine*, "The American Scene: Cleveland's Farmers Markets," also credits Dill with responding to a connoisseur market, including a healthy demand for fresh herbs and growing specialty produce of the time, like spaghetti squash, yellow cucumbers, and winter melons for his Asian customers.

All the while the smaller commission houses continued to close, were torn down, and the wholesale food trade consolidated into one area, with six large commission houses existing today under one roof. Produce still arrives by rail, but deliveries by refrigerated freight trucks are more common, and all the vendors who sell fresh produce year-round rely in some measure on the resources of the food terminal.

Market butchers would get whole steer, half steer, whole hogs, goat, and lamb from the Cleveland Union Stockyard on W. 65th, a processing center that provided meats through the 1970s and in terms of volume, rivaled

Above, from top: Anna Mae Grady at her cheese and butter stand, 1950s; Butchers Larry Vistein (left) and Emil Churchin wait on the loading dock for the Gibbs truck to arrive, 1970s

the stockyards of Chicago. The Union Stockyard's proximity to the Market ensured a constant flow of fresh meat for the vendors, important in an era when animal protein was the focal point of every dinner and a Sunday supper always featured some kind of beef roast. When the stockyards closed in the late 1970s, the Market's butchers were forced to seek out packinghouses to supply what they needed.

Domestic cheeses that filled the cases of the "butter, egg, and cheese" vendors like Holger Penttila, the Simmelinks, and Gordon Wendt, came from Wisconsin and Ohio. Janet, Penttila's daughter, recalls hundred-pound blocks of Amish Swiss from Middlefield and forty-pound wheels of Cheddar, which needed to be reduced to a more manageable size with cutting wire, and imported cheeses that arrived from Holland, Switzerland, France, Italy, and other foreign places. Local dairies like Hillside brought their milk, specially-made cottage cheese, and heavy cream to the Market.

"The heavy cream used to come in large stainless steel milk cans and when my dad worked for Simmelinks, it was his job to fill the bottles to sell at the stand," she said. Maple syrup from local producers came that way, too. "It always worked out that there wasn't enough milk or syrup in the bottom of the cans to completely fill one more bottle, but just enough for him to take home to my mother."

"Sixty-eight pound slabs of butter were the norm," she says, "and they all had a very high butterfat content. Everyone sold quality butter." Laid on ice in giant tubs, it was cut to order and used by many home bakers to achieve a flaky piecrust or as the secret ingredient in their special cookie recipe.

Eggs would arrive direct from local farms, already cleaned, but it was the vendor's job to "candle" them, holding them to a special light to look for signs of age, blood spots, or double yolks. Once farmers began to rely on distributors as an easier way to get their eggs to the Market, candling equipment was no longer necessary at most dairy stands.

The scent of freshly-baked breads, pastry, cookies, cakes, and pie filled the Market, especially in the early hours of the day. Throughout the history of the Market, these aromas accompanied the deliveries of these goods prepared at off-site bakeries. Inside the building, on the main floor or in the basement, no

Memories

"It was a tradition to go to the stockyard on a Monday, which was a slow day at the Market. We would pick out the sides of beef we would need. Then we would go to Windy's, a local tavern on Storer Avenue, for a cheeseburger or a sandwich and a beer."

—*Chuck Maurath, former vendor*

"The Market butchers were very particular about the meats they would pick out to sell at their stand. Sam Santner was one. On the days when the Market was closed, he would take me to Sandusky Packing or to Earl C. Gibbs at the stockyards and show me how to pick out the best hind- or forequarters. He would look for the marbling in the meat and the fat covering. Sam used to buy a lot of cows (as opposed to steer). The fat was butter yellow and had a high calcium level. He also knew just by looking at the swinging beef if it was a cow. Cows ribs are curved like a rainbow, while steer ribs are straighter. Guys like Sam and Arnold Fernengel didn't like electric saws to break down the beef. They used hand saws."

—*Dennis Belovich, former employee*

baker ever had an oven or a workroom to produce the quantities needed to satisfy the many customers. In 1966, Hungarian-style napoleons, *doborschtorte*, and *gerbeauds* arrived from the Farkas Bakery on W. 28th Street in Ohio City. Robert Jensch recalled the trips he made to the Market to deliver the baked goods from his Uncle Albert's bakery on Ridge and Pearl Roads.

> "Parma Home Bakery was owned by my Uncle Albert Jensch from 1929 to 1974. We prepared everything from scratch and I delivered it fresh every market day All the breads, the rye and white, Vienna, raisin; German-style pumpernickel that looked like a small brick and had to be sliced very thin on a special slicer; dry and soft rye; Jewish egg breads; Easter bread with raisins; hot cross buns; French breads and hard dinner rolls went into wicker baskets with lids. We also sold lamb cakes for Easter, big sheet cakes with buttercream icing, all kinds of German pastry and kolache, Danish kolache (the difference is in the dough), strudel, bear claws, lady locks, turnovers, cakes, kuchens, whipped cream pies, date nuts cakes, cream puffs, and éclairs. We had fifteen bakers working in the shop but only a couple at the stand. In 1939, I was driving a full-sized panel truck to make the deliveries. I would get up at 4 AM before school to make the deliveries. Most of our delivery boys didn't know a lot about the Market, except that if they wanted to avoid a fight with the produce guys, they had to get to the loading dock early."

Today, bakery still arrives at stands like Vera's, Michael's, Michelle's, Theresa's, and Spanos from bake shops throughout the northeast Ohio area. Most stands bake a portion of their goods off-site and contract other bakeries to broaden their selection. John and Paula Mitterholzer's great uncle started a bakery in Old Brooklyn in 1974 and the business is still there, still run by members of the family. They expanded with a stand at the Market, opening Michael's Bakery in 1980. "We do old-fashioned hearth baking," says Paula, "and make things like Euro-style breads, traditional German tortes, and Hungarian nut rolls. We produce everything we sell at the original Broadview Road location and deliver in the morning to the Market."

Memories

"My mom bought from eleven different suppliers. I remember there were three Italian bakers, a Jewish one, a Bohemian, and a Lithuanian—he had the best sourdough. He delivered it still hot and the vendors would snap up the loaves, get some unsalted butter, and that was their breakfast. She paid around sixteen cents a loaf, and sold them for twenty-four, twenty-five cents. She had an agreement with all her suppliers that they wouldn't sell the same stuff to her competitors. So there were a few vendors buying from the same bakeries but everybody got different products."

—Beverly Tabacco, former employee

"I remember the Fritches. They had the first egg stand outside the Market with the produce vendors. All he sold was eggs and he had an electric light bulb hanging by the stand so the customer could hold the egg up to the bulb to see if it was good. If the air cell is too big, that meant the egg was old."

—Larry Calabrese, former vendor

STRETCHING THE FOOD DOLLAR
Rushes, Rationing, & Real Deals

THE MARKET WAS designed to welcome and serve all, not just the wealthy or the privileged. It was where a homemaker could stretch a modest food budget by buying potatoes in a fifty-pound sack or splurge on pricier exotic fruits sold by the piece; where ground beef was at a bargain price if purchased at the end of business on Saturday; or if money was no object, prime-aged tenderloin could be ordered anytime. It was where the cheaper day-old bread, although not warm from the oven, was still soft and delicious. Everyone's food dollar is welcome.

Today, there are lines that snake around the Market at lunchtime for Steve's Gyros, a hefty ten dollar Greek sandwich made famous by the Food Network. In the 1940s, during World War II, lines also formed around the Market and out the door as people waited their turn to buy limited supplies of beef and butter, one of the rare times in Market history where the supply of food was limited or restricted.

He (Gordon Wendt) also remembers the butter rush of Cleveland during World War II which seemed to draw people like the gold rush of the old west.

"Butter was rationed in those days. The market was the only place Clevelanders could obtain it fresh daily," he said. He pulled old photos from under his counter to show the swarms of customers.
—*Cleveland Press,* April 25, 1970

"The War years took a toll on the vendors. Meat and butter were rationed and some vendors just couldn't earn enough and lost their stands. Others had to let their kids work for other families, whose own sons went off to fight. Lots of families lost boys. We had a customer who bought so much meat that one day my brother asked her why. She told him she took in boarders and fed them all. There were three shifts of sleepers for every bed."
—**Alvin Stumpf, former employee**

Above, from top: Marie Guenther takes butter from a crock for a waiting customer, 1950s; A vendor and customer talk over an empty counter
Opposite: A ration book from World War II

Ann Churchin recalls that it was hard to get real butter to use for even the simplest pleasure of buttering bread and it was doled out sparingly at the dairy stands as customers presented their ration coupons.

"If people didn't get the real butter, they bought oleo, big blocks of white margarine and some yellow coloring," she recalls. "You would mix it together to make it look like butter."

Churchin and her husband Emil owned a butcher stand at the time, and she remembers that all the meat vendors were limited by rationing programs that spelled out how much meat they could sell to their customers.

"People might only be able to buy $2 worth of meat at time," she says. "That might last you three days. You got whatever the ration ticket said." Even the butcher's family went without. "In the days of rationing, you would buy whatever you could get for your customers," she says. "Lots of times we would run out of meat and didn't have any for ourselves."

Charles "Bud" Leu Jr., whose family owned a lunch meat stand, said that there was a limited supply of bologna, hams, and other cold cuts and that much of the product was being canned and shipped overseas to the troops. "Every vendor was only allowed to get so much from the packinghouses," says Leu. "The government was involved in pricing the stuff, too. Some of the vendors would try to take advantage of the shortage so the government inspectors would come around and make sure the prices were reasonable."

Families learned to "make do" during food shortages and tough times have always required stretching the family food budget. One way was to look for good buys. Many vendors were able to provide them.

Tony Anselmo grew up at the West Side Market and in the family produce business alongside his father, Nate Anselmo. Today he operates his own specialty food distributorship and finds himself back at the food terminal, among vendors from the Market that all still carry on the business of buying produce and looking for bargains. "When a vendor gets a good deal, they pass it along to their customers," he says. "It could be as simple as the salesman at the food terminal owes him a favor, so they work out a one-time deal on a pallet of onions or lemons. Or maybe the pallet tipped over and some of the product spilled out. The rest is good but now he has a deal for the customer."

Sometimes, a "stressed product," one that is at its peak of ripeness, like flats of strawberries, comes in to the terminal. "They're dead ripe, but too ripe for a grocery store to buy because they have to store it and then distribute it to their stores and that doesn't happen fast enough for grocery chains," says Anselmo. "So now the commission house has a pallet to sell and they look to the produce vendors at the Market who can get them to the customer

Memories

"My dad used to talk about the meat shortage and food rationing during World War II. It was a different way for people to shop for food at the Market. There were lots of lines and it was the start of the numbering system. People had to take a ticket and wait till their number was called. My dad recalls one lady who was unfamiliar with the process and when it was her turn, she shouted, 'What did I win?' "

—Charles "Bud" Leu Jr., former vendor

faster." And it's up to the vendor to tell the customer that these strawberries are wonderful today—and should be used immediately, maybe for freezing, jellies, or jams. "It's only a value if the customer can use them right away and they appreciate the honesty of the vendor," he says.

Then there's the end of the week deal. "Vendors are better off making their customers happy with a good price on produce that still looks good at the close of business on Saturday than repacking it and putting it in the cooler," says Anselmo, "because by Monday, it's not going to look so good."

"This is the beautiful part of the Market atmosphere, something grocery stores can't do," observes Anselmo. "They don't have hustlers and hawkers mingling with the crowd. There it's visual, here it's hands on. Nothing is wrapped and people get closer to their foods. It's still like the old days at the Market where you can get to know your vendors, trust them to sell you quality produce, and share a good deal."

"There are always vendors who only buy top-shelf produce and then there were the bargain hunters. Customers are like that, too. None of us were ever big enough to take advantage of volume buying like a grocery store could. So it was always to our advantage to find a deal. It's the classic story of the Market."
—Jack Gentille, former vendor

"When I offer something at a real bargain price it's because it has to be used right away. There's a reason it's cheaper. It won't last and I always tell people that. They don't always listen."
—Tim Ducu, vendor, Ramos Produce

"I'm okay with haggling on price for produce. Sometimes I have pears and their stand life is short and they get bruised so easily, so I'll tell people to make me an offer. I have to sell them cheaper. Someone will buy them to make wine.

Lots of time people who complain about the quality of the product don't understand what they are getting when they buy the cheap stuff. It's not rotten, it just won't last."
—Hany Xenos, vendor, Mena's Produce

"We would put together boxes of broken carrots, celery, and onions and sell them as soup vegetables. At the end of the week, we would gather all the loose muscatel grapes that would be in the bottom of the boxes and sell them to someone who would use them to make wine, and they would always bring us a bottle. If the tomatoes were soft, I would put them in smaller container and sell them at a good price. Lots of the vendors did this. It wasn't bad stuff but it just wasn't going to keep so it needed to be used right away. And the customers needed to know that."
—Nate Anselmo, former vendor

Above, from top: A Market shopper at the Boutrous Brothers produce stand; Joey DiBlasio tempts customers with a cluster of fresh grapes, circa 1980
Opposite: The H. F. Hoehn stand, 1950s

"My mother often told me of the times she went to the Market during the Depression and picked up the bruised, discarded fruits and vegetables in the alley between the produce stand and the Market. She would take them home, clean them up, and serve the food to her family. Times were tough and she had to be resourceful."
—Bonnie Mytnick

"My grandparents, Alexander and Maria Derrico, emigrated from Italy to America in 1908. They had a fruit and vegetable stand at the Market in the early years. My grandmother would tell us stories of working there, relating how people that were new to visiting their stand would come and 'test' the vegetables and squeeze the fruits to see if they were fresh, ripe, and tasty before buying. She would describe how she tried to be patient for a sale, while some customers would take many 'samples' and eat their fill and then walk away without buying anything. Sometimes she would get upset but she would also consider that it may have been their only meal of that day because times were so lean."
—Loretta Storch

"My uncle Bill Wapinski had an outdoor lettuce stand which straddled the curb between the street and the sidewalk on the south side of the Market. I gladly helped him on Saturdays, all day, for the sum of two dollars. For a kid in the late fifties, that was a lot of money. One of my jobs was to walk up and down the produce aisles every hour and see how much other vendors were charging for lettuce, then report back to my uncle who would promptly take a paper sandwich bag and post the new price on it, usually a cent less than his competitors."
—John Karpinski

In the early 1970s, the news of a possible beef shortage may have sent customers over to the chicken stands, but in the minds of many vendors, both those still selling at the Market and those who sold there then, the event didn't have much of an impact and barely seemed newsworthy. John Rolston, a poultry vendor at the time, recalls that a local television reporter came in and wanted to do a story on the shortage but couldn't find a good example. "This reporter was desperate to craft a story," said Rolston, "so he had the crew shoot the empty cases of a beef vendor who was on vacation."

Business at the Market never wraps up neatly at closing time. There are the customers who know that if they wander in during the final hour they might score a good buy or be able to strike a deal with a vendor. Tom Nagel, a longtime Market employee, has worked at a number of meat stands and is familiar with the end-of-the-day and end-of-the-month bargains to be had. "Remember, the vendors are selling a perishable product and they make money only if they sell it. The consumer makes out since he gets good meat at a good price and the vendor can put out fresh stuff the next day. That customer knows he cannot 'order' what he wants but could end up with a lot of great T-bone steaks one time and roasts and ground chuck another."

WHERE'S THE BEEF?

In 1973, retail beef prices hit an all-time high and the nation braced itself for a shortage of its favorite meat. President Nixon imposed a price ceiling on beef, pork, and lamb, but the price of animals bought at live weight was not controlled; packers found they couldn't afford to buy at uncontrolled prices and sell at controlled ones, so a shortage ensued.

"During this time, some West Side Market butchers closed their stands early and took unwanted vacations because of the shortage. Sommer, Hartman and Vistein Meats would close their stands before noon. The beef shortage was a result of packers who couldn't get enough cattle…Some counters substituted more expensive prime grade for the choice grade they typically stocked but couldn't get…consumers were confused."

—*Plain Dealer,* August 25, 1973

Chris Sommer Krisak worked at the family stand from the 1960s through '80s. People with larger families came in often looking for bargains. "It was a mutual feeling, they helped us and we helped them," she says. "Except there was this one fellow that came in, and the only thing he ever bought were left-over lamb chops. He really haggled when we had already lowered the price considerably, and he would start 'making deals.' He would only talk with my Uncle Edgar, so I would say, 'Monty Hall, your lamb chop guy is here to see you.' He usually took all that we had left."

The seasons, as well as the weather, come into play when it comes to pricing. Vendors notice when the weather is hot, people don't eat as much and consequently don't buy as much, so shoppers might find good buys for their freezer. Don't look for great deals on steak or ribs before a summer holiday, but that could be the time for a great discount on stew meat or chuck roast. Conversely, in the winter, cooks want the slower cooking, heartier meats and vendors don't sell steaks as quickly.

"When it was a really slow week, or say a snow storm, and we really got stuck with quite a bit, we had a few customers we could call and give them a decent price on items to fill their freezers," says Sommer Krisak. "My grandfather used to say that 'a good transaction was when both sides felt that they came out well, and everyone was happy.'"

"In the 1960s, Hildebrandt meat products went to supermarkets in the area, which were growing and buying tonnage of our meat. So what we were sending to our stands at the West Side Market at that time—the hot dogs, spiced ham, bologna—was the same product, same ingredients, but maybe had a little blemish or was part of a broken case. If we were in the carpet business, you would call these remnants, but the frugal West Side Market shopper of the time didn't care, they wanted a bargain. Basically, we were like the broken cookie stand of the Market, only we were selling hot dogs."
—Bill Hildebrandt, former employee

"I had a lady customer who used to have me hold onto her food stamps, back when they issued the actual stamps. That way she knew she would always be able to buy meat."
—Vince Bertonaschi, vendor, Vince's Meats

"There was one customer, a bar keeper in the area, who knew that the best deals were the last few Saturdays of the month. He would buy about everything in the stand; chops, steaks, and roasts. He would mark the price on the packages and take the stuff back to his bar and

Above, from top: Angie Tabacco at her bakery stand, 1950s; Closing time at the Market was a good time to strike a deal on baked goods

sell it. At times, he would tell the vendors that the price on 'that roast is too high' since another person would charge him less. He only dealt with a few stands so he could maximize his benefits."
—Tom Nagel, employee

"My father had a section of the stand he called the 'BK counter.' We didn't know what it stood for but this was the 'scratch and dent' corner. He was able to buy all the hot dogs and smokies that had little flaws, like if the casing had a tiny tear or a bubble. He would buy it at a reduced price and pass along the savings to the customers. When first-grade meat would go for fifty-nine cents a pound, we could sell the ones with defects for forty-nine cents a pound. It was exactly the same as what was in the case a few feet over, just not perfect."
—Ed Badstuber, former employee

"There are also the people that will travel to the Market through a blizzard on a Saturday. They know they can stock their freezer because vendors don't want to get stuck with meat, but we also know that if they came all the way down to the Market in a snow storm, they came to buy."
—Tim Jeziorski, employee

"Steve Sikula worked for my dad for many years. By the time I knew him he was in his seventies, a real grizzled old curmudgeon. One Saturday, in the late afternoon, we had a lot of whole chicken legs left. We were pushing hard to sell them all because our stand was not open on Mondays and my dad sold only fresh stuff, never frozen. So Steve was yelling out to shoppers, offering ten pounds for nine dollars. A woman walked up to him and said, 'I want just the drumsticks, not the thighs.' Steve replied, 'Sorry lady, it's like when I got married. I didn't want my mother-in-law but she was part of the deal.' He got a laugh and a sale out of that one."
—John Coyne, former employee

The Market and the vendors, as a group, rarely advertised or published what was on sale; rather, they used hand-printed signs taped to the front of the case. Organizing one cohesive marketing campaign has been attempted many times but has been difficult to sustain. Each business is different, vendors have their own ideas, and unadvertised specials are the norm.

"We tried coupons once, too, but that didn't last long either," says Charles "Bud" Leu Jr. "The best advertising for any of us was word of mouth and the quality of the product itself."

Above, from top: Shoppers toting their purchases head north on a snowy W. 25th Street; From left, Edgar Sommer, Chris Sommer Krisak, Janice Sommer Arkangel, and Arnold Sommer dressed in 1912 attention-getting garb

FEED THE VENDOR
Eating on the Job

THERE'S AN OLD SAYING about the shoemaker's kids having no shoes, but at the Market the butcher's kids ate steak and the poultry vendor's family ate chicken. Chuck Maurath remembers that his dad Fritz, who had a beef stand in the 1970s, was always bringing home lunch meat and cuts of beef to feed his seven children. "We ate so much of that stuff, sometimes, we just hoped we would get invited to someone else's house for spaghetti," he says.

The butcher's family ate whatever was left on the counter. "Once it's cut, you sell it or you eat it," says Ann Churchin. Her husband Emil was a butcher at the Market from the end of World War II up until 1982. "Very seldom did my three boys ask for seconds because we ate so much beef." Too much of a good thing led to a conversation Churchin overheard between her boys and the neighbor kids. "They were complaining that we were having steak for dinner—again. They didn't appreciate the way we ate until they found out they were the envy of all their friends who wanted to eat steak."

Vendors were also very good at feeding themselves and each other on the job. In their world, the best foods were either in their own cases or across the aisle. Working long hours meant that breakfast was a Johnny Hot Dog and more than a few lunches and dinners were made behind the counter and in other corners of the Market.

A bucket of hot tap water is a pretty basic cooking technique, but vendors were very creative, often preparing impressive feasts with a minimum of equipment and combining the best of ingredients from their own stands.

> "Nick Roberto had the stand next to ours. When Market wasn't busy he'd make lunch for us on a hot plate. He'd get meat from one guy, vegetables from another, buns from me. Everyone who contributed got to eat. My favorite was a pork and fennel sandwich. He had a beat up aluminum coffeepot. He'd tell me to get 25 cents from my mom and go to the café and ask them to fill it with coke, no ice. Those were the best of times. Sometimes I watched his stand while he took a break—sometimes they were long breaks. He 'paid' me every Christmas with a five pound bag of pistachios."
> —Beverly Tabacco, former employee

Memories

"We would eat a lot of chicken. And if business was bad, like a snowstorm, we ate more chicken. My family ate very frugally, soups, stews—and a lot of chicken."

—Bill Pawlowski, former vendor

"Christmastime was so busy! It took all eight employees behind the counter to take care of everyone picking up hams…but we always had our egg nog behind the counter at the end of the day."

—Becky (Stumpf) Fitch, former employee

"I started as a cooler boy for Bob Stumpf when I was twelve. When I would bring up a cart loaded with meats from the basement, Grant Lance would always stop me and tell me to give him some bratwurst. I didn't want to because I thought it would get me in trouble. Finally Grant just started taking them. He would cook them in water straight from the tap. That's how hot the water in the Market is. He would always make one for me."

—Michael Turczyk, vendor, Turczyk's

Customers often feed their favorite vendors by bringing th___ tastes of what they've cooked or baked using ingredients fr___ s. "It's fun for us to feed people but they are alwa___ ___ary Pell. She exchanges recipes freque___ ___ and season-ings where sh___ ___ pickles and chutneys to c___ ___ndors, the Market is also ___ ___ket, I was never afraid to t___ ___nd lamb fries (testicles)."___ ___ckfire.

"In 1955, my___ ___ts.
All around the___ ___ks
of plump hot d___ ___.
In the case you c___
rolls of creamy g___
pure white pigs' fe___
smoked ham and b___

On a particularly s___
he needed to sample___
to do the job of a mea___
every single customer v___

So he did. He bit off a___
down a brat, poked his fi___
on a large cracker, and or___
sampling and when the bos___
him off with, 'I'm not that h___

When his shift ended at 6___
Transit System] bus and head___ ___an, 'Oh,
my gosh! What have I done?' l___ ___s.

He limped home from the bu___ ___ushed to the family bathroom where we didn't see him for more than an hour.

Since that fateful August day fifty-five years ago, Chuck testifies he has never eaten bologna, salami, bratwurst, blood sausage, or most cuts of pork ever again."
—Annie Star

Above: Hildebrandt employees at one of two stands that served customers at the Market for close to sixty years, 1950s
Opposite, from top: Ann Pawlowski holds son Bill in front of the Sebek Poultry truck, which the family used to get to church on Sunday, 1947; Nicky Roberto behind the family's stand that carried pasta, beans, rice, and grains

Memories

"I'm two hundred and fifty pounds because of my customers. I learn about their lifestyles through how they cook. They explain to me what they are cooking with things they buy and they share their recipes, which I cook myself. One of my favorites is couscous with pork. They also send me 'care packages.'"

—**Matt Minyard, vendor, Edward Badstuber & Sons**

"A lot of my meat comes back to my stand. Customers bring in the different foods they make…the Lebanese bring in stuffed grape leaves and the Arabs bring in lamb and rice with a yogurt sauce that they use for weddings or big gatherings. It's nice to taste the foods of different cultures and get the recipes and learn about all the different spices they use. It helps me understand the cuts of lamb and goat they are looking for."

—**Michael Turczyk, vendor, Turczyk's**

A TISKET, A TASKET
Foods That Fill the Baskets

HASTILY SCRIBBLED OR neatly ordered, a shopping list from fifty years ago would have hinted at what someone had in mind for Sunday supper; what would fill a lunch box or go into their holiday baking.

While advertising was not a routine practice for the Market, in 1962, for the fiftieth anniversary celebration, a special section was created for the *Plain Dealer* that offered a snapshot of what the Market offered.

Pot roast from Fernengel's, 55¢/lb.
Badstuber's pure meat wieners, 45¢/lb.
Homemade Krakow Sausage from Radeckis, 79¢/lb.
Steer ox tails from Steve Pawlowski, 25¢/lb.
Stewing chickens from Kaufmann Poultry, 19¢/lb.
Ehrnfelt's had beef patties, 8 for 59¢/lb
3 pounds of Selezanu's Old Kentucky-style sausage was $1
1 pound of coffee from Roberto's Grocery 45¢
Simmelink's had 3 dozen eggs for $1
Chocolate chip cookies from Dolores' Kookie Korner were 39¢/lb
…and a Johnny Hot Dog was only 15¢[6]

They were foods that would feed a family. The ingredients were nothing exotic but it was the cook who turned them into something special.

"We would go to the Market for a special dry cottage cheese. My father would use a meat grinder to combine it with butter. Then he'd blend that with a mixture of egg yolks, sugar, and vanilla, and pack it into little clay flowerpots lined with cheesecloth and put a weight on top. We called it *pascha*. It was served with *babka*, a sweet bread. My aunt used to bake it, but after she died we bought it at the Market."
—Kristina Kuprevicius

emories

"We always carried ducks' blood for czernina. We would mix it with vinegar. My mom would tell me it was chocolate soup because it was so sweet."

—Bill Pawlowski, former vendor

"I can remember my mother using those cracklings on top of noodles mixed with cottage cheese and sour cream. I think she cooked a lot like Paula Dean."

—Valeria Check, former vendor

"I used to be able to sell a ton of crack-lings. They hardly ever made it to the counter because I had standing orders from Hungarian churches."

—Miklos Szucs, vendor, Dohar Meats

"Each item she [my mother] brought home was instrumental in making the most mouth-watering meals ever. The yeast used for her kolach, a braided sweet bread, enabled the dough to rise to heights I have yet to see anywhere. The eggs were used for her crepes, or *palacinke*, which is the Slovak word for them. The cheeses and bacon were important for her famous *halushki*, another Slovak meal of potato dumplings covered with fried bacon and shredded cheeses. During tough times when it was hard to put meat on the table, the *halushki* made for a hearty meal.

Dad made his own kielbasa so seasonings, casings, and pork were a must when shopping for those special dinners. The Market offered a potpourri of wonderful food and mom's meals were a testimony to the vendors who took pride in making sure that everything they sold was the freshest possible."
—Ellie Behman

There were also the ingredients, less mainstream and definitely less common, that satisfied ethnic shoppers—like ducks' blood, the primary flavor of a traditional Polish sweet and sour soup. It is a "discontinued item" at the Market, likely to remain so along with a collection of others for which there's now little demand.

Valeria Check and her husband Steve Sr. operated a beef, lunch meat, and pork stand at the Market for more than fifty years. In the 1950s and '60s, Hungarians went to the Check stand for their "cracklings," a traditional ingredient in Eastern European households, particularly those of modest means.

"We would take the pork fatback with the skin, cut it up into small pieces and slowly fry it in a big cauldron to get the fat out," she describes. "Then we would strain it, let it cool and salt it. They would use it as flavoring for their biscuits.

When pork became the "other white meat," leaner than before, and people began rethinking their intake of rich and fatty foods, cracklings faded from the Market, and lard, the rendered fat, also became harder to find. "There was a time when we all cooked with animal fat," Check recalls. "Everybody had bacon grease and chicken fat to use. We didn't have the oils like we can get today." Lard, also called leaf lard, was the key to success for flaky *kifles* and pastry for many Hungarian bakers.

"We would get in fifty pounds of lard and I would have to break it down into one pound cartons. I couldn't go home on Tuesdays or Thursdays until it was done. It was pure white. That is what people baked and cooked with…it gave great color to pie dough."
—Charles "Bud" Leu Jr., former vendor

Above, from top: From left, Steve Jr., Valeria, and Steve "Jay" Check Sr. at their pork stand; Henry Pawlowski gestures from his poultry stand, 1970s

"We would go to Dohar/Lovaszy and buy *szalonna*, or roasting bacon," recalls Marge Vamasey. "My dad would skewer chunks of the bacon on a long fork and catch it on fire over an open barbeque. My mother would make a tray of sliced rye bread covered with finely-chopped green pepper, radish, green onion, salt, and pepper. When the bacon would start to fry, he would let the fat drip over the sliced bread. Every Hungarian remembers what it is. It was peasant food but so good."

Miklos Szucs is also Hungarian and remembers this treat as one he both indulged in and provided for others at what is now called Dohar Meats, a stand that has specialized in Eastern European smoked meats for over fifty years. "About ten years ago, I put an ad in a national magazine for meat processors looking for the fat back I needed to keep making this," he says. "I got one call from a producer in Idaho. The shipping alone made it unaffordable."

"Greasy bread" by today's health standards sounds deliciously dangerous, but it was a summertime treat for many Hungarian families years ago. Once again, skinny pigs and changes in how people view their fat intake makes this preparation and *szalonna* roasts just another food memory.

Live chickens were also sold, first on the curb by street vendors in the early years, and later at the poultry building adjacent to the West Side Market. Although it wasn't truly part of the Market and closed in the early 1980s, the experience of picking out dinner there was unforgettable.

> **"My favorite recollection is that of the trips mom took to purchase chicken for our Sunday meal. Chicken noodle soup was a must but when I was old enough to realize how that chicken got from the grocery bag onto the plate, I was a bit reluctant to try it."**
> —Ellie Behman

> **"If you wanted a really 'fresh' chicken, the Market is where you went …when the platter of chicken paprikash appeared on the table, we forgot about the chicken's fate. If it was used for soup, there was no need to add 'chicken cheater' to enhance the flavor."**
> —Dorothy Tharp

Above: Emery Lovaszy with customers, 1960s

Emerson Batdorff wrote a story for the *Plain Dealer*, "Everything From Eels to Oxtails," that offered a snapshot of foods still available fifty years after the Market opened: "Oxtails…and trotters, peanut butter that the man grinds before your eyes…garlic on the hoof; horseradish roots, for people who grind their own…homemade headcheese; eels in gelatin; salt stroming (*sic*); lingon; bread made of actual wheat instead of whipped chemicals and it isn't afraid to have a tough and tasty crust."[7]

Many of the foods Batdorff mentioned are still around—like oxtails, once a soup bone, now elevated to gourmet status by roasting and eating the marrow inside—as well as breads with chewy, rustic crusts. Headcheese, made from the meat of a pig's head, is one food that hangs on by a thread. "I would put

the quality of the meat up against any hot dog," says Miklos Szucs, the only vendor in the Market to still make the cold cut.

"Ninety-nine percent of my customers who buy this are older," says Szucs. "If I hear them talk, I can guess which country they came from." While there's still a taste for headcheese, there's not as much demand. "Twenty five years ago, we made and sold eight hundred pounds a week," he says. "Now I sell seventy or eighty pounds a week, but it's still an item I have to have. If I sell out in a day or two, I have some very angry customers. If I could call it something else, I could sell a lot more."

Inside the Market, vendors have wrapped up all kinds of unconventional requests from customers.

> "We had a man buy fifty pounds of beef tongue for his fiftieth wedding anniversary. People have also requested steer hooves and someone's granddaughter would buy her grandfather veal brains for his birthday every year. We also got in orders for whole [animal] heads a lot."
> —Wally Ehrnfelt, former vendor

> "Our Hungarian customers would buy pigs' feet and cook them up until the meat fell off the bone, then they would make a gelatin and pour it over the meat. When it was all gelled, they would eat it with a little splash of vinegar. It was called *kocsonya* (sic)."
> —Valeria Check, former vendor

Memories

"When the holidays roll around, we still have people coming in looking for eels but they are much harder to find now. I've been here twelve years and I've never seen a barrel of eels. Some things are really scarce in the fish world and not that easy to come by."

—Kate McIntyre, vendor, Kate's Fish

"It was a heavy snow day and we decided to close at noon because the place was empty. Just as we were about to leave, a man in his late sixties comes in and wants a half-pound of headcheese. He said it took him three hours to drive in from Brunswick—just for headcheese! I didn't charge him and told him to be careful going home."

—Miklos Szucs, vendor, Dohar Meats

"I went to buy headcheese for my dad at Dohar's. He loved the stuff. Me? Not so much. When I told Chuck Hokey, the guy behind the counter what I wanted, his face went blank. It took me a while but I realized that he didn't think I knew what headcheese was. He apologized and confessed, 'You don't look or sound like our regular headcheese customer.'"

—Marilou Suszko

THE CORNER GROCERY

Within the building there existed "grocery" stores, small, out-of-the-way places tucked into corners. If the Market was the main entrée, these stores were the side dishes.

Victor and Marge Roberto owned and operated the stretch of grocery store between the fresh fish stand and the entrance to the Market floor for many years. They sold sodas, canned goods, cereals, snack food, and plenty of odds and ends. The store was patronized mostly by those who worked at the Market. It was the model of neighborhood convenience stores that would appear elsewhere many years later.

Once area supermarkets extended store hours, business slowed and the last owner, Sam and Maha Zayed converted the space into a falafel sandwich stand.

At the other end of building is Mediterranean Imported Foods or as the owners, Konstantinos "Gus" and Maria Mougianis like to call it, "the specialty aisle." It's always been a compact grocery, a real mom-and-pop store. Maria's parents, John and Ifegenia Kantzios bought it in 1967 and ran it as a family business. "My dad did the ordering," says Maria. "There was a language barrier between him and his customers, but he understood the international language of mathematics." Her brother George helped, her mother did the cleaning and selling, "and Gus is our engineer who cuts cheese."

Every inch of shelf and counter space is filled with foods from all over the world: olives, cheeses, and oils; dry aged salamis, schmaltz herring, German brick bread, and Lithuanian sourdough rye, and poppy seed ground to the perfect consistency for baking. Gus speaks a few different languages, "most just well enough to fill an order," but many more are spoken here on the packaging alone: Dr. Oetker (baking products from Germany); *Krufki* (Polish Fudge candy); *Lutenitsa Todorka* (Bulgarian tomato and red pepper paste); Spanish Marcona almonds; *Vlaha Trahana Hylopites* (Greek egg pasta); *Verjus du Perigord* (green grape wine vinegar); and Romanian *Zacusca* (vegetable spread).

It has always been its own little store, part of the Market and yet separate, with two entrances, one inside the building and another on W. 25th Street (no longer used) which allowed them to open on nonmarket days.

"We're called the Greek store because we're Greek," says the handsome shopkeeper with a strong accent, "but all the ethnicities shop here." He and Maria have watched the succession of ethnic groups as they met in the tight aisles—Eastern and Central Europeans, Arabs, Germans, Scandinavians, and the eclectic mix of people living in nearby Ohio City and Tremont neighborhoods who use the store as their "coffee house," a place where they can come to mingle and find imported foods from all over the world.

"Chicken livers? I had no idea people would eat those. Working at the Market made me realize that odd things were important in the way different cultures ate."
—Tom Hamm, former employee

The Market is still home to many old world foods, a few of which have experienced makeovers to keep them interesting for the next generation of shoppers or "foodies." Some vendors find ways to make what is old seem new and exciting again.

Up until the mid-1950s Myrtle Chappell, the Market's "Horseradish Lady," ground the pungent root for lines of customers just outside the doors of the Market. It was just horseradish, pure and simple. Today, most horseradish is sold already bottled, but at Rita's the freshly-harvested root is still ground and ordered by weight as well as intensity: "3X" strength has a kick, but "5X" kicks harder.

Customers have snacked on J & J Czuchraj Meats smokies for generations—when a smokie was just a smokie. Today the question isn't, "How many smokies would you like?" but, "Which kind? Classic, Mild, Barbeque, Cajun Hot, Jalapeño, or Turkey?"

Grant Lance, owner and butcher at Lance's Beef, pulls out the beef chart and a pen to show exactly where hanger steak comes from. "It used to be the 'butcher's cut,' one he would take home for his own family," says Lance, a reference to leaving the better, more expensive pieces for paying customers. "Today, it's one of the pricier cuts because each animal yields only one and chefs and the Food Network have made it popular."

One of the most dramatic changes might be in everybody's favorite Eastern European dumpling—the pierogi. Many Clevelanders were raised on the traditionally meatless doughy pillows, once made at home to fill the bellies of large families for just pennies. No *baba* worth her salt would have ever considered buying them when the ingredients were right there at the Market, but Pierogi Palace set up shop in the 1980s and brought them into the mainstream as a heat-and-serve food.

Owner David Blaha says that the leagues of little old ladies who sat at tables years ago pinching made-from-scratch pierogis around humble fillings of cabbage, potato and cheese, mushroom, and *lekvars* have been replaced with leagues of "little young ladies" who still hand pinch. The original twenty varieties they sold have given way to more than seventy-five, including "designer" pierogis labeled Bourbon Meatball, Philly Cheesesteak, Szechuan Green Bean and Chicken, and Refried Bean. It might make purists shake their heads but it keeps the pierogi on the plate for the next generation.

"My Asian customers like the fruit, cabbage, mushroom and chicken, and the Italians like the fillings that remind them of their ravioli," says Blaha, "but don't be fooled. I still sell pierogis to older Polish, Slovak, and Russian women who say they are as good as ones they used to make—but don't tell anyone."

Some foods don't change because their simplicity is good enough. "Fresh ground peanut butter is a nostalgia food and something people always want," says dairy vendor Ed Meister, who up until 2000 ground hundreds of pounds of the coarsely textured butter right in front of his customers. "When the new

Above, from top: Myrtle Chappell, the "Horseradish Lady"; Pierogis from the Market
Opposite, from top: Thousands of products from around the world fill the shelves; owner, Gus Mougianis behind the counter, 1970s

cases were installed the grinding machine wouldn't fit, so it's now ground downstairs and brought up in big tubs. Some people still come with their own containers to fill."

> "When my mother was pregnant with me in 1953, she craved home ground peanut butter. At the time, the West Side Market was the only place you could buy it so my father would drive from Brecksville (a distance in those days) to purchase it for her. To this day, fifty-eight years later, peanut butter is still one of my favorite foods!"
> —Susan Tiedman

> "I grew up on Scranton Road. My mom always bought our peanut butter at the Market. I didn't know that peanut butter came in jars at the store."
> —Millie Evens

As the world gets smaller, the cuisines of other cultures get closer. Foods that come from all around the world are no longer foreign to the eye or the palate. Some blended into the mainstream of the Market long ago.

> In 1956, [Dave] Weisberg's parents, Ted and Rae, bought the [Buechler Jaeger] meat stand in the Market.
> The stand originally sold ethnic European meats but gradually, "we introduced corned beef, roast beef and a fresh pepper beef," said Weisberg. "Corned beef was my father's forte and we got the West Siders used to it by giving away free sandwiches. Soon they were buying pounds of it. We started by cooking a few pounds of corned beef in the basement of our home and ended by cooking thousands of pounds."
> —*Cleveland Jewish News,* **January 14, 1994**

It's hard to image that something as familiar as corned beef was once a new discovery for Market shoppers. It's true of many foods considered common today including hummus, Mediterranean olive oil, and tofu. As the shoppers and the vendors at the Market change, so will the foods bought and sold here. First generations of immigrants will continue to arrive and rely on the Market for the spices, seasonings, produce, and proteins that remind them of home—and others will discover them, too. The selection in the cases, on the shelves, and in the bins will constantly evolve with the way people eat and how they cook—or no longer cook. It will always be the place where the frugal cook can shop next to the gourmand, and where the adventurous eater will be as satisfied as the ones who choose the same products week after week. This will always be how food creates history at the West Side Market.

Notes

1. *Cleveland Press,* Jan. 29, 1953.
2. *Plain Dealer,* May 31, 1981.
3. Ibid.
4. *Plain Dealer,* Aug. 23, 1962.
5. *Cleveland Leader,* May 1, 1902.
6. *Plain Dealer,* Sept. 30, 1962.
7. Ibid.

WEST SIDE MARKET SHOPPING LIST

A century's worth of newspapers, magazines, radio broadcasts, and television programs have served as invaluable resources for creating this "shopping list" of bewildering varieties of foods that people shopped for and bought at the Market. Listed here is just a fraction of the names of food, delicacies, or oddities mentioned over time along with a probable definition. Some might sound familiar, others bizarre, and still others, like "Shoe Soles" completely impossible. Some are still available at the Market; others are a part of history and were enjoyed while they lasted.

Cod roe paste: a Swedish sandwich condiment
Sweetbreads: thymus gland of a calf or lamb
Mountain oysters: bull testicles
Lamb fries: lamb testicles
Kapusta: common Eastern European term for sauerkraut
Lingon: refers to *lingonsylt* or lingonberry jam, which has a taste like cranberries
Schmierwurst: spreadable German pork sausage
Blood tongue sausage: Bavarian sausage and a classic part of *Aufschnitt*
Garlic knockers: garlic sausage or hot dogs
Gjetot: Norwegian goat cheese
Houska: nutmeg- and mace-laced sweet bread
Sap Sago: Swiss grating cheese that has a green hue
Raclette: Swiss cheese, melted and scraped onto the plate
Kuchen: a German coffee cake
Shoe soles: flaky oval pastries shaped like a shoe sole
Marzipan: confection of sugar and almond meal

Mandel splitters: chocolate with almond chips
Krakowska: Polish sausage seasoned with allspice, coriander, and garlic
Leberwurst: German for liverwurst
Schwartenmagen: German headcheese
Presswurst: chopped ham and pork sausage
Weinsauerkraut: sauerkraut in wine
Šunka: Czech ham
Lekvar: thick jam or fruit butter
Kolache: fruit-filled pastries
Palacinke: variation of a crepe with a sweet or savory filling
Salted sprats: preserved fish
Salt Stromming: also called *Surströmming*, canned fermented herring
Gelbwurst: German "yellow" sausage flavored with ginger and nutmeg

Memories

"As a child in the nineties, my mother and I would make monthly trips from Pennsylvania to see my grandmother. On the way we would make several stops and always end up going to the West Side Market. We would head into the meat department to find all the ethnic foods of my mother's childhood. We would always go to the candy vendor but my mom would give me the run around before we would 'accidentally' end up there."

—Natalie Shipula

"As a kid we would occasionally have 'West Side Market' for lunch. Dad would get pickled or creamed herring while we just held our noses. We would buy fresh rye bread and salami for sandwiches, and a mustard pickle on the side, and our last stop was the magical candy counter where we would get peach stones or lilac-flavored candies, red licorice whips, too, in small brown paper bags. There were tons of candies to choose from but those were the ones that went with our West Side Market lunch."

—Liz Scholz Donahower

CHAPTER FOUR

MEMORABLE MOMENTS
at the Market

OPEN FOR BUSINESS
Red Letter Occasions 1911–1915

Previous pages, clockwise from top: The centerpiece of a customer's pig roast is carried to the car; The Apple Queen in front of Larry Calabrese's produce stand; Vendors and employees in a 75th anniversary portrait
Above, from top: The unfinished building hosted a trade expo in 1911; "It's a beauty!", from the *Plain Dealer*, September 2, 1911
Opposite: The view from Market Square Park, late 1970s

IN THE SUMMER OF 1911, laborers put the finishing touches on the market building's exterior. Even though much remained to be done inside, the structure was officially dedicated on Founder's Day, July 22, as part of an annual citywide celebration marking the 1796 landing of Moses Cleaveland and his band of surveyors at the mouth of the Cuyahoga River. Both Mayor Baehr and Public Service Director Lea were on hand, along with throngs of spectators gathered to witness H. W. S Wood of the West Side Chamber of Industry accept the Market on behalf of the community.

> According to Public Service Director Lea, who delivered one of the principal speeches at this ceremony, the structure is the finest market building in the world.... The mayor, in turning the building over to the people, declared that it was an enterprise that represented a fight of the West Side. After reviewing the difficulties that had barred the progress of the work, he advised that the West Side citizens rejoice in the accomplishment and forget the rest.
> "Let the new market house become the center of the activities of a progressive people," he said in conclusion.
> —*Plain Dealer*, July 23, 1911

Less than six weeks later, the Market hosted a trade expo sponsored by the Chamber of Industry. The huge empty interior was the perfect setting for hundreds of booths promoting businesses located on the west side of the city. The populace turned out in droves, eager to get a peak inside the building, as well as view the exhibits, watch the sideshows outside, and enjoy a variety of entertainments.

An electric sign on the top of the tower spelled out the word EXPO in eight-foot letters. Installed beside it, a searchlight cast a bright beam visible for miles in every direction. A parade featuring 20 floats, 150 horse drawn vehicles, 150 automobiles, 6 brass bands, and marchers from 20 fraternal organizations kicked off the week-long event on Friday night, September 1.[1] Beginning at W. 14th and Lincoln Park, the parade traveled a five-mile route, and finished by passing a review stand set up at the Market for public officials, community leaders, and their wives. Mayor Baehr called it the greatest day in the history of the West Side, and told residents they had reason to feel proud.[2] The Expo opened at 7:30 PM on Saturday evening, with a boom and a burst of light: a cannon was fired and a thousand lamps in the Market and on storefronts around the district were turned on. An estimated six thousand people, including many from the east side, according to a newspaper report, entered the hall within the ninety minutes.

Booths were "presided over in many instances by daintily gowned young women." Manufacturers and merchants presented their products. The People's Savings Bank table held a replica of their headquarters. The Anti-Tuberculosis League created a miniature woodland scene to emphasize the value of fresh air. Members of the Woman Suffrage party passed out handbills. One kiosk featured heaps of pumpkins, corn, beets, cucumbers, and other vegetables grown by students on the Willard School farm. The German singing club, eighty-five voices strong, performed and so did The Royal Hungarian Gypsy band. Roy La Pearl, a baritone noted for his exceptionally loud and resonant pipes, appeared with Dockstader's Minstrels, a touring blackface vaudeville troupe. He did a solo from the top of the Market tower, accompanied by the rest of the group gathered below on the corner of W. 25th and Lorain. Friday's amusements included a baby show, with prizes given out for the prettiest, best-dressed, and best-behaved tots.[3]

Behind a temporary fence, midway attractions took over the space where the produce arcades now stand. Among the more thrilling spectacles were an Indian encampment populated by members of a tribe from Wisconsin, complete with teepees and warriors, and a twenty-foot oval velodrome, where the Daredevil Volo and a trio of motorcyclists sped around a banked course. Even a downpour on September 5 didn't put a damper on the turnout.

MARKET SQUARE: A PLACE FOR THE PEOPLE

When Josiah Barber and Richard Lord deeded the 183 square foot parcel to the city, they stipulated that it should always be used for a public market but over the years that proviso has been loosely interpreted. After the old Pearl Street Market house was razed in 1915, people sold flowers and produce from temporary stands. A 1934 survey done by the Civil Works Administration for the City Planning Commission shows a shelter house (a covered, open-sided pavilion) and small brick building on the site. In 1976, when William Gould, an architect and urban planner, was hired to redesign the corner, the brick building housed a bakery, a deli, and a public transit waiting room, and was surrounded by a parking lot for merchants from the Market. He got rid of both and created a park addressing the broad intent of the bequest for a community gathering place, rather than its specific requirement. Every summer since 1997, there's a Saturday festival held there featuring arts and crafts vendors and live musical performances.

 Memories

In the past, stalls in the Pearl Street Market were "let to the highest bidder;" vendors transferred their leases, even after they'd expired, to whomever they wished. In the fall of 1912, Server Springborn announced that this would no longer be tolerated. He told a reporter that a new system would be tested for one month "allowing market dealers in the new West-side market to retain stalls only for the term of good behavior." After that trial period, he announced, "there will be a canvas of the market situation and rules will be formulated to govern all [city] markets.... If a stall holder gives up his stand, a retail price will be fixed for that and if there are more applicants than one, the stall will be let by lot...[5]

West Siders themselves were surprised at the magnificence of the display and of the beauty of the new market house.... The crowd came thronging through the turnstiles and there were exclamations of delight from many.... The building in itself is well worth going to the West Side to see even though there was no exposition.

—Plain Dealer, *September 3, 1911*

BEFORE SHOPPING CENTERS

The new market house was the superstore of its time, offering people the convenience of a wide variety of products under one roof. Plans for the space included a druggist and an area for the sale of flowers. Shoppers in 1912 could buy butter, eggs, fresh and salted (cured) meat, poultry, game in season, smoked fish and pickled herring, crackers, cakes, and bread. The corner spot under the tower, later home to Johnny Hot Dog, was a place to sit and wait for the street-car. In 1950, a dentist had his office upstairs on the north side, in what had been intended as a live-in suite for the market manager.

It rained in the neighborhood of W. 25th-st and Lorain-av yesterday—rained hard and much—and the water trickled down the necks of the ballyhoo men on the midway of the West Side exposition and made the Hindoo priest, who has his uncle's spirit canned in a mason jar telling fortunes, keep his ancestral canning factory under cover to prevent the spirit from dissolving in moisture, but in spite of the inclement weather large crowds were on hand all day to view the exhibits.
—*Plain Dealer*, September 6, 1911

The doors were locked at midnight on September 9, the Market hall went dark and quiet, and "there was only limp bunting which waved spectral-like in the wind."[4] Roustabouts packed up the midway. An estimated 110,000 had attended the Expo and it was considered a stunning success. The West Side Market wasn't big news again until the fall of the following year.

The official ribbon-cutting was scheduled for Thursday, October 31, 1912. When it became clear that the scales would not be delivered in time, some suggested postponing the event. They were overruled—the public could not be disappointed yet again. So on the appointed date, local government dignitaries gathered to mark the completion of the long and costly project with a fanfare of music. The headline in the *Cleveland Press* was "RAH! West Side Market's Open." On Saturday, November 2, 1912, the scales installed, the merchants were ready for customers. One hundred and ten stands were piled high with a huge selection of food and most of it was gone by the end of the day. The Market Master, Charles Kamp, dressed in a new brown suit with a red carnation in his buttonhole, welcomed shoppers into the marvelous new facility.

Streetcar conductors on West Side lines rubbed numerous sore spots and bruises when they came in off their runs Saturday night. All afternoon and evening they had been jostled and prodded by market baskets in the hands of thousands of West Siders who flocked into the West Side Market to select their Sunday meats and vegetables from the spotless marble counters for the first time…Dealers wrapped up meats, groceries and other products to the strains of *Everybody's Doing It*, *Dixie*, and other airs played by Kirk's Military Band. The fragrance of flowers mingled with the smell of sausages and cheese as the building had been tastefully decorated.

Every face in the market were [*sic*] a smile when Market Master Kamp opened the place for business at 10 o'clock with the exception of the young girl in a stand in the southwest corner. She had been grating horseradish and the tears were streaming down her face. Unlike the other dealers every new purchase during the afternoon and evening brought fresh tears.
—*Cleveland Leader*, November 3, 1912

That weeping child was Myrtle Schenk. She'd been helping her German immigrant father sell ground horseradish across the way at the Pearl Street Market "since she was old enough to tell a dime from a nickel."[6] After he died, she ran the business with the help of her husband, Herbert Chappell. She'd set up shop on the curb and was a familiar figure for decades, popular but never welcomed inside again, due to the pungent nature and unfortunate effect of her product.

Since opening day, millions of people have come here to work, to buy, to browse, to eat, to chat, to campaign, to film, and, of course, to be amazed. But in the early years, after the initial rush of interest and enthusiasm, the West Side Market had to sell itself to the public. Market Master Kamp proposed a pageant and street fair unlike anything Clevelanders had ever seen and enlisted support from area boosters and businessmen eager to promote the entire community. They formed the United Market Square Carnival Committee and put together a jamboree in 1915 that lasted from June 21–26. The festivities followed the demolition of the decrepit Pearl Street Market house and organizers hoped to spread the word about the neighborhood's progress and its desirability as a place of residence and retail commerce.

> "Deserving merit because of merit," is the slogan of the men [at] back of the massive carnival. Civic pride, they say, will come as the result of an inspection of this section of the city, its wonderful conveniences... and its allurements for those who desire a residence in the most beautiful as well as the most popular section of Cleveland.
> —*Plain Dealer*, June 20, 1915

To say that the Market group went all out is something of an understatement. No expense was spared to make the carnival a spectacular event. A writer dubbed Kamp "the Aladdin of things along the amusement line," and reported that under his guidance "a wonderful city of joy is rapidly rising...a miniature New Orleans at Mardi Gras time."[7]

Opposite, from top: The Market Packing House stand (now Fernengels); the R. J. Hildebrandt stand on opening day
Above, from top: In the early years, before there were cases, meat hung from hooks and was displayed on open counters; Illustrations from an article about the Market Square Carnival, *Cleveland Leader*, 1915

A CARNIVAL WEDDING

Even a wedding was on the Carnival agenda, complete with 22 young ladies, selected by the flower committee, to strew roses in the aisle. All were friends of the bride, Miss Elsie E. Wuertz and employees of West side stores. She and her fiancé John Spilker, both residing on Bridge Avenue in Ohio City, were selected from a pool of applicants to take their vows on the bandstand. Spilker admitted feeling nervous, but not about getting hitched.

"I don't like the idea of having the ceremony performed in the middle of such a crowd of girls," he said Saturday. "But I'll go thru with it if I have to be held up by my best man."

"At least he will be there—and the pastor."

The pair were pronounced man and wife June 24th. The groom wore a blue suit, white straw hat, white tie with a diamond stud, and high tan shoes. The bride was dressed all in white, with an aigrette flower hair ornament. She carried a bouquet of lilies of the valley and roses. The couple received furniture for a five room house from the Market Square committee. Other donations from area tradesmen and stores included wallpaper for two of those rooms and the services of a photographer and a moving company. Market vendors donated seventy-five orders of meat and groceries to keep the pair well-fed for months.

—*Cleveland Press*, June 19, 1915

Free streetcars ran to the west side between Ohio City and Rocky River and to the east side from Harvard and E. 53rd. Thousands of yards of colored bunting, flags, and electric lights decorated shop windows and lampposts. Canvas tents surrounded the market house. An outdoor stage was put up on the empty lot where the Pearl Street market building had stood for fifty years. The public was promised "stunts of every description for father, mother, and the little ones."[8] Each day offered a special entertainment: acrobats, midgets, and vaudeville acts; Restivo the Accordionist, a saxophone quartet, band concerts, and choral recitals; hayrides, a popularity contest for young ladies, gymnastics demonstrations, seventy-nine Iroquois Indians, and performances by trained animals and strong girls. A ladies orchestra played inside the Market. Among the Midway games were two with intriguing titles, "ringing pegs for pillows" and the bewildering "throwing balls at babies." Other star attractions included Ethel Rollins, a skimpily-clad female wrestler who took on all comers, and Little Elsie, a champion lady high diver. She dove into a pool from atop a ninety-foot ladder every day at 4 and 10 PM.

Fraternal associations paraded through the neighborhood on Friday night, competing for cash prizes in two categories: best uniforms and largest number of participants. A masked ball followed, with awards given to adults and children for the best-dressed couple, the most original costumes, and the most comical. Men and boys also had a chance to win money for their Charlie Chaplin impersonations.

The market house was open daily and at night throughout the Carnival for inspection, with tour guides available to point out noteworthy features. The restrooms for men and women in the basement got special mention in one newspaper story, "as one of the real pleasures to be enjoyed during the stay of the carnival at the West Side." The article went on to explain the particular merits of the modern, municipally-owned facility.

> Whether you have or haven't seen it, doesn't make a particle of difference. You are going to be given an opportunity...to make yourself at home in the most remote nooks of the finest market in the United States.
>
> The entire place will be in spick and span shape, as it always is, and will prove a very interesting building to those unfamiliar with it and its policy of offering consumers the very best things for the table at prices they can afford to pay....
>
> Thousands upon thousands of dollars are spent annually at this market, which is scientifically arranged for the purchase and distribution of goods. Thousands of Clevelanders depend upon it every week for their food supply, and while many thousands point to the great structure with a great deal of pride, there are many thousands more who have never seen the inside of one of the most elaborate and useful buildings the city owns.
> —*Plain Dealer*, June 20, 1915

MARKING THE YEARS
Anniversaries

THE MARKET HAS always been proud of its age and the staying power of the merchant tenants. Commemorating the passing years prompted festivities, ceremonies, contests, media trips down memory lane, group photos, speeches, giveaways, and special deals. The first formal birthday event was in 1937, the Market's twenty-fifth anniversary. The Great Depression was a daily reality, but no doubt the six day party lifted public spirits, offering free music and food samples, meat-cutting demonstrations and carnival amusements. Vendors gave away several hundred dollars worth of merchandise as gifts and prizes, a meaningful gesture when work was hard to find and so many were going hungry.

Mrs. Walter Schaefer, the former Elizabeth Hahn, was a guest of honor. The mother of two girls was just a year old in 1912 when she showed up in a wicker buggy and won the best baby competition, earning herself a silver spoon. Speaking to a *Cleveland Press* reporter Mrs. Schaefer said, "My mother told me in later years that she was the most surprised person in the world when I came home with the spoon. My sisters entered me in the contest for lack of anything else to do."[9]

The festivities came to a close Saturday evening.

> **Crowds that at times reached 10,000 milled and churned through the West Side Market Building last night to climax the week's celebration...From 6:30 to midnight visitors surged through the building and overflowed out into Lorain avenue and W. 25th street....Now celebrating its silver anniversary, it is still said to be one of the finest municipally owned markets in the country.**
> —*Cleveland Press*, October 29, 1937

The Market's Golden anniversary in 1962 was a big bash held a month ahead of the official 1912 opening date. A parade kicked off the festivities on Saturday morning, September 29, with an estimated hundred thousand people watching. In the lead were two of the oldest tenants and founding members of the Merchants Association, Walter Simmelink Sr., a dairyman, and butcher Arnold Sommer. The Governor marched with them, along with a senator, the mayor, an ex-mayor, bagpipers, a drum and bugle corps, a troupe of Indian dancers, and various nationality groups dressed in traditional costumes.

Antique cars also cruised the route, but perhaps the most unusual feature was a stagecoach with two horses, two riders, two drivers, and a man with a shotgun. When the parade came to a finish, the riders dismounted and unloaded a strongbox onto the stage. The lock was shot off, the box opened, and Mayor Ralph Locher was presented with keys—gold, of course—to the Market. He gave an address, and then cut the five-hundred-pound cake, a replica of the building. Slices were passed out to patrons all day and throughout the week, until the monumental dessert was nothing but crumbs. This was, however, a less-enlightened time, so in the handout to tenants about the week's plans, organizers wrote, "We hope that the ladies of the market will find time in their busy schedule to serve the cake to their friends and favorite customers."

From top: Icing the 50th anniversary cake, 1962; Victor Rini and his father Joseph pose next to the 25th anniversary cake, 1937; Mayor Ralph Locher and a "babushka'd" shopper at the 50th anniversary, 1962; butcher Arnold Sommer celebrating a birthday with Market family, circa 1960

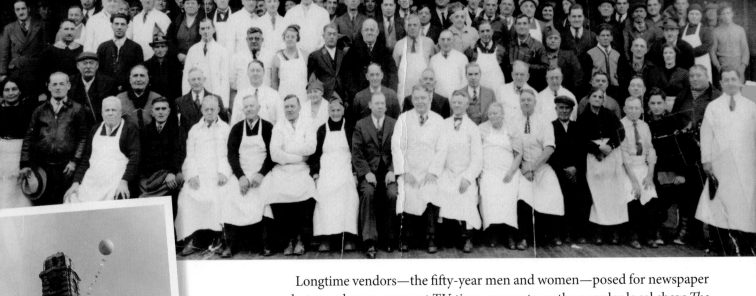

Longtime vendors—the fifty-year men and women—posed for newspaper photos and some even got TV time, as guests on the popular local show *The One O'Clock Club*, with Dorothy Fuldheim and Bill Gordon. Observations and recollections were not in short supply.

> [Arnold] Sommer has a very favorite patron. "I have one customer who has been buying a rump roast of veal from me every Saturday for the last 42 years. Now that's what I call a steady customer."
> —*Cleveland Press*, September 24, 1962

> "We didn't even have ice on the stands in those early days," [Edward J. Weigel] recalls, "and customers would handle every joint in sight before they'd decide which piece to buy."
> —*Plain Dealer*, September 30, 1962

> One of the other old timers in the vegetable business is Joe Tramer, 83, who moved over from the Pearl Market and has been at the business since he was fifteen. "I got grandchildren of my old customers coming to me now," he said. One of the big problems never changes. "I still gotta ask people not to squeeze the tomatoes," he sighed.
> —*Plain Dealer*, September 30, 1962

Balloons with prize certificates attached were released, and planes dropped specially-marked ping-pong balls that could be redeemed for market merchandise. There was a drawing on the last day for the grand prize—an all-

Memories

"During the Depression, one of the big department stores donated blankets for the needy. People could pick them up at the West Side Market. I went there with my mother to get some. I remember they were stored in a room at the bottom of the tower, and I was allowed to climb up the steps—there were so many—to the top of the tower and look out the windows. That's something I've never forgotten."

—*Ruth Sitko*

"I was born in 1926 and grew up in Cleveland, just over the bridge from the West Side Market. I had three older brothers and in the 1930s, when times were hard, they all got part-time jobs at the Market to help out. They worked for people who sold fruit and vegetables outside. It didn't pay much, but they got to take the trimmings home. Mom could always turn those scraps into something good. She shopped at the Market, too. I pulled the wagon for the packages. As a reward she'd buy me a brown paper bag filled with potato chips. It cost 5 cents. There was a man that fried them right there. They were so good."

—*Gladys Wozniak Smolio*

expense paid trip for two to Disneyland. For reasons now unknown, and that bear no connection to significant Market dates, vendors donned Gay '90s costumes (that's 1890s) striped vests and derby hats for the men, bonnets for the ladies. While not historically relevant, the look was certainly festive.

Some ethnic communities got their own day in the spotlight: Italians on Monday, Russians on Tuesday, Germans on Wednesday, Thursday for Hungarians, and Friday for Poles. In a nod to everyone else, Saturday was dubbed United Nations Day. Local celebrity emcees introduced the entertainment: ethnic music and dance performances, contemporary orchestras, and popular singers. Two TV personalities beloved by northeast Ohio kids, Lawrence "Jungle Larry" Tetzlaff, and Ronald "Captain Penny" Penfound, took the stage. They were popular Channel 5 regulars from 1955 to 1971. Seeing them in the flesh would have been a big deal, especially for a six-year-old. The fashion show and beauty pageant sponsored by Fries and Schuele, the upscale department store across the street from the Market, with lovely local ladies in bathing suits and heels, attracted its own appreciative audience.

For two teenagers, there was only one important event on the schedule. "There may have been a lot going on at the West Side Market's fiftieth anniversary celebration," says James Ziga, "but I was focused on winning the dance contest. There was this big stage out front and one hundred and fifty couples danced the Twist."

His partner was Dolores Ziga (no relation). James lived on Bridge Avenue and both he and Dolores were part of the large Hungarian community that resided there. He was fifteen, she was thirteen, and the two were friends. "We knew each other from the neighborhood," says Dolores. "Maybe he was a distant cousin. Even if you weren't related, you considered yourself a cousin. The stage was in front of the Market. The contest started at five or six and ran a couple of hours."

"It was down to the two finalists," James recalls. "One of the three judges turned to the other couple and said, 'Sorry, you lose.'" The prize for their winning moves was a stack of records.

Anniversaries came and went with much less fanfare after the fiftieth. For the sixtieth, held September 10–16, 1972, people who could show proof that they were born in 1912 got a souvenir gift, courtesy of the anniversary committee co-chaired by Robert E. Stumpf, one of the Market's elder statesmen. In 1982, the slogan that appeared on banners and buttons for the three-day anniversary party was "West Side Market...Still Fresh after 70 Years." A seventy-foot submarine sandwich, reputed to be the world's longest, was made in the park across the street, with ingredients from the Market. Mayor George Voinovich cut the first piece and the remainder was sliced and sold in small portions. There was a drawing on Saturday for the grand prize—a hindquarter of beef. Anyone celebrating their seventieth birthday that year got a carnation. Congresswoman Mary Rose Okar and Ward 14 Councilwoman Helen K. Smith, both regular Market shoppers, stepped to the other side of the counter, along with local TV and radio personalities to work side-by-side with the vendors.

Above, from top: Swimsuit competition, 50th Anniversary; The Curiale family dresses up for the 50th anniversary celebration
Opposite, from top: West Side Market Tenants the year of the 25th anniversary, October 27, 1937; An 8 foot weather balloon was launched during the 50th anniversary festivities; An officer and spectators await the 50th anniversary parade

WQAL radio host Larry Morrow broadcast live from the Market all morning on October 3, 1987, for the seventy-fifth anniversary, and then served as Master of Ceremonies for the afternoon rededication ceremony, which included remarks from Mayor Voinovich, Councilwoman Smith, and Tony Pinzone, President of the West Side Market Tenants Association. Some vendors were not in a celebratory mood. James Sperano, President of the Outdoor Tenants Association, was invited to be on the program but refused. Sperano was protesting the lack of investment in upgrading the produce aisles, still a miserable freezing place in winter, at a time when money was being spent on improvements for other parts of the facility. He told a reporter that the conditions inside the building, compared to those outside, was like the difference between the Taj Mahal and the Bowery.[10] The winner of the grand prize drawing—a $750 Market gift certificate—surely went home happy. Five years later, Michael White was Cleveland's mayor, but he was out of town for the eightieth anniversary nod on October 4, 1992, which was little more than a chorus of Happy Birthday and a market-shaped cake.

In the Market's Centennial year, marked with a neighborhood festival, a parade, and a gala fund-raising dinner to kick off a capital campaign, there's a renewed respect for its history, a deeper understanding of its role, and an increased awareness of its value and meaning. "The soul of our city resides in the West Side Market," says Councilman Joe Cimperman. "And we have to take care of it."

Above, counterclockwise from top: Radio personality Larry Morrow visits the Market; Captain Penny and Jungle Larry entertain crowds at the Market
Opposite: Sunday at the Market

Ⓜemories

"Families serving families. That's what the Market's all about. My family's been down here for four generations. We've enjoyed a good life…, a hard life but a rewarding one. I think I've reached out and touched more people than any President of the United States, any politician. I think I've made more people happier than most in show business…. We are the envy of all the big cities in the country. They don't have a market like this. And we've survived by holding fast to what it was and what it should be for 80 years. I'm proud of it and I wish it stays around until long after I'm gone."

—*Nate Anselmo, former vendor, WWWE interview, August 12, 1995*

DAYS TO REMEMBER
Special Events, Holidays, & High Points

WITH A HUNDRED YEARS of history, there are bound to be quite a few unforgettable dates and stand-out happenings. Some made headlines or were chronicled in official records, while others are preserved as snippets of fact, cherished personal memories, and the kind of yarns sure to get a laugh or prompt a tear. String them together, like charms on a bracelet, and they tell a story like no other.

For one night, a Sunday, in September 1971, the market hall was converted into a party center. "Romp with the Bard," a benefit for The Great Lakes Shakespeare Festival, was the rare fund-raiser held inside the building for an outside organization. Fifteen hundred guests feasted on an international buffet, featuring many products from Market vendors, and boogied in the aisles to live music from eight bands. Governor and Mrs. John Gilligan joined in the fun, along with State Representative (and future governor) Dick Celeste. Ladies could buy a dance with a leading man from the Lakewood-based repertory company for a dollar; sketch artists made quick portraits; and a photographer shot Funny Fotos of people with their faces framed by life size cardboard characters in Shakespearean attire. There were no tubs of butter or ground beef by the pound available but bargain hunters could purchase a jade cat, a Wedgwood platter, bronze bookends, and busts of the great playwright himself at the rummage sale.

The revelers could also find some very unusual clothes. Reporting on the event for the *West Side Sun News*, Denise Rochford took note of a pitch man with a circus barker's flair. "Get your Halloween costumes here," he called. "Every one guaranteed worn by an actor." Among the items available were a red chiffon belly dancer's outfit, a Lady Macbeth, and a lion from *A Midsummer Night's Dream*. "…[S]ome of them were most elaborate, complete with

ALIVE AND SWINGING
Letters

Your August 11th article on Cleveland's West Side Market stated "the market doesn't seem to be dying just yet"—as if it might soon follow the demise of other such markets in major cities.

Far from it! On the weekend of Aug. 6–7, our four Kitchen Maid Meat stands enjoyed nearly the greatest volume ever recorded in our 50-years of business there. (And this goes back to when I used to sleep under my father's stand as a boy of six).

…For the information of your readers, the West Side Market will be open for the first Sunday of its entire history—on Sept. 26th—when it will be taken over by the Great Lakes Shakespeare Festival Women's Committee for an international buffet with music, dancing, fun and games…

Cordially,
Robert E. Stumpf
President, West Side Market
Merchants Association[12]

headdresses and ornate adornments. Teen-agers had a hey-day picking over the offerings. Many of them were planning to wear their [*sic*] 'buys' for every day apparel…not just at a costume ball!"[11]

On an ordinary day, everyone at the Market concentrates on food. But polyester knits, white patent leather, and "a perky Indian print poncho" were the focus in April 1973, when the hall was filled with women who weren't there to pick up something for dinner. As volunteers from the U. S. Navy Finance Office and Cuyahoga Community College, they modeled for Goodwill Industries Swingin' into Spring Fashion Show. A crew filmed the ladies as they sashayed past the stands for a segment that aired on television.

> **The Goodwill show features fun and kicky new styles of the "NOW" generation…The models zipped through the wide aisles, posing with vendors, youngsters whose mommies were shopping and bakers whose specialties are tall elaborate wedding cakes.**
> —*Call and Post*, April 7, 1973

A 1974 promotional stunt in the Market's parking lot put produce in the spotlight. Don Samsel, Cleveland district manager for Heinz USA was the tosser-in-chief for his employer's attempt to assemble "the largest salad ever made in Cleveland," on Wednesday afternoon, October 30. To achieve this raw vegetable milestone, Samsel used 600 heads of lettuce, 27 pounds of cucumbers, 20 pounds of cut green beans, 18 pounds of carrots, 18 pounds of celery, 18 pounds of cherry tomatoes, 18 pounds of onions, 14 pounds of green peppers, 8 pounds of grated Parmesan cheese, and 10 gallons of Heinz salad dressing, all collected in an oversized plastic swimming pool. The great mix-up took place in the parking lot at 2 PM. Portions were offered to the public at no charge.[13]

Sunday at the Market, motivated by the same desire that inspired the 1915 Carnival, was an event-driven effort to publicize the Ohio City community. The first "Sunday" was held July 6, 1980. Subtitled "An Astronomical Gastronomical," the summer street fest ran from noon to eight at night. Admission was $1.00 and the main draw was restaurants selling sample-size portions. Chefs were positioned outside in the Market's produce arcades, passing paper plates and bowls to crowds that thronged the alleys on either side. The menu

Above, from top: Cleveland's biggest salad; Governor Dick Celeste and first lady, Dagmar, circa 1983

Memories

"*During World War II, there was a meat and poultry shortage so the government issued colored tokens, like food stamps, to the public. The customers would have to have the money to buy the product as well as a token. I recall them coming in two or three colors, which determined their value. On Sunday after church, our family would sit at the dining room table and count up to ten tokens in a stack and put them in something that resembled an egg carton. The next day we would take them to the bank and exchange them for cash.*"

—*Charles "Bud" Leu Jr., former vendor*

"*In term's of our city's crown jewels, the West Side Market is the biggest, brightest diamond in Cleveland's tiara.*"

—*Anne Bloomberg*

was eclectic, with a few ethnic specialties—everything from barbecued ribs, fries, steak on a skewer, apple pie, and cheesecake to German sausage sandwiches, bouillabaisse, tacos, West Indies crab salad, and baklava. There was a wine-tasting booth, and stands for soda, beer, and lemonade.

A New Orleans-style jazz ensemble jammed in Market Square, and the sidewalks all the way down to W. 28th Street were used for other bands, plus antique and art shows. The sun shone down on competitors in "The Bastille Day Waiters Race." Professional servers made their way through an elaborate obstacle course set up along the north end of W. 25th Street in timed heats, with an audience cheering them on from the sidelines. "Each contestant had to run to around a maze of tables to various stations," remembers Hap Gray, then an Ohio City resident and one of those who spearheaded the "Sunday at the Market" project. "They uncorked wine, poured glasses of champagne, picked up various items, and had to carry the stuff on trays without spilling anything."

Gray, owner of the now-closed Watermark Restaurant, worked in partnership with the Ohio City Redevelopment Association, the forerunner of today's Ohio City Incorporated. "At that time the Market, like the area around it, was looking old and tired," he says. "Neither had gotten much needed reinvestment. We thought 'Sunday' would be a way to get people here, draw attention to the great assets in our community and raise some money to help it."

The fund-raiser became an annual event that continued into the late eighties. In its third year, says Anne Bloomberg, who lived in the neighborhood and worked as a "Sunday" volunteer, the building was opened to host a Salon of Culinary Arts. "Teams created beautiful platters in categories like Cold Food, Hot Food, and Pastry that they set up on the vendors' counters for judging. I think it brought many people inside the Market for the first time." Chefs, their apprentices, and students from multiple cities participated, vying for prizes. Sanctioned by the American Culinary Federation, pros could earn points needed to qualify for the International Culinary Olympics, and therefore all entries had to be edible, and parsley and watercress were not allowed. That same year, "Sunday at the Market" also featured ice carving inside and a string quartet playing on the Market's loading dock. A beer slide was set up on Market Street in 1984 and the world's largest apron was attached to the Market tower.

Memories

"*I was working for Arnold Fernengel in the 1970s. I had worn my best bell bottoms and didn't want to get them dirty because I was going out after work. I bent over and split my pants. So I ran across the street to Fries and Schuele [the department store] and bought a sewing kit. I took my pants off and was trying to sew up the split but Arnold kept calling to bring meat upstairs. I had my cooler coat on and started making trips up and down the steps in my underwear, no pants. I would come back down, sew a few more stitches and then have to make another trip up. While I was gone, one of the guys downstairs took my pants and threw them up on a catwalk where the electric meters were. When I saw what he did, I jumped up to get them and split my head wide open. Now blood is running down my back and I gotta go get stitches. So I run down the street to Lutheran West Hospital, where they shave my head and stitch me up. Back at the Market, Arnold wants to know where I am. Someone tells him I'm at the hospital. Arnold is livid and I'm on the verge of getting fired—except he didn't because I was such a hard worker.*"

—Tony Pinzone, vendor, Pinzone Meats

Joanne Lewis wrote and self-published a book about the Market in collaboration with photographer and designer John Szilagyi. *To Market, To Market* was published in 1981. The Market hosted an autograph party on November 21, complete with a twelve-piece Slovenian accordion ensemble—the Maple Heights Button Box Club—playing in the balcony. Essentially an oral history, Lewis let her subjects tell their own stories, in their own ways. Her interest in them, her method of tape-recording lengthy interviews, and the book that resulted showed a respect for the merchants that they weren't used to receiving.

"I realized the importance of the building, the location, and the people of the West Side Market," Lewis recalls. "Many of the vendors were suspicious of my intentions at first. They thought I might be from the IRS or connected to an ex-wife trying to get their money. It took a lot of diplomacy to get people who worked there to talk to me. They didn't see the place as a national treasure or anything especially interesting about their lives. They were just trying to earn a living. But gradually I won their trust."

Lewis's portraits reveal an interesting contradiction. Merchants who'd been there the longest took pride in their multi-generational connection to the Market, their toughness, skills, and work ethic. Lewis describes them as a kind of Market aristocracy. They loved the place and wanted it to continue unchanged, and recognized the bond between their family business and the families they served. But these entrepreneurial men and women also wanted their kids to get an education, do something else, something easier that paid better. Many did just that, and still ended up behind the counter, a phenomenon that's still evident today.

The West Side Market did a star turn in the movie *Telling Lies in America*. Joe Eszterhas wrote the semi-autobiographical script and insisted that it be filmed in Cleveland, where he grew up. The film was shot on location over twenty-four days in August 1996.

The story, set in 1961, revolves around Karchy Jonas, played by Brad Renfro, a Hungarian immigrant and high school kid who is struggling to find his place in America. Kevin Bacon, as a shady, swaggering radio DJ, befriends him, bedazzles him and then involves him in the illegal pay-to-play scam that was endemic in the music business at the time.

ⓜemories

"I have no idea how my stand got in this movie. They rented it for two days. I still had the original cash register my dad used. They didn't have to change anything because the film was set in the 1960s and we hadn't changed much since then."

—Bill Pawlowski, former vendor

"The West Side Market has this real, warm ethnic vibe. It's naturally inclusive. Tourists may come to see it but unlike other similar kinds of places, regular people still do their shopping here. It exists for them and because of them."

—Joe Eszterhas, screenwriter and author

"My brother John and I got jobs with Robert Stumpf of Kitchen Maid Meats during our high school years at St Ignatius, 1973–79. We both left Cleveland soon after (military service) and have not been back since. I have lived and worked in Germany for many years now and will never forget one late night, I was up watching a movie with Kevin Bacon and Calista Flockhart, filmed in Cleveland. I recognized the interior of the Market and a stand very close to the delivery ramp. I was so excited, I woke my wife up yelling 'I used to work RIGHT THERE!!'"

—Paul Westerh, former employee

Though he never actually worked there himself, Eszterhas has the characters of Karchy and Diney, and the girl he pursues, portrayed by Calista Flockhart, working at the Market. "I put the West Side Market in my movie," Eszterhas says, "because it's a part of my history, a part of my heart. To me it was another character in the story. [Kevin] Bacon did not have any scenes in the Market, but during the shoot I told him about it and took him there. He fell in love with the place. He's a pretty sophisticated guy and he's been all over the world but he was totally knocked out. I saw him six or seven years later and we started talking about Cleveland and he wanted to know how the West Side Market was doing."

The film was shown on opening night of the Cleveland International Film Festival in 1997. Eszterhas and his wife Naomi, who had moved back to the area after his stint in Hollywood, were there, along with director Guy Ferland and actor Maximillian Schell, who played the role of Karchy's father.

The Market got another cameo in the promotions for the twenty-fifth Cleveland International Film Festival a few years later. In a nod to the organization's location in Ohio City, across the street from the West Side Market, the theme for the 2001 Festival was "In the Market for some Fresh Film?" The silver anniversary trailer and program book cover were shot inside the market house and the seminal image for both brought the old and new world together—an elderly lady wearing the classic shopper's babushka, clutching a movie reel.

There's the same mix of past and present just before Thanksgiving, Christmas, New Year's, and Easter. People come in search of the traditional foods they remember from their childhoods, rare and fine ingredients, and unusual products to put on their holiday tables. The seasonal decorations, musical entertainment, and distinctive aromas wafting through the market house are added benefits for the reliably large crowds.

It's not uncommon for musicians to set up in the balcony to entertain the shoppers below. But what happened on Saturday December 18, 2010 was anything but ordinary. The West Shore Chorale, a local non-profit arts organization, turned its free performance of the Hallelujah Chorus from Handel's *Messiah* into a flash mob event, part of the nationwide Random Acts of Culture initiative launched by the Knight Foundation. Mobilized to gather in the Market via social media and word-of-mouth, a huge crowd stood shoulder to shoulder, filling

Jeremiah Wiencek: The Fourth Generation

Thirty-one-year-old Jeremiah Wiencek is the fourth generation of his family to have a stand at the West Side Market. His maternal great-grandfather, Robert Stumpf, was among the original 1912 vendors. "Other than delivering papers, working at the Market is the only job I've ever had," says Wiencek. "My first job was as a cooler boy for Lance's Beef. I started on a 4th of July weekend. I was thirteen, scrawny—under a hundred pounds. Grant Lance told me if I survived that Saturday I'd be okay and I did. I was with him for six and a half years, through high school and then while I was going to Case Western Reserve University studying mechanical engineering. A stand became available behind Grant and I took it over on March 1, 1999, my twentieth birthday. It was a big decision, but not a hard one. I felt at home in the Market. I'd enrolled in college because it was expected. I liked the idea of continuing the family tradition. I specialized in beef because that's what I knew. Now I have a second stand selling poultry. Eleven years later and I have no regrets."

Opposite, from top: Cleveland International Film Festival poster, 2001; John Szilagyi's photo of Rose Thomas

ⓜemories

"There's only five feet of counter space to a single stand. We fit seven people back here at Easter. That's our busiest time of year. There's a system—you tap the person next to you on the shoulder whenever you move, otherwise there'd be chaos with everybody walking into each other.

—**Jerry Chucray, vendor, Czuchraj Meats**

"The local public television station WVIZ made a documentary about the West Side Market in 2000. It was the best thing that ever happened to us. We got so much attention. Business was phenomenal after it aired. I could have put a pair of old shoes on the counter and I would have sold them."

—**Patrick Delaney, former vendor**

"This is the best place my nose has ever been."

—**Kieran Harper, age nine, walking through the Market at Christmastime**

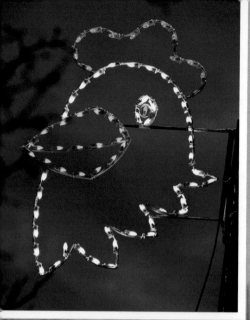

the aisles. For a few minutes, no business was transacted, as every face turned toward the singers up in the balcony. Some in the audience joined in, others just listened awestruck by the magnificent sound reverberating through the hall.

For one local family, a seasonal excursion has become an annual shopping spree and an essential part of how they celebrate. In 1932, Edwin and Margaret Haas made a trip with their infant son Edwin Jr., born November 4, to the West Side Market on the Saturday preceding Thanksgiving. They went to buy things for the holiday meal and came home with all the trimmings, plus a selection of delicacies for a spontaneous feast that same night. "I am seventy-nine years old," says Edwin Haas Jr. "I have done this every year of my life, with my parents, brother, and sister, and later with my wife, Gene Alice, and children and now our grandchildren. The sights, the sounds, and of course the wonderful smells are always the same."

In 2011, twenty adults and seven kids, ranging from toddler to teenager, went on the Haas Market outing. "We got lots of meats and cheeses and pickles to make the best Dagwood sandwiches," says Edwin, "just like we usually do. That's the best part of our Saturday night spread if you ask me. And ever since it opened, we go to the popcorn stand. The little kids love that."

It's also popular place to bring out-of-town guests, an interactive, 3-D kind of entertainment that never fails to astonish first-timers, and a way to show off the city. Ex-Clevelanders like Stephanie Simon, who currently lives in Durham, NC, return like homing pigeons. She went to the Market regularly with her mother and sister in the seventies and eighties. Visiting family in November 2010 for the Thanksgiving holiday, she brought her husband and young son to the Market. "We live in a world where so many things have changed so much. It's nice to come back to a place that's stayed essentially the same."

Lois Rose has been shopping at the Market since 1968 and has become a self-appointed tour guide. "I came to Cleveland from New Orleans as a grad student. One of my professors at Case Western Reserve University took me there and introduced me to all his favorite stands and vendors. I've done the same thing with other newcomers hundreds of times. I love the look of astonishment on people's faces. Most have never seen anything like it. For many people who are from other countries, especially Russians, where store shelves can be almost empty, the abundance can be almost overwhelming."

Ⓜ emories

"I remember one year when the Market hired a Santa Claus at Christmas. The guy got pretty tanked and kept pulling down his fake beard for the kids. Kenny Loucka had a stand next to my dad. Once during Christmastime, he found Christmas carol books. So he thought it would be nice if we sang a few songs. He brought in some of the bums and homeless from outside to sing along. The Market commissioner had a talk with us the next day."

—Chuck Maurath, former vendor

"Thanksgiving was a really busy time for us. Dad would rent a second cooler to hold all the turkeys. At Easter we'd sell ducks and geese. When we closed up on the last shopping night before a holiday, dad, me, and my brother-in-law, who also helped out for awhile, always went to Ferris steakhouse at 70th and Detroit for a nice dinner."

—John Coyne, former employee

"We would always make a stop on the Saturday before Christmas when polka bands played and Santa Clauses would dance through the balcony."

—Debbie DeMaria

A BIRD IN THE BAG
Poultry Dead & Alive

LIVE CHICKENS LOOM large in many people's recollections. The birds were never sold inside the market house, but in the first half of the twentieth century they were available from street vendors. Later, poultry—in all its squawking glory—could be found in a separate building, located next to the West Side Market but never affiliated with it. It was in operation under various owners until 2001. By the 1950s, shoppers commonly chose live birds and returned later to pick them up—dead and de-feathered. But in earlier times, a fresh chicken was one that met its fate on a backyard chopping block. Shoppers took journeys with their birds from W. 25th Street to pots and ovens all over town.

> "My Grandma would buy one live chicken a week. They would wrap the chicken in newspaper and put a rubber band around it and the head would stick out. She would keep the chicken at home for a week, then we would have it for Sunday dinner and she used the feathers to make comforters.
>
> One time we were coming home on the streetcar (which cost 10 cents at the time), and Grandma's chicken was tucked under her arm with the head facing backwards. We stood, as there were no open seats. A fella behind us tapped Grandma on the shoulder and said, 'Ma'm. Would you mind turning your chicken around? It keeps pecking me.'"
> —Henry Dunasky

> "I'm ninety years old but I still remember the day my mother let me carry the duck home from the Market. It was 1926. I was four years old. The farmer put a string around her wings so she couldn't fly away, wrapped her up in newspaper, and tied her feet together. I was so happy to hold that duck. I loved animals. But my father worked in a slaughterhouse and he taught me not to feel sorry for them. He said they're here for us to eat and that's just the way it is."
> —Ruth Sitko

> "In the forties, the streetcar would stop at the West Side Market and the ladies with babushkas would get on with their live chickens, turkeys, or

Opposite, from top: In 2011, Ohio City resident Fay Harris gathered donations to buy new food-themed holiday lights to string up on lampposts around the Market; Christmastime at the Market
Above, from top: A goose headed for the Christmas dinner table, December 23, 1928; The live poultry business next to the Market

Above, from top: Streetcar passing the site where the Pearl Street Market once stood; Streetcars brought many shoppers to the Market for decades

ducks. What a melody we listened to the rest of the trip—the clucking, gobbling, and quacking of the birds. One by one, the babushkas got off and by the time we reached Brooklyn Avenue, the streetcar was quiet."
—John M. Busch

"I have no idea how mom mastered that feat on her trips to the Market, carrying heavy shopping bags filled with produce and meats with one hand, while the other held a struggling fowl, but she seemed to do it with ease.... On some occasions when I accompanied her, she was like a juggler, trying to keep me from slipping away and also make sure the chicken was not pecking at the string that tied the top of the bag.

I smile as I wonder what the conductor or passengers would have done if the chicken had managed to escape confinement on that old streetcar.

My best guess is mom would have had me sit still while she chased that chicken up and down the aisle.... I'm sure she would have had me collect the feathers fluttering about as she used them to stuff pillows. Nothing from the Market was wasted in those days."
—Ellie Behman

"In the mid-sixties, to help make ends meet, mom began working at the chicken coop building [beside the West Side Market]. The owner's name was Harry. The building stood behind the fruit stands, across the alleyway. There were cages and cages of clucking chickens unknowingly awaiting their destiny at the hands of Willie. Customers came in, many with broken English, but they knew how to convey which one was their prize pick. The bird was plucked from the cage and hurried to the processing station of the store for Willie to prepare it. There was a window where my brother and I stood and watched, standing witness as we squealed and squirmed. It's too graphic to describe, but I could tell you every detail of what it took to get that bird onto your dinner plate. Once it was slaughtered, cleaned, and cut, it was passed through the window to my mom where she displayed it to the customer for approval, wrapped it, and rang up the sale on a big brown cash register with lots of buttons. The gleeful customer bid good day to her and no doubt proceeded to the vegetable stands to select a side dish to serve with their prize pick of the day from Harry's."
—Laurie Goyetche

This same building, once live poultry's last stop, was completely gutted, renovated, and repurposed as the tank room and distillery for Market Garden Brewery, which opened in 2011. The owner, Sam McNulty, feels a connection to the neighborhood, the West Side Market, and this particular piece of real estate that dates back to his childhood. "The whole family regularly piled into the station wagon for a weekly shopping trip to the Market," recalls the thirty-seven-year-old. "I thought it was great, like going to an amusement park of food. I have vivid memories of the chicken place next door. My brothers and sisters and I took turns choosing the bird to buy."

RAVE REVIEWS
Accolades, Awards, Praise, & Shout-outs

EVEN BEFORE IT officially opened near the end of 1912, the West Side Market was earning kudos. Stately and beautiful, a symbol of achievement for Cleveland, it was a model for other cities: modern, hygienic, and well-organized with symmetry of form and function. More recently the Market's longevity, constancy of purpose, and the unchanging, Old World, old-fashioned atmosphere are what garners attention and applause. Throughout its history—as newspaper and magazine articles, TV coverage, and shopper testimonials make clear—the selection of food, the ethnic mix on both sides of the counter, the social interactions, and the personal service are what inspires devotion and compliments.

Formal recognition first came on December 4, 1972, when City Council passed an ordinance making the West Side Market an official Cleveland Landmark. The following year it was listed on the National Register of Historic Places. The American Planning Association (APA) named the West Side Market one of the Great Public Spaces in America for 2008, citing its utility as both a neighborhood gathering place and fresh food market; the engaging atmosphere; and its role as an Ohio City anchor that stimulates nearby commercial and residential activity. An article about all the honorees that year got the Market a mention in the November 2008 issue of *Travel and Leisure Magazine*.

Above, from top: Bread at Mediterra Bakehouse; The Market celebrates its designation as a historic landmark

Memories

"My family decided to have a pig roast for Labor Day weekend in 2010. It was our first one. We ordered a thirty-five-pound pig from Whitaker at the Market and I got the job of picking it up. I went with the baby and there was no way I could get it to the car by myself. One of the guys behind the counter threw it over his shoulder and walked it out to the parking lot for me. The legs were too long and it wouldn't fit in the cooler. Luckily, I brought a plastic garbage bag filled with ice just in case and he put it in there. While he was doing this, he told me some firefighters had ordered a 150-pound pig the week before. Four guys, dressed in official looking clothes, arrived to pick it up. They stuffed the pig in a body bag and wheeled it out through the produce aisles on a cart. According to the guy from Whitaker's, rumors instantly started circulating that somebody had died at the Market."

—*Cherry Bochman*

In his book West of the Cuyahoga, journalist George Condon writes that the Market merits classification as a civic monument, noting "it is no overstatement to describe the building as a municipal masterpiece."

BEING THE BEST

Megan Driscoll, a freelance producer, came to the Market at the end of March 2010 to do some scouting and preliminary filming for a new Food Network show called *America's Best*, hosted by Alton Brown. I followed her and the crew around, eavesdropping as they chatted with shoppers and vendors. Not all these comments made it into the show, but I captured them in my notebook.

"It's like having our own personal butcher."

"They know what I want when I walk up to the counter before I even open my mouth."

"It's like *Cheers* [the TV series about the Boston bar, 'where everybody knows your name']."

"It's not just what they sell here. It's the quality, the freshness, the fact that things aren't wrapped in plastic. And that you really get to know the people you buy from."

Michelle Vigh, who operates Michelle's Bakery, faces into the camera and gives the nutshell version of her story. "I've worked here for thirty years, ever since I was thirteen. I've tried to leave, gotten jobs somewhere else, but I always come back to the Market. There's nothing else like it."

After a couple of hours of this, Driscoll turns to her cameraman and says, "This place is amazing."

—Laura Taxel

Above: America's Best crew filming at Michelle's Bakery
Opposite, from top: Chef Michael Symon; The line at Steve's Gyros

To earn the APA designation, the Cleveland City Planning Commission and the Cleveland Landmarks Commission had to answer a number of questions. Asked to name specific characteristics that distinguish the Market and make it different from other places in the community, they wrote:

> In an age when the majority of people do their grocery shopping in sterile and homogenous supermarkets, the West Side Market still offers a visitor an authentic and very human experience. One does not find shelves stocked with pre-packaged goods at the West Side Market, but instead specialized vendors willing to share their expertise…A visitor can purchase anything from freshly made pasta to an entire pig. There are few other places where a person can purchase Chilean Sea Bass, homemade Lithuanian sausage, European cheeses and freshly baked bread all under one roof….Cultures from around the globe are represented by both vendors and the shoppers they attract.

In September 2010, after christening it the country's "Best Food Lovers' Market," the Food Network featured the West Side Market in a series about America's top food destinations. *Frommer's* dubbed the West Side Market one of the thirteen best public markets in the country in 2011. In February 2012, *USA Today* published "11 Reasons to Visit Cleveland" on its Pop Culture blog. The West Side Market was Number 4.

Over the years, many individual vendors have been singled out in the local press, especially the old-timers. Butcher Bob Leu briefly became the face of the Market and the most widely known vendor in the eighties.

> Bob Leu has become something of a media personality. Last year the New Cleveland Campaign featured his bright smile and balding head on a poster that was circulated internationally.
>
> That, coupled with a television commercial that shows him promoting Cleveland, has turned Leu into the most recognizable personality at the Market. He seems to enjoy the role.

"There are actually Germans who come here from Germany and take my picture because they saw that poster," says Leu, who is of German and Swiss heritage. "The kids are the ones who remember me from the television commercials."
—Bill Miller, *Plain Dealer*, May 13, 1981

In 2007, Steve's Gyros was voted best gyros in the country by *Maxim Magazine*. Over the years, *Cleveland Magazine* has spotlighted the best the city has to offer. Narrin's Asian Spice and Sauce, Kaufmann Poultry, Maha's Falafil, and Campbell's Popcorn Shop have made it into the annual lineup.

A sign at Czuchraj Meats proudly proclaims, "Michael Symon picked our beef jerky for the Food Network's *The Best Thing I Ever Ate.*" Symon, a national celebrity who calls Cleveland home, is an award-winning chef, restaurant owner, cookbook author, and popular TV personality. People pay attention to what he says and what he likes. "Thanks to Chef Symon, who loves it, our beef jerky was featured on The Food Network in 2010," says Jerry Chucray. "They came to the Market and filmed for four hours and then did more filming where we make the jerky. We set up a website and got more than six hundred prepaid orders within the first two hours after it aired on January 28. We weren't ready with enough product. We didn't expect that kind of response."

In a piece for *Gourmet* in August 1995, well-known and well-respected food writer Evan Jones penned a love note to sausages and shoppers, the handsome structure, the multi-ethnic mix, and the long history and personal relationships that defined commerce there. "Sunday at the Market," he writes, "seems to be a way of crystallizing the spirit of *Gemütlichkeit* and joie de vivre that characterizes regular shopping days. Throughout the year, though, many Clevelanders continue to rhapsodize about this shoppers' landmark."

Other mainstream print mentions have followed. Two different writers inked travel pieces titled "36 Hours in Cleveland" for the *New York Times*, in 2005 and 2009, and both included a description of the West Side Market. The Market garnered the number three spot on the *Saveur* 100 list for 2001, the national food magazine's annual round-up of noteworthy culinary people, places, and products. Editors advised readers, "Go for groceries;

Ⓜ emories

In October 2011, award-winning restaurant critic, author, and former editor-in-chief of Gourmet *Magazine, Ruth Reichl, came to town for a lecture at the Cleveland Public Library. When her flight home was cancelled, she made an unexpected visit to the West Side Market and wrote about the experience on her blog. "It's a vibrant place that reminded me more of the great markets of Europe than anyplace I've seen in America… they're still turning out old-time, hand-made smoked meats and charcuterie that's hard to find anywhere else. I arrived home with a suitcase filled with obscure German and Hungarian sausages—a fine way to remember Cleveland."*

Above, from top: Irish eats at Reilly's; The red tile floors inside the hall show little wear despite a century of use

leave with a taste of Cleveland's history." The list, which appeared in the January/February issue, was a salute to mastery and experience, to "the practiced, the confident, the authentic." An item in the April issue of *Better Homes and Gardens* the same year had a similar theme, noting that the Market offered an experience of food shopping as it was done in the early 1900s. The Market showed up again in *Saveur's* pages in 2010, in a piece by Jane and Michael Stern entitled "The Best Places to Eat in Northeast Ohio."

It's a feat to get out of Cleveland with any appetite at all if you spend time grazing around the city's sprawling, century-old West Side Market, where temptations include the West Side Market Cafe's fried fresh walleye sandwich and Reilly Irish Bakery's triple-chocolate, six-pint Guinness Stout cake, not to mention a plethora of fresh produce, stone-hearth breads, and German kuchen (fruit- and cheese-filled pastries).

Amy Eddings is a Cleveland-area native, now living in Brooklyn. A reporter and the host of National Public Radio's *All Things Considered* on WNYC in New York, she does a weekly segment on seasonal eating, and blogs for the station at "Amy's Food for Thought." In one post she wrote that Cleveland's West Side Market is her favorite foodie paradise, adding that a trip home isn't complete without a stop there. She especially loves the loud, lively atmosphere that is part of its essential character.

My first visit to the West Side Market took place when I was a teenager, and it was a visual and aural shock. The high, vaulted ceiling, with its regal herringbone brick pattern, the buzz of conversations and multiple transactions coming from the rows of stalls—I wasn't used to shopping for food in such a grand, busy environment. Up to that point, I had only experienced the blandness and anonymity of suburban supermarkets, where your interactions were limited to the guy at the deli counter and the lady at the cash register.

At the Market there's an electricity in the air of pride and competition. I always feel guilty when I sense a vendor catching me moving away from his stall and toward his competitor's. But I also feel

emories

"*The West Side Market gives Cleveland huge bragging rights. When visitors come, it's part of my version of a local culinary tour. It says something about who we were and who we are. It has that real Midwest broad shoulders attitude, a kind of pushy old school, blue collar rough-and-tumble hardworking immigrant bargain-hunting spirit.*"

—**Jonathon Sawyer**, *Cleveland chef*

"*I was impressed with the huge variety of meats and cuts. We tried some outstanding Polish and Hungarian foods. It's amazing that the Market has survived these hundred years, and it does feel like we've come full circle, since much of what they're doing there is now being touted as 'artisanal,' when they've just been doing this all along.*"

—**Kate Heddings, Deputy Food Editor, Food & Wine Magazine**

adventurous. I enjoy the hunt for the best taste, the best deal, the best service.

During my last visit to the Market, strolling through the produce arcade, I felt like a woman walking past workers at a construction site. "Hey, lady, you lookin' for fresh broccoli? I got it!" "Miss, miss, whaddya need?" "I got great tomatoes! C'mere, try a slice!" The West Side Market has the energy of the chase, for both shopper and seller. There's a mood, a vibe, that can't be found in supermarkets.

Journalist Maryann Haggerty came to Cleveland for the Bruce Springsteen exhibit at the Rock and Roll Hall of Fame. While in town, she made a trip to Ohio City and was pleasantly surprised by what she found.

There's something appropriate about going to Cleveland to pay homage to Bruce Springsteen, the poet of Rust Belt rock. What I didn't expect in that much-maligned city was a fun neighborhood of historic bed-and-breakfast inns, up-to-the-minute restaurants and one of the best traditional food markets I have ever visited.
—*The Washington Post*, September 24, 2010

Getting national media exposure, compliments, and endorsements from people who drop in for a visit is nice. But the most meaningful recognition for the West Side Market comes from those who really know the place and make it part of the fabric of their lives. Daniel Thompson, the first Poet Laureate of Cuyahoga County, is a member of this group, and he enshrined his connection in a piece called "Fruits and Vegetables." The words were inscribed on a tile and incorporated into a 1985 sculptural installation in Market Square Park, located directly across W. 25th Street. A 2012 reconstruction project totally changed the look and the landscape of the park, but the tile, along with others made by neighborhood residents, has become part of the new design.

Above, from top: Minnie Zarefoss grins widely for the customers at Jim's Meats; A vendor offers a smile with a customer's bag of produce; A shopper checks out fresh watermelons and cantaloupes

FRUITS AND VEGETABLES
Daniel Thompson (1935–2004)

It's raining, I'm on the West Side to get my thumb x-rayed. Was it Lutheran
Where Uncle Art died? I cut through the Market, through decades of fruits
And vegetables to World War II. There I am again with Sis on the way to school
In this same arcade, where everything's alive and tells a story
Like poor, young Sweet Potato, after telling Cherry Tomato they cantaloupe
'Cause he's squeezed dry making payments on that lemon they're driving
Goes out with the boys for a spinach, pulls up to the nearest pumpkin
You help us? We need asparagus. Beet it, cries a big grape, who looks like
He belongs in the zucchini see we're closed, and throws Corn out on his ear
I'd call that a cauliflower, Artichokes with emotion and swings open the car door
Avocado, desperado. The boys jump out swinging like Tarzan and the apricots
I don't wanna die-ah, says the Papaya. Call me a cabbage. I'm leaving. Too late
After the Rhubarb wires home to Lima for beans, the boys're bailed out of jail
And they sail off to work. But it's not up to parsley, so the eggplant's out
On strike. Pears of goons on celery stalk picket limes, peppering them with insults,
You dirty radishes, this is the last strawberry the hatchet or we'll squash you, we'll
Mango you, we'll string your beans up by the nectarines, we'll brussel your sprouts
Turnip tomorrow, you'll get more than the raspberry, you'll go home with a pineapple
Up your ask me no questions, I'll tell you no lying sweet talk, says Sweets
And pulls out a banana, splits open those sons of peaches, pits and all
He really creams them, so Broccoli surrenders to the Onion, love is everywhere
Sweet Potato grabs Tomato, Yam nuts about you, honeydew, lettuce tangerine
You can see I know my peas and cucumbers, and no unrhymed orange
Nor crazy plum could have made me hum that day happy as a watermelon
Only carrots, loud and hard as nails. What's in the bag, kid? Updoc
Bugs Bunny on the streetcar, I eat my roots, roll my eyes heavenward and salute
Now, lucky me, I'm two wars older, running late as usual
Where is everyone? O, it's Thursday, the Market's closed. Our friends
The fruits and vegetables are off today. The arcade's almost empty
There are only those crossing guards who wish to keep dry and these gentlemen
Who do not, the morning body count. Are you my lost uncle, my brother
Itinerant artist, veteran of the starvation army? Last night was it the slammer
Or a hallelujah flop? And you, old man, you know by heart those nameless dogs
Where your dead soldiers lie. Why are you so grave, soldiers? You've tailor-mades
I see. You've no part, no muscatel. Well, you've come together this day unsaved
A black-toothed crew—tattooed, blue, open flies, eyes of salt and humor, surviving
Wars and rumors. I catch images of myself, my breath in the bad air, hurry on…

From *The Big Book of Daniel*, reprinted with permission.

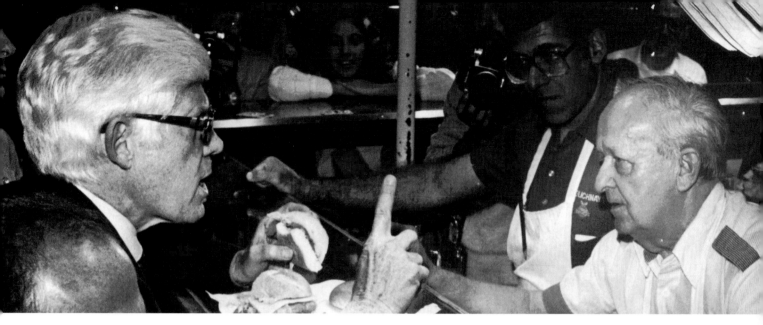

VIP VISITORS
Celebrities, Politicians, Big Shots, & Odd Ducks

MARKET MERCHANTS TAKE pride in recognizing their customers and remembering their names or other personal details about who they are and what they like. But the fact is some of those standing on the other side of the glass-fronted case or the displays of produce are simply more notable than others. Not all of them come to shop: when the beautiful, the famous, and the high-ranking arrive, their presence is often an event in itself.

The Pearly King and Queen must surely have turned heads among the Saturday crowds when they toured the Market on June 2, 1962. Following a practice that dates back to the late nineteenth century, the royal visitors wore outfits covered in thousands of mother-of-pearl buttons arranged in elaborate designs. Although they appeared to be dressed for Halloween, Mr. and Mrs. J. H. Marriott were real Cockney monarchs.

They came to Cleveland from London, England, as representatives of the Pearlies, a British society of street hawkers known for their charitable works. Every borough of London had its ruling family whose titles were inherited. Traditionally, the eye-catching costumes were worn to distinguish Pearlies from other street vendors and help them gather donations. The Londoners weren't the only "royals" to make an appearance at the Market.

Above, from top: Former Congressman and Presidential candidate John Anderson talks with vendors Dave Weisberg, left, and Louis Sliwa; London's Pearly King and Queen pose for pictures

Memories

Before he retired, Walter Simmelink served some noteworthy customers. Lorin Maazel, conductor of Cleveland Orchestra from 1972 to 1982, used to buy his cheese from him. When First Lady Betty Ford came to town in 1976, the chef at the Marriott Hotel where she stayed, knowing her preferences, stocked the room with her favorite cheeses, purchased from Simmelink's.[14] King Khalid of Saudi Arabia was at the Cleveland Clinic for heart surgery in 1978. Members of his entourage went to the West Side Market to get him "French Roquefort, Holland Leyden, Danish fontina, domestic Gouda, and Wisconsin Cheddar" at Simmelink's stand.[15]

"One of the boys from St. Ignatius that worked for me [at Euclid Sausage] wrote the essay for his college application about one single day at the Market when he met an NFL player, Senator Mike DeWine, and the local TV weatherman."

—*Patrick Delaney, former vendor*

Above, from top: Billy Graham and John Rolston; Apple Queen Terry Drake with produce vendor Louis Stein; Walter Simmelink Jr. and Senator John Glenn

Dressed less elaborately in a short skirt and a tiara, the Apple Queen didn't have to do more than smile to attract attention when she walked through the produce arcade in October. The goodwill ambassador for Ohio, Michigan, and Pennsylvania apple growers was actually Terry Drake, an airline stewardess from Lakewood. She toured the Market as part of National Apple Week

Celebrity sightings, though often unexpected, happen with regularity. Vendors aren't shy about name-dropping and tell their stories with pride.

"In the mid-1960s, Jim Brown, the fullback for the Cleveland Browns, used to shop at my dad's stand. One Saturday morning he comes to the counter and buys a big rump roast. Elmer, a funny little guy who used to work for my dad, hands it to him like he was passing off a football, points at the exit sign about two hundred yards away and says to Brown, 'I'll bet you can't make it to the exit sign in thirty seconds.' Brown looks down the aisle jam-packed with people shopping, and says, 'No way.'"
—Larry Vistein, vendor, Vistein Meat

"Ann Margaret came to the Market while in town filming a movie. At first, I didn't recognize her. She walked by the stand [Rita's Pickles] and I offered her a pickle chip, just like Rita would. She bought a pound, and as I bent down to scoop them into the container, I see her chest, right there, through the glass case. I recognized that chest! I've been a big Ann Margaret fan since I was a kid. When I finally looked up, she was smiling at me. I said, 'If I didn't know better, I would think you are Ann Margaret.' She was impressed that someone my age would know her. My knees were knocking and I was at a loss for more words."
—Fritz Graewe, former vendor

"My parents had been in a terrible car accident. My mother broke her neck. On this particular day, dad was working at the Market and she was recovering at home. He was on the phone with her and said, 'You'll never believe who's in the Market right now—it's Billy Graham.' She replied, 'I wish I could be there.' At that moment Graham was walking past our stand, so my dad calls out to him, 'Billy, speak to my wife,' and hands him the phone. Graham came over, took the receiver, said hello and then prayed with her. They were so touched that he took the time for this.

Years later I asked my father what Billy was really like in person. Dad said he exuded such magnetism and charisma that if the man had told him to take off his apron and follow me, he would have done it."
—Suzette (Rolston) Martin, former employee

"My wife met Billy Graham in Toronto. He was working with a youth group. She was a big fan, so talking to him when he was at the Market was very exciting. His organization sent us the photo of him on the telephone with her. It was a lovely gesture.

We had so many celebrities and politicians come by. Too many to remember. I do recall chatting with the singer Pearl Bailey. It was early on a Monday morning. I told her I loved her music. She told me her feet hurt."

—John Rolston, former vendor

"I still have the dollar Ronald Reagan's daughter Maureen gave me as a tip when I worked at the [West Side Market] cafeteria. It's one of my treasures. She was at the Market with her father and as nice as she could be. Her mother was Jane Wyman, Reagan's first wife. I almost got to shake his hand but some woman with a baby got in front of me. Hillary Clinton also came into the cafeteria and Ed Kennedy was there two times. Dr. Ted White, the famous brain surgeon from Metro, was a regular customer of mine. He was always nice, very polite. He traveled all over the world and sent me postcards."

—Mary Hunt, former employee

"John McCain likes hot sauce. He came to the Market during his campaign, stopped at my stand and bought some. My relatives in Cambodia were sitting in a café and saw it on CNN. Al Roker stopped by to look at the hot sauces, too. Bobby Flay, the famous chef, came to the Market when he was in town to do a tailgating party for TV [*FoodNation*, 2002]. He bought all his spices from me and mentioned me on the show. When Chef Michael Symon needs something special in a hurry, he gets it from me and Robin Swoboda [local TV personality] is a customer of mine, too. It's fun and exciting when these big name people buy my things or mention me. Of course, it's good for business, too."

—Narrin Carlberg, vendor, Narrin's Asian Spice and Sauce

"Nick Meyo was known as the Market photographer and he worked for my dad at his poultry stand, so some people called him Chicken Nick. His hobby was taking pictures of people at the Market. He shot celebrities and ordinary customers. He'd print the photos and write the person's name, where they were from, and anything else he'd found out about them on the back. If he saw them again, he'd give them a copy. Many of his shots ended up on the wall at the Johnny

Above, from top: Betty Hunter, left, and the rest of the Market restaurant "girls"; Nick "Shutterbug" Meyo celebrates his birthday at the Market restaurant

Memories

Alex Trebek, the host of the popular television quiz show Jeopardy, *visited Cleveland in the late 1980s on a search for contestants. He was walking around the Market and stopped at Hartman's to look at the meat in the case. Longtime Market employee and a master of one liners, Tim Jeziorski happened to be working at the stand that day when Trebek asked him, "Where does your beef come from?" Tim's quick response, echoing the game's signature answer-followed-by-question format was "Uh, what is…cattle."*

John Rolston and Pearl Bailey had their conversation in September 1976. The vocalist and special United Nations "Ambassador of Love" was in Cleveland to speak at a benefit for Goodwill Industries of Cleveland, held at the Sheraton Hotel ballroom on a Saturday night. But she did more than make a speech. Guests paid $100 to dance with the famous lady and there were plenty of takers. That would certainly explain her sore feet!

Above, from top: Tony Pinzone with Senator John Glenn and his wife, Annie; Clara Chucray

Hot Dog stand. Jose Mesa [former Cleveland Indians pitcher] and his wife were regulars with us. Mesa loved Nick. He gave a big check to his widow to help out when Nick died."

—John Coyne, former employee

Politicians are a distinctive group of luminaries that flock to the West Side Market. Whoever hopes to be elected—whether to municipal judge or American president and every office in between—finds it the perfect spot to connect with voters. Vendors greet these appearances with mixed emotions. A few minutes of chit chat or glad handing with a famous candidate could be a thrill, but the disruption caused by the media entourage and the onlookers often meant less money in the till.

Toledo Blade reporter Jack Torry describes a 1994 episode of real retail politics. "Amid mountains of fresh bananas, sweet corn, and Hungarian kolbasz, Democrats Joel Hyatt and Mary Boyle, and Republicans Bernadine Healy and Eugene Watts shook hands with customers and had their pictures taken by delighted vendors as they stalked for votes in the crowded aisles of the West Side Market…Tony Peters of Peter's Produce saw Mr. Hyatt and cried out that if he wanted a vote he would have to "spend a buck. You can't just go by and shake hands." When Mr. Hyatt handed over $1 for eight oranges, Mr. Peters said, "I hope you make it." Elsewhere in his piece, Torry notes that Healy, a cardiologist, also made a purchase—six bananas and four skinless chicken breasts. "No cholesterol for her."[16]

"My mother was very forward, very honest, and outspoken. People loved her for it. Senator Ted Kennedy came to the Market when he was running for President in 1980. When he didn't stop at our stand, my mom shouted out, 'You just walked past the best kielbasa in Cleveland.' He smiled but kept on going. That wasn't good enough for her. So she stepped out from behind the counter, chased him down and said, 'You come over to my stand. You try my smokies.' She grabbed his arm and escorted the candidate back to our place. He couldn't say no. The Secret Service didn't know what to do with her. She was an unstoppable little old lady."

—Jerry Chucray, vendor, Czuchraj Meats

"I got to meet a lot of famous people: Ronald Reagan, John Glenn. I had a hot dog with Ted Kennedy in his limo. He was going around the Market, shaking

Memories

Nicholas Meyo began taking photos of people at the Market in 1954, while helping his father Rocco, who sold sausages and hams for the Hildebrandt's. And he was still doing it in 1997, right up until a couple of days before he died at age seventy-four. In between, Nick worked as a sales rep for a couple of large food companies and for fifteen years as a wedding photographer. He returned to the Market part-time after retiring and was a familiar figure behind the counter and the camera. He got pictures of Hillary Clinton, then-Representative Mike DeWine, and Dr. Bernadine Healy, former head of the National Institutes of Health. But his enthusiasm for taking portraits made everyone— from shoppers and their children to Market employees—feel important.

"I went to Slovenian school on Saturdays, and afterwards to the West Side Market with my parents. I'd always get a salt stick and some prasky—a holy marriage of bologna and salami. The vendors who remember my parents treat me like family. But they're also my constituents, which gives them the right to yell at me. I don't mind. The Market gave me many happy memories and now, as a Councilman, it's my chance to give back."

—*Councilman Joe Cimperman*

hands, and came by our produce stand. I was ten or eleven. I offered to show him around. He said sure so of course I took him to Johnny Hot Dog. He invited me to sit with him in the car while we ate."
—Tony Anselmo, former employee

"The Market was exciting at election time. In 1980, Ronald Reagan came there. At our stand [Farm Queen Poultry] he went behind the counter and shook hands with my father. Dad got a real kick out of that. I remember he said that Reagan had a firm handshake."
—John Coyne, former employee

There was never a more enthusiastic fan and docent than former Cleveland councilwoman and member of Congress Mary Rose Oakar. She recognized the Market, with its ethnic diversity, as a politician's dream and a great representation of the city and the country. She brought John Glenn and his wife Annie to the Market when he was campaigning for a Senate seat. "Annie didn't just walk around smiling and shaking hands," Oakar recalls. "She bought stuff. The vendors loved her for that." Oakar took the Metzenbaums, too, and Howard's wife Shirley also endeared herself to the merchants by shopping. Rosalynn Carter came to Cleveland and Oakar made sure their market expedition included a stop at Rita's stand so the wife of the nation's goober-growing presidential contender could watch the nuts being freshly ground into peanut butter.

Above, from top: Johanna Ratschki and daughter Ilse Sheppard of Frank's Bratwurst shake hands with Hillary Clinton, circa 1992; Member of Congress Mary Rose Oakar shopped at the Market whenever she came back to her district

Ⓜ emories

"All the political requirements are to be found in a people-gathering place like the West Side Market, and the scent of votes mingles nicely with the aroma of the fresh fruits, meats, and baked goods. Little wonder that candidates find the fragrance exuded by the old marketplace to be absolutely irresistible."

—***George E. Condon,***
   West of the Cuyahoga

"I've been going to the West Side Market since 1960. When I was a meat eater, I would buy from the Ehrnfelts. I became a vegan in 1995 and for me the Market offers every possibility. On my last trip there, I had a falafel sandwich, and I always buy bread. The market is a campaign stop for many politicians, but first it's a place to get great food."

—***Dennis J. Kucinich, former Congressman***

"The sign of a great city is first, a great market. That makes Cleveland like Paris."

—***Anthony Bourdain, chef, author, and TV personality***

"When Rosalynn Carter was here, the FBI came in the morning, towed cars away, roped off the area and stopped the Market completely. She showed up about 3 in the afternoon, made a 20 minute speech and left. It killed the whole day at the Market.... John Glenn... now Glenn is a politician but he was an American hero first. He was really glad to give me his autograph."
—Nashur Romano, former vendor, *Plain Dealer*, November 22, 1981

"In 2000, John McCain came to our stand with his wife when he was campaigning to be the Republican presidential candidate. There was a clip of it on the *Jay Leno Show*. It was a Saturday so the place was really busy, and the aisles were extra crowded with people waiting for him to show up and all the reporters, photographers, and cameramen from the newspapers and TV stations. Our customers couldn't get near the counter for hours. We lost a lot of business that day, but at least McCain bought our bacon and smokies."
—Jerry Chucray, vendor, Czuchraj Meats

The emergence of food-focused television programming brought another kind of VIP to the Market. These superstars are on the job—with cameras rolling—when they wander the aisles. Rachel Ray filmed a segment for the show *$40 a Day* at the Market that aired in April 2004. She oohs and aahs over the selection inside and out, enjoys a date from Mena's Produce, and snags a sample from the Pierogi Palace.

Today Show meteorologist Al Roker did a live broadcast from inside the Market on June 12, 2009, his enthusiasm for the place clearly evident. He became a fan during his tenure as a Cleveland weatherman on WKYC, from 1978–1983. His production team arrived at 4:30 AM to set up, beating even the early-bird vendors. A year and half later, Roker and Adam Richman, the insatiable host of the Travel Channel's *Man v. Food*, bonded on air over their mutual appreciation for the West Side Market.

Richman was promoting his just-released book, *America the Edible*, a chronicle of ten American cities and their unique food offerings. The West Side Market is prominently featured in the chapter about Cleveland. Richman

Above, from top: Senator and presidential contender John McCain draws a crowd; A bulging jumbo gyro from Steve's

Memories

"My father Jesse Bradley worked at the West Side Market for over thirty years as a dock foreman. Every week he did the weekly shopping for us—there were six kids—and his brother, three sisters, and their families too. Dad is no longer with us, but my wife Lorraine and I continue to shop the same stands that he purchased from, and many times take our grandsons with us.

My sixteen-year-old grandson George loved coming to the West Side Market just as much as we did. I will forever remember one special trip with him. He informed me that he was going to get lunch from Steve's Gyro's. I asked him—what do you know about that stand? He said that they sold the best gyros in the city. Well to my shock when we got there the line was maybe thirty people deep. He just smiled at me. That moment was priceless. I realized he had done some research. Seeing how much he enjoyed eating it on the way home made it worth the twenty minute wait in line."

—*Joseph Bradley*

got to know and appreciate the city's culinary landscape while a resident actor at the Cleveland Playhouse. He writes that the Market is one of his "favorite places on earth," and describes it as a "Disneyland-like fantasia" of artisanal and imported foods.

On the segment of *Man v. Food* that originally aired June 23, 2010, Richman tells viewers the Market is "jam-packed with awesome eats," and is "a melting pot of C-town flavors from fully loaded bratwurst sandwiches to thick cut beef jerky." He got especially eloquent after biting into one of Steve's Jumbo Gyros, two pounds of savory-spiced lamb and beef cooked on a spit, layered on grilled and buttered pita bread, and doused with the Vasdekis family's secret sauce. "In the pantheon of Greek food," Richman announces, "Steve's gyro is Zeus."

The sandwich scored again with celebrity chef Anne Burrell. She stopped by for a bite in 2011 while travelling the country for the Food Network's *The Best Thing I Ever Ate-Road Trip*.

No Reservations, a Travel Channel program, also focused an episode on Cleveland. Host Anthony Bourdain was enticed here by his friend and verbal-sparring partner Michael Ruhlman, the locally-based and nationally-renowned food writer. "I wanted him to see this city the way I do," Ruhlman explained, "and give him a real taste of my hometown."

The schedule—and the show—included a Saturday shopping expedition to the Market on a chilly January day in 2007. Accompanied by a production crew, the pair collected ingredients for a Sunday dinner they planned to prepare together.

"It was a real pleasure introducing Anthony Bourdain to the West Side Market," Ruhlman says. "We picked out the food for a meal that we made at my house—pigs' ears, bacon, and more pork, but we did buckle and bought some leafy greens, like chard, and shallots. He was genuinely impressed by the size, scope, and unusualness of the Market. This, in a city that, he joked, was at best farmland and an uncomfortable place with no indoor plumbing. Yet when he saw the Market, there was no snarkiness, no snide comments, no, 'We do this better in New York.' He has a genuine respect for this place."

Above, from top: Author Michael Ruhlman shops the Market with celebrity chef Anthony Bourdain; Bacon can be found thick cut, Hungarian style, or applewood smoked

ROMANTIC INTERLUDES
Stories of Love, Marriage, & Stolen Kisses

THESE MEMORIES NEED little introduction or explanation. From brief flirtations and passing fancies to proposals and nuptial festivities, the Market's been the backdrop for expressions of ardor and affection. The stories are treasured like a pressed corsage, a wedding gown wrapped in tissue paper, or a scrapbook of snapshots, and best told by those who hold them dear.

"I met my wife Helen Zak at the Market. She was Polish and worked at a bakery stand. We got married in 1943. I was twenty-three years old. Ten years ago I walked past that same stand and saw another pretty young girl behind the counter. I told her to watch out because it was a dangerous spot unless she was looking for a husband."
—Alvin Stumpf, former employee

"My husband Al worked as a cooler boy for Phil Dryer in the late thirties and by the time he was a teen he was working behind the counter. Every Saturday, this girl would come in and hand him a note with her meat order which always included her phone number and a few enticing words. Al would write a note back to her on the white butcher paper he used to wrap her order. This was a ritual every week for a while, although he swears he never went out with her. So it was a love affair carried out on butcher paper."
—Pat Deucher

"My husband and I got married on Monday, December 13, 1948. Market people got married on Mondays when the Market wasn't busy.

Above, from top: Kevin Artl holds aloft a wedding gift from a fruit vendor; Valeria and Steve "Jay" Check Sr. *Opposite, from top*: Russ and Patricia Schwark; Mr. and Mrs. DiBlasio, 1980s

Memories

"When a new girl would start at the Market, there would be thirty-five to forty guys in competition for her affections."
—**Bill Pawlowski, former vendor**

"We lived in what's now known as Tremont, just over the bridge from Ohio City. It was 1981 and I was seventeen. I was outside hanging out laundry and Jimmy drove by in a patrol car. I guess he liked what he saw because he started coming around and got friendly with my mother. She encouraged me to go out with him. We dated for five years and then got married.

I was working at Angie's Bakery when we met, for pocket money, first on Saturdays and then full-time after I turned eighteen. Jimmy would come and visit me there. I bought the nut stand in the corner about sixteen years ago and then Jimmy became the beat policeman for the neighborhood. Now he and Gus [Mougianis, of Mediterranean Imports] own the West Side Market Café. I guess you could say the Market's always been part of our life together."

—*Regina Traynor, vendor, P-Nut Gallery*

When we got back to work, our friends got a 4-wheeler and Mrs. Grady cleaned the tubs that held her preserves, olives, and pickles and put them on the cart for us to sit in. They carted us up and down the aisles with a 'Just Married' sign attached and everyone threw rice at us."
—Valeria Check, former vendor

"I was a shy child and at age nine my dad, Harvey Hoffman, insisted I work at his beef stand, E8. I was reluctant at first, but it became my favorite thing to do and my personal adventure. I loved the people and the excitement of selling. While most of my friends went to college, I was perfectly content being dad's business partner. The biggest bonus of working for dad was that I met Elroy, my future husband, there. He was home from Ohio State on break and working for another vendor. He came up to our stand, wanting to talk to me. He asked if I would be going back to school soon. I told him no, this was my full-time job. He didn't care that I wasn't a college girl and we started dating. We were engaged in 1952, and were married in 1955, after he came back from Korea. We've been happy together and our life has been good. We have three wonderful successful children. I am now eighty years old. Every time I go by the Market, I thank God and look back on my blessings with a grateful heart."
—Elaine (Hoffman) Schaedel, former employee

"It was Mike's eighteenth birthday and he went down to the coolers to get two baskets of beets. I had a horrible crush on him. As he was coming up the stairs, I planted a kiss on his lips and ran away. We've been married forty-five years."
—Roseann Anselmo DiBlasio, former vendor

"When I was working at the Market in the 1960s, I was getting ready to propose to my girlfriend and bought her a ring. I wanted to show it to Rita Graewe before I gave it to her. As I unwrapped it, the ring fell right into Rita's sauerkraut barrel."
—Bill Retzer, former employee

"I am from Cambodia. I was living in a refugee camp in Thailand when a family from Geauga Country sponsored me. I came to US in

emories

"My best friend Joy introduced me to the Market in the late 1960s. Our husbands were in the Marine Reserves and we wanted to make a great meal for them after their meeting one weekend. I was waiting for the results of a pregnancy test and used the pay phone at the entrance of the Market to call the doctor. Indeed, I was, and I can still picture the phone hanging on the wall as I jumped with 'Joy' upon hearing the news. At the end of my pregnancy, Joy and I once again went to the Market. It was May 7, 1971. We shopped all afternoon. My son Brian was born only a few hours after I got home. The Market brings beautiful memories of 'new life' to me and I will always hold that connection very dear to my heart."

—Marti Schaffran

"I met my wife Patricia at the Market. I hired her, then I married her."

—Russ Schwark, former vendor

1981. I was eighteen. When I met my husband-to-be, I was manager of the seafood department for a grocery store. He brought me to the Market on our first date. It was February 1992. He had been coming every week for the past ten years and introduced me to all his favorite vendors. I had never been inside before. I started going there with him regularly. Soon I began thinking about getting my own stand. We were married in 1995 and I opened Narrin's Asian Spice and Sauce in April 1997."
—Narrin Carlberg, vendor, Narrin's Asian Spice and Sauce

Narrin Carlberg encouraged Sopheap "Sophie" Heng, another Cambodian refugee and a friend, to start a Market business. Like many tenants before her, Heng, who came to America in 1998, was an immigrant with little money and shaky English. She had to wait two years to get a spot after putting in her application. Heng sells prepared Southeast Asian dishes that she cooks herself. She's been successful, expanding to a bigger location in the Market and achieving longed-for financial independence. But Sophie got something else too—a husband. It was a courtship that began with spring rolls and pad thai.

Charles Barrett, a native Clevelander and expert in historic timepieces, bought his food at the Market and did volunteer repair and maintenance on the tower clock. As he begins to tell the couple's story, he looks often at his wife, wanting her to confirm the facts or maybe just to take in her beautiful, happy face.

Charles: I had been going to the Market to shop every week for years. It was my Saturday morning ritual. My parents and my grandparents had always gone there, too. But not in my wildest dreams could I have ever imagined meeting the woman who would become my wife at the West Side Market. Sophie opened her stand in 2005. By early 2006, my main reason for going was to visit her. The food was fabulous. So was the chef.

Sophie: I noticed him. He'd buy something, then go off in the corner and stare at me while he ate it. I was thinking, what's with this guy who eats all these spring rolls? Is he on a diet? After a long while, he finally asked me out. Charlie said my spring rolls reeled him in.

Charles: It took me months and months. I wasn't looking to get involved. But we'd started talking, her on one side of the counter, me on the other, and despite the obvious differences we discovered we had a lot in common. We were both divorced and neither of us planned to marry again. She'd had such a hard life, no family in Cleveland, and my heart went out to her.

Their early dates were for lunch. He took her to the Rockefeller Greenhouse for the first one. She loved it there, and liked his choice and what it revealed about him. He was impressed by her positive attitude, despite an incredibly difficult past, and captivated by her warm and charming personality.

Sophie: Lots of guys tried to talk to me at the Market. But Charles was different. Very polite. Interested in what I had to say. And I still

Above, from top: Jimmy and Regina Traynor; Sophie Heng
Opposite: C. C. Halloran and Kevin Artl

am a very traditional Cambodian in many ways. I liked that he didn't take me to a bar at night.

Charles: We started out as friends. Then it bloomed into romance. One thing led to another and we were married June 9, 2007. The pastor who officiated at the ceremony ended up becoming Sophie's customer and a regular Market shopper.

Sophie: Many of my customers sent cards and gave us gifts. They remember our anniversary. A few of the guys say things like, "Your husband's a lucky man" or "Too bad I didn't ask you to marry me."

Charles: Meeting each other was the start of a new chapter for both of us.

Sophie: The Market means so much to me. It changed my life.

Neither C. C. Halloran nor Kevin Artl ever worked at the West Side Market. But they decided to have their wedding photos taken there. The couple, who wed April 25, 2009, got some unique images and much more.

"I grew up in Shaker Heights," says Halloran. "When I was five or six Dad and I started doing errands together on Saturdays and one of our stops was the Market. He'd give me a few dollars and let me choose what to buy. It was a larger-than-life kind of place, and very exciting, especially to a child. I loved these times with my father and the place has a lot of sentimental meaning for me. So when James and Gen [James and Genevieve Nisly, wedding photographers, who often shoot in unusual, urban settings] suggested it as a possible location, I was thrilled."

"We had our ceremony in the afternoon and then did the photos," recounts Kevin. "The Market was crowded when we arrived, even though it was near closing time. Everyone there—the customers and the vendors—kind of joined in the spirit of the occasion, smiling, cheering, calling out congratulations."

"The first person we met going in was selling watermelons," C. C. adds. "He handed a small one to Kevin."

"I hoisted the melon high and carried it around for awhile," Kevin continues, "because I didn't know what else to do with the thing. Then C. C. told me to get rid of it because she didn't want it in every picture."

"As we walked through the produce aisle, the sea of customers parted for us," C. C. recalls, "and there was a wave of applause. Inside we got hugs and handshakes. All these strangers became part of our special day. It was wonderful."

Notes

1. *Plain Dealer*, Sept. 1, 1911.

2. *Plain Dealer*, Sept. 2, 1911.

3. *Plain Dealer*, Sept. 3, 1911.

4. *Plain Dealer*, Sept. 10, 1911.

5. *Cleveland Press*, Oct. 1912.

6. *Cleveland Press*, Dec. 10, 1947.

7. *Plain Dealer*, June 20, 1915.

8. *Cleveland Press*, June 19,1915.

9. *Cleveland Press*, Oct 25, 1937.

10. *Plain Dealer*, Oct. 4, 1987.

11. *West Side Sun News*, Sept. 13, 1971.

12. "Alive and Swinging," Letter to editor, Robert E. Stumpf, 1971, from the private collection of Becky (Stumpf) Fitch.

13. *Plain Dealer*, Oct. 28, 1974.

14. *Cleveland Press*, Oct. 20, 1976.

15. *Cleveland Press*, Sept. 29, 1978.

16. *Toledo Blade*, May 1, 1994.

CHAPTER FIVE

THE MARKET EXPERIENCE
Then and Now

BACK IN THE DAY
Rules, Regulations, & High Standards

THE WEST SIDE MARKET is a feast for the senses: the visual splendor of the building and the enticing displays of food; the feel of a perfectly ripe fuzzy peach in the hand followed by a burst of sweet juice on the tongue; the heady aromas of spices, smoked meats, and fresh fish; the sounds of laughter, huckstering, and conversations held over the counter. It's not much different for today's shoppers than it was a hundred years ago. While so much seems to stay the same, the place has also evolved with the times, achieving a delicate balance of continuity and change.

Practices and standards enshrined in law and tradition influence how things are done. Relationships—who you know and who knows you—and the mix of merchants shape what happens at the Market. Everyone brings their own style, stories, accents, and attitudes and it all blends together to create the distinctive day-to-day energy and atmosphere that defines the West Side Market. That's what makes this place so different than anyplace else.

In 1912, Cleveland's Department of Public Service was responsible for the Broadway, Central, and West Side Markets. The department's main goal was to provide Clevelanders with easy access to fresh, affordable foods.

Conditions were mandated to ensure fair treatment and sanitary settings, and guaranteed that patrons would get full value with every purchase. Stalls were rented for only three months at a time, which made it easy to get rid of dishonest dealers and others who failed to comply with the rules. The city even had the right to evict vendors before their leases expired. Tenants were required to "keep their counters, meat block, stands, and refrigerator lockers clean at all times" and were held responsible for their employees "in so far as conduct, cleanliness, and honest dealing with the public is concerned."

Previous pages, clockwise from top: One young shopper admires fresh pasta while another perhaps ponders a stop at the candy counter; Young, stylish shoppers make their way through the arcade; A vendor serenades produce shoppers with accordion tunes, circa 1979
Above, from top: Hanging scales at the ready along Lorain Avenue, circa 1960; Shoppers at Urban Herbs

Profane language was strictly prohibited. Prospective tenants were required to include references with their applications and the Market Master had final say in deciding whether someone would make a "suitable and satisfactory" renter.[1]

Additional ordinances governed the newly-built West Side Market, including one forbidding the use of sawdust on the floor and another requiring all deliveries to be made through the rear entrance only. Vendors were not allowed to have telephones, make home deliveries, or extend credit—all services that could drive up food costs. Rent was inexpensive and large two-sided scales were required equipment. Fred C. Alber, the Superintendent of Markets wrote, "With these various regulations applied and enforced, I believe we have contributed every possible aid to making this Municipal Market what it should be—a place where the people of Cleveland can come with confidence and purchase fruits, vegetables, meats, etc., at a great saving."[2]

Market Master Charles Kamp penned a 1913 article outlining the fundamentals of good planning and governance. "High rents," he wrote, "destroy the purpose for which markets are intended." Minimizing all sources of expense, including delivery services and charge accounts, he explained, would lead to savings for the public. He insisted that the custom of giving trading stamps redeemable for prizes—an incentive program offered by many private grocers at the time, should be prohibited because customers would be better served by discounted prices. Further recommendations included an emphasis on regular and frequent inspection of weights and measures, foodstuffs, and sanitation; a requirement that vendors use fifteen-inch double-sided scales hung so that one side of the large numbered dial faced the customer; having a market master and assistants with "several years of actual market experience, making them conversant with general conditions and the tricks prevalent in the marketing trade;" and "a location which is readily accessible to most of the car lines of the city."[3]

Kamp's official 1914 report to the city makes clear that the approach he advocated was good for the public coffers and the public good. Attendance

Above, from top: The Packing House Market was one of the original stands in 1912; View of the loading dock area, circa 1965

Memories

"In every section of this country there is more or less agitation against the high cost of living.... Having studied this problem carefully for the last twenty years, I have come to the conclusion that the inhabitants of our large municipalities must adopt the only solution that will afford them a possibility of relief—the municipally controlled public market.... A city can well afford to operate a market at cost where a private concern must earn dividends on its investment.... The municipal market that operates under the conditions I describe is a blessing to any community and makes itself felt not only to the patrons...but also to a great many people who do not patronize the market but live within a radius of two or three miles of it for the difference in prices must influence prices in the whole community."

—*Charles Kamp, Market Master,* **The American City,** *January–June, 1914*

"I have memories of long ago—getting on the Clark Avenue streetcar and going to the Market with my mother, always late on Saturdays when food costs were cheaper. A lot of people did the same thing."

—**Marcella Huber**

LADIES ON THE JOB

A campaign backed by 12,000 Cleveland women, members of the Federated Women Clubs and the Consumers' League to have the civil service examinations for city food and market inspectors opened to women, was announced at the monthly meeting of the executive board of the Consumers League at the Goodrich House yesterday.

Cleveland Leader, March 11, 1914

WOMAN MAY INSPECT

It is thought that a civil service examination for women may be secured and a woman inspector appointed who will look after the girls working in the market stalls, some of whom are said to be under age, and who will also keep an eye on the condition of exposed fruit.

Plain Dealer, March 11, 1914

Opposite, from top: Newspaper ad for West Side Market; John Anselmo, former produce vendor, at eight years old, circa 1929; Newspaper ad for city markets

at the Broadway, Central and the new West Side Market for the previous year was reported to be 75,000 and he said "it is plain to be seen that from 250,000 to 300,000 of our population are benefited by our Municipal Markets." He credits the West Side Market with boosting that number by 50 percent and attracting customers from Lakewood and other nearby communities. His report goes on to note that there was a waiting list of two hundred vendor applicants. The convenience of the comfort station and waiting room were appreciated by many, and the not quite finished refrigeration plant for public use was filled to capacity and anticipated to be the city's "best money earning utility, considering the investment."

Businessmen in and around the Market banded together in 1914 to promote it, forming the Retail Merchants' Board of the Chamber of Industry. The *Cleveland Leader* covered their efforts in a three-column article. " 'The people don't realize what a splendid thing we have here,' said Charles Myers yesterday, 'What we want to do is get them to visit the market once—then our work of converting them will be easy... We have one of the greatest institutions in the country... and we want to parade its advantages before the people of the East and West sides and every one in northern Ohio.' "

Headlined "Time and Coin Saved at West Side Market," the story goes on to mention the great variety of goods available, reasonable prices, and easy access via the new Harvard-Denison bridge. One more asset worth remarking on, then as now, were the specialty vendors. "Waldemar Meckes is another enthusiastic booster of the West Side market house.... 'I never knew there were so many different kinds of sausages until I visited the market one day and looked over the stock of one of the dealers. He had about 100 different brands and kinds and I could not begin to mention the names. And just as he had the best in sausages other stand-holders have the best and greatest varieties in the specialties they sell.' "[4]

One persistent myth is that ice deliveries determined the schedule for the West Side Market. Not only did the Market produce all its own ice, but the city decided when each of its three municipal markets would be open. In 1912, all did business on Friday and Saturday, the biggest shopping days,

---

Ⓜemories

"Each week during the last year an average of sixty thousand of Cleveland's citizens have entered the broad doors of the [West Side] municipal market to purchase foods at glass counters. Concrete floors, glazed tile walls... high, well ventilated ceiling, and thorough sanitary conditions make this market a pleasant place in which to shop. And the cost to the merchants—one hundred and forty to one hundred and sixty dollars a year for a stall, including pipe-cooled counter refrigeration at the butter and egg stands—makes it possible to [sic] the consumer to enjoy genuine reductions in prices."

—**Technical World Magazine,** *September 1914*

"In the years before World War II, the Market stayed open until after 10 on Saturday nights. People came late because they could get good deals. The last ones to show up collected the scraps that couldn't be sold to give to the nuns and the needy they cared for."

—*Alvin Stumpf, former employee*

but alternated weekdays. The West Side Market was closed on Tuesdays and Thursdays, when people could go to the Central and Broadway Markets. This gave consumers access to food six days a week—Sunday was never considered an option for retail merchants until quite recently—and also made it possible for some vendors to maintain stands at more than one location. The West Side Market, the only surviving of the three, continues to operate on Mondays, Wednesdays, Fridays, and Saturdays. Vendors, who wear many hats as small entrepreneurs, use the other days to take inventory, place orders, prepare products, and handle piles of paperwork.

The hours of operation have often been a topic of debate. Despite the deeply-held belief among many current vendors that the hours have been the same since day one, the historical record tells a different story. The "Rules and Regulations Governing Municipal Markets for the year 1912" state that the hours of operation for the Central, Broadway, and West Side Markets would be from 5 AM to 2 PM weekdays and 5 AM to 10:30 PM on Saturdays.

By 1932, the Market remained open an hour longer on weekdays but closed much earlier on Saturdays. Some thought it was high time for a change. Increased traffic was noted in the vicinity of the Market and merchants discussed the idea of extending the closing hours to 6 PM on Mondays, Wednesdays, and Fridays, and shortening Saturday hours to 9:30 PM.[5]

According to a report compiled for the city in 1950 by the T. W. Grogan Company, the Market was in operation from 7 AM to 5 PM weekdays, and Saturdays from 7 AM to 8 PM. Twenty years later, the Market was locking the doors at 4 PM on Mondays and Wednesdays, 6 PM on Fridays, and 7 PM on Saturdays. In 1977, 6 PM was closing time on both Fridays and Saturdays, just as it is today.

With the approach of the Centennial, discussions of whether or not the Market's current days and hours should be updated to better reflect patrons' twenty-first century lifestyles often ignited heated debate among merchants. The truth is that the hours of business have constantly evolved over a hundred years—and will probably continue to do so.

Memories

"Back in the 1950s and '60s, the Market opened at 7 AM but customers came in the back door at 5 AM and we would wait on them. Today, the building, and even the vendors, wake up at 7 or 7:30, even on a Saturday, and the customers are arriving later. It used to be that people getting off work from the steel mills and factories stopped at the Market on their way home. As industry in Cleveland changed, so did the customers and so did the times when we conducted business."

—*Mark Penttila, employee*

"When my dad John Anselmo was a little boy in the late 1920s, his family had a produce stand on the Lorain Avenue curb. It was a lot of work setting that stand up and taking it down. They would often stay overnight, sleeping in the truck. That was the lifestyle. When I was a kid in the early 1950s, we didn't stay overnight but I did sleep on the sidewalk underneath the stand. I can still remember seeing people's legs and shoes."

—*Roseann Anselmo DiBlasio, former vendor*

MONEY MATTERS
Making Change is Hard

MARKET POLICY DIDN'T allow merchants to extend credit, but nonetheless some vendors made exceptions, as a favor or a charitable gesture. "Back in the day money was tight, like it is now," says Ricky Calabrese, the third generation of the family to operate a produce stand. "Customers still tell me that they shopped here because our family took care of them. If they were short on money, my dad Richard or my Uncle Larry would let them slide until the following week. It was credit before credit cards." Ricky still extends the same courtesy to some of his customers. "You can tell as they count their money; it's in their eyes that they don't have enough," he says. "I tell them, 'See you next week,' then I hand them their purchases. Sure, we're stiffed every once in a while but not often."

For others, extending credit was just how they did business, regardless of rules and regulations. It's a practice shopper Theresa Kuehn recalls as far back as the 1950s. "It used to take hours to shop with my Italian mother," says Kuehn. "She had to stop and talk to each of the vendors. I remember her shopping for produce with the Rinis—only the Rinis. She would tell them to put it on her 'tick'—that was her credit account."

ⓜemories

"Dolores Michaels had the little corner stand next to Frank's Bratwurst. When I was in high school, she decided to give up the stand and asked me to help her clean it out. She let me take the old National Cash Register that only rang up to 50 cents. It had four slots for coins, only one for paper money, and weighed ninety pounds. Inside was a stamp that said Thelma's Cookies, probably the owner before Dolores. That's how you find out about the history of the Market."

—Gary Fougerousse, former vendor

"During the summers as a teenager, I'd go in alone on Mondays to give my mom a day off. I rode the bus, carrying $25 worth of change for the register in the morning and all the day's proceeds, usually around $100, after closing at 4 in the afternoon, hidden in a paper bag underneath a loaf of bread."

—Beverly Tabacco, former employee

For most of the Market's hundred years, cash was king. In the early years, the day's take went in pockets, cigar boxes, or home-made cash boxes. At the DeCaro Produce stand, the original wooden cash box built in 1934 by Augustino DeCaro is still in service, worn smooth by more than seventy-five years worth of currency and fingers reaching in to make change. Lashed tightly to the stand with a bungee cord so it doesn't fall or "walk off," there are three original slots, one each for pennies, nickels, and dimes. "Quarters were big money back then," said Joe DeCaro. There's only one slot for paper bills, rarely used then, but now stuffed on a busy market day.

Like the DeCaros, some continued to do business this way long after cash registers came into widespread use. George Novak worked for his mother's brother, Joe Boubin and his wife, Mildred. He remembered that his aunt and uncle had a brass cash register at their meat stand in the 1930s and '40s, equipped with a four-inch white marble shelf where the customer's money stayed until their change was made and handed over. But Beverly Tabacco, whose mother owned Angie's Bakery, recalls that even in the 1950s many merchants still preferred the old-fashioned approach. "They didn't want receipts," she says, "and only reported what they wanted to."

Vintage cast-metal and wooden machines are still in use at some stands, alongside credit card terminals, PIN pads, and other electronic devices. Jerry Chucray of J & J Czuchraj Meats says his mom stuck with her familiar push button register long after more modern models were available. "She never felt comfortable with credit card machines," said Chucray. It was a way of thinking that slowly changed from one generation of vendors to the next.

When Diane Dever took over her mother Irene's dairy stand in 2000, one of the first things she did was accept credit cards. Breaking the news to her mother didn't go over well. "I remember the first time I came home, proud to tell her I had added a credit card machine to the stand," recalls Diane. "It was the worst yelling I ever got from her in my entire life!" Over the next six months, Diane brought the books home daily. Irene stopped complaining after she saw the improvement to the business's bottom line.

Above, from top: Boubin's meat and sausage stand; Angie Tabacco at her bakery stand, Angie's
Opposite, from top: Busy day behind the counter at Berchtold's beef and pork stand; Vintage wooden cash register used by Dolores Michaels at her cookie stand

Memories

"My grandparents, Marion & Theresa (Lizzie) DeGrandis had the corner produce stand at the Market where one corridor bent into the next. My grandparents always said that they had "the corner on the Market"... and they did! It was an ideal L-shaped location! They put their money in a large handmade wooden box with a hole cut out of the top. Money was just dropped in there... and every once in a while you had to lift the lid to make change. Almost all of the wares were priced so that only coins were needed. It was a hard life... but they loved it."

—**Joanne Marie (Pilla) De Fiore**

"Once I went to Sears and was 10 cents short. They told me to go home. That's the difference between big business and family businesses like us."

—**Ricky Calabrese, vendor, Calabrese Produce**

GETTING CARRIED AWAY
Totes, Bags, & Carts

IN THE PRODUCE AISLES, fruits and vegetables are bagged in brown paper or plastic. But there's an artistry to how the butchers, cheese sellers, and fishmongers turn sheets of paper into tidy packages, folding them like origami experts, no matter how odd the shape of what's inside. Amateurs cannot easily duplicate the snug smooth wrapping. Once they were also masters of the knot, but tape has taken the place of string for finishing off each parcel.

Toting purchases is a timeless challenge at the Market. The best and long-favored strategy is to arrive with extra hands to carry heavy bundles. In the early decades of the twentieth century, most folks used wicker baskets. In the late 1930s gusseted, flat-bottomed paper bags had become cheap to manufacture, and supermarkets, which were prevalent by then, provided them to customers at no charge. The West Side Market merchants started providing the same amenity to their customers. Later, plastic shopping bags replaced paper. At various times, signature sacks made of paper and cloth and bearing the Market's name have been given away or sold.

These days, shoppers arrive with reusable totes and even backpacks. Wheeled wire carts have replaced wagons, but it's not uncommon to see baby carriages and strollers, with or without a baby on board, serving as ad hoc shopping carts. Many Market memories feature descriptions of lugging, carting, carrying, and even "walking" dinner home.

"In the forties when I was a little girl we lived next door to my grandparents on Jefferson and Professor, in the area now called Tremont. Every Saturday, my grandfather John Prociw, who was Ukrainian, would put me in a wagon and take me across the Abbey Road Bridge to the West Side Market. He did all the family shopping. The last stop was the live poultry market next door. He'd choose a chicken, then tie a string around its neck. He pulled the wagon, loaded with food, and I'd walk that chicken all the way home. What a sight that must

have been! My little sister and I would play with the chicken until my grandmother made it into noodle soup for Sunday dinner. My sister wouldn't eat it but I did. I didn't let myself get attached. My stomach came first and it never bothered me to eat our 'pet.'"
—Lee (Wojdacz) Laurenty

"I was born in 1932. From the age of seven, until I was seventeen, it was my job to help mother carry the groceries home from the Market. My father supported us by gambling. He'd give ma an allowance for food and that's all she had to spend. It would take us a long time to shop because she had to be careful with the money. She went often and bought a lot. We were Italian. She cooked everything from scratch and put out abundant meals. So the bags were always heavy. The ones they gave you were brown paper, with these thin handles that cut into my hands. We only lived two blocks away but I'll never forget what it felt like to carry those blasted bags and I'm glad I don't have to do it anymore."
—Theresa Kuehn

"I remember one dark, fall rainy day, trying to waddle up the street with all of these packages strewn around our arms, bodies, carts, and our necks. The oranges started to fall down from one of my rain-drenched bags. Panicked beyond belief because traffic was coming from both Lorain Avenue and W. 25th Street, I started gathering up everything I could off the ground. I finally held up my hand to stop traffic. I was nine years old, mind you, and traffic did stop, as I continued to gather each orange off the street."
—Kathy Bencze

Above: A customer and produce vendor share a laugh
Below: Market shoppers make their way across W. 25th Street
Opposite, from top: Buying and toting produce purchases from the alleyways around the arcade, circa 1960; A shopper fills her wicker basket with eggs and cheese, circa 1920; Wagons come in handy at on big shopping days

HELPING HANDS

In the early 1990s, the West Side Market's Merchants Association formed a partnership with the Cleveland Metropolitan Housing Association to create Helping Hands. Youth that lived in the agency's apartment complex north of the Market were recruited to help patrons carry their heavy shopping bags as they made their way around the Market. Although the program was viewed as a way for the youth to get service experience, patrons gladly tipped for the "helping hands."

Above, from top: Customers appreciated "Helping Hands" during shopping excursions; Herbert J. Spuhler beef stand, circa 1960

"In the late 1970s, Dad and I would hop in the car a few times during the summer and head to the West Side Market, an exciting adventure for a suburban kid used to traditional grocery stores. Walking through the produce aisles inundated my senses. I politely accepted wedges of shiny plums and fuzzy peaches, so sweet and juicy you would swear you were standing in the farmer's field. The summer breeze blowing through the aisles blended the fragrances of ripe strawberries, cantaloupe, and watermelon together. I can still hear the 'snap' of brown paper bags as they were opened to hold your produce."
—Beth Wiblin

"In 1951, our Croatian family immigrated from Austria. I was nine years old when I went with my mom to the West Side Market to help her carry the bags. Being very small in stature, I remember walking the crowded corridors with the old ladies pushing, shoving, and hitting me on the head with their full bags. It was unintentional; they didn't know. One day I came home crying and begged Mom to please never ask me to go with her again or to take my taller sister Manda instead."
—Violet (Dosen) Bosiljevic

"In the early 1960s, my Uncle Ray would drive over to pick up Grandma about 5:30 AM. He had to carry Grandma's groceries, as well as his own, if no one else went with them. It wore him out. He knew Gram would spend time talking with each vendor she visited. If I stayed at Grandma's for the weekend that meant I could carry her bags. Once back at home, Gram would start the coffee and fix us a big breakfast while Uncle Ray and I put things away.

I lived in Louisiana for many years. On a visit to the Market after returning home, one of the vendors said I looked familiar and asked if I was a 'Jewel' (grandma's last name). There I was, nearly forty years later, and the vendor remembered my grandmother and began telling me what a lovely person she was. What a blessing!"
—Helena Hoogstraten

"I grew up going to the Market with my dad and my grandmother on Saturdays. They'd shop for both households. We'd make multiple trips to the car and they'd always bicker in the parking lot over how to divide things—who should get the extra head of cabbage or more lemons."
—Chef Jonathon Sawyer

SIGNS OF THE TIMES
Express Yourself!

PLACARDS, BANNERS, AND POSTERS promoting products at individual stands reflect cultural trends, changing demographics, and contemporary eating habits. Michael Turczyk sells halal goat and lamb, animals slaughtered and processed in accordance with Muslim dietary laws. Foster's posts a notice when local grass-fed beef and heritage-breed pork is in stock; Annemarie's Dairy announces when fresh eggs from a nearby farm are available. Christopher's Bakery has a gluten-free selection, clearly marked among the traditional loaves of Russian Rye, rustic Italian, and crusty whole grain. The Basketeria advertises its focus on organic produce and the sign at Whitaker's Poultry promises "All Natural. No Hormones. No Preservatives," reflecting their customers' personal standards and preferences.

There were, and still are, vendors who don't see the need for a sign to call attention to a special product they carry. In the early 1980s, a *Plain Dealer* reporter interviewing Dave Russ of A. A. Russ, a stand specializing in lamb, asked the butcher, "How come you don't have a sign that says you carry mutton?" Russ replied, "Customers that want mutton, Lebanese and Greeks, they know we got it."[6]

There are timeless signs that can help visitors find their way around the West Side Market: a simple depiction of a finger pointing down to the restrooms; neon letters that beam in the southeast corner, spelling out an invitation for shoppers to come in, sit down, and have something to eat.

First-timers, and even regular market goers, often end up casually wandering from stand to stand or relying on landmarks, like the clock that hangs on the east wall or the balcony facing it from the opposite end, to maintain their bearings. While the vendors at the Market change, the basic floor plan has not.

From the Market's balcony, the layout is easily discerned. Four long avenues run west to east, from the balcony to the clock. The left and right sides of

Above, from top: Tending to customers at Michael's Bakery stand; The ornate clock on the east wall of the Market keeps shoppers and vendors on time.

Melissa DeCaro Lau entertains customers with a regular change of costumes

EXPRESS YOURSELF

Every merchant is their own advertising agency and coming up with attention-getting signs, slogans, and saying is a an art.

In 1971, a placard on the wall above the grinder at the nut stand in the corner proclaimed "Peanut butter is better than pot."[7]

A yellowed, handwritten piece of paper over the counter at Kaufmann Poultry reads, "Art Modell Special: Spineless Chicken with No Guts," a reference to the former owner of the Cleveland Browns, infamous for moving the team to Baltimore.

Larry Schade, proprietor of Kaufmann's penned a sign for a tray of skinless boneless chicken that read: "Our Elvis Special: Love Me Tenders."

A bumper sticker stuck over the entrance of the fresh fish stand encourages shoppers to "Promote Catfish. Run Over a Chicken."

A sign at Bistricky's once hinted that the customer might not always be right: "This is not Burger King. You can't have it your way."

each avenue are identified alphabetically: A and B; C and D; E and F; and G and H. The avenues are intersected by a series of numbered aisles running north to south. This pattern creates an "address" for each stand inside the Market, from Johnny Hot Dog at A2 (there is no A1) to Maha's Falafil Stand at H13. The "addresses" are clearly posted on the corners of each stand's marquee or signboard; simply look up. The foods that line the counters and fill the cases have always pulled the shopper's gaze elsewhere and the letters and numbers are often overlooked.

The outside produce arcade consists of two long aisles forming an "L." Stands are in numeric order, beginning with number 1 at the W. 25th Street entrance and ending with stand 85 at Lorain Avenue. Even-numbered stands are on the south and west sides of the arcade; odd-numbered stands stretch along the north and east sides. Most produce vendors occupy two or more stands. The DeCaro and Calabrese families have been in the same spots for more than seventy years.

Several merchants have used creative self-expression to enhance their visibility. John Rolston, a poultry vendor, was frequently seen behind the counter in his trademark Nova Scotia short-brimmed fedora and Karen Curiale Torreiter always remembers her dad Banjo Curiale wearing a paper butcher's hat. On special occasions, Walter Simmelink Sr. would wear a black top hat to compliment his cooler coat and Emil Churchin was frequently seen in his distinct cotton butcher boy hat. Many vendors only wear one hat, so to speak, but Melissa DeCaro Lau has worn many more—about three hundred the last time she counted.

"I have a collection that includes Chinese opera hats, a Hershey Kiss, a Russian naval hat, an Alaskan rabbit hat," she rattles off. "I'm kind of following a tradition my grandmother Rose DeCaro had at our stand." Rose always wore a hat for function and warmth. Melissa's hats are for entertainment.

"It started out as being lazy," she confesses. "I didn't want to bother fixing up my hair in the morning, so I used to shove it under a hat. It got to the point when I wasn't wearing a hat, the customers would ask why not? Then they started bringing me hats."

Melissa has even gone a step further to promote her presence. "Once when I was about thirty-two, I wore a Superman outfit at the stand and someone from the local newspaper took my picture," she says. "From there, the costumes started." What began as lark turned into a not-so-subtle marketing device. "I would dress up in Halloween costumes in October and for Thanksgiving, I was a pilgrim, turkey, or an Indian," she says. "During the month of December, it's Christmas outfits. I wear costumes for St. Patrick's Day, Easter, July 4th, Valentine's Day, any holiday you can dress up for." People still make it a point to come to the stand to see what Melissa's wearing and she'll likely sell them some fresh produce while they're there. "More than the sale," she admits, "I'm after a smile."

INSIDER ADVICE
Shopping Strategies

FINDING THE BEST parking space and navigating up and down the aisles is only the beginning of the experience. The art of shopping the Market requires patience and practice. No visit here is ever quite like any other. There are more than a hundred stands to choose from and even more personalities behind them to get to know. The selection of foods range from the familiar to the unusual. The temptation is to buy more than what's needed or to bring home things that weren't even on the list. It's hard to resist a bargain, or the allure of a wonderfully marbled porterhouse or a decadent cream pie. The beauty of the building and the fascinating mix of people moving through it can be distracting. Knowing how to meet these challenges and get the most from a trip here separates the novices from the regulars. It's wise to learn from the pros.

Vendors, like Miklos Szucs, can spot a first-time visitor to the Market with ease. "Just by the way they look at everything," he says, "and sometimes they seem a little lost. It can be an overwhelming experience."

While he's handing them a taste of Hungarian sausage or paprika-coated bacon, he also doles out advice. "I usually tell them that they need to make three or four visits," he says. "It will make them a shopper, not a buyer. I tell them to ask for tastes at other stands. I always want to make sure when someone comes to my stand, whether they are a new or regular customer, that when they go home and they open the package, they will not be disappointed." Advice is cheap, but priceless when it comes from the vendors.

> "Every week, someone new comes to my stand. I don't expect them to buy right away. I know they are just looking, seeing what's good. My advice? Just go around and try to talk to as many vendors as you can. Chances are though, one of them will talk to you first."
> —Don Whitaker, vendor, D. W. Whitaker Meats

"I had this really nice lady come up to me and she said she hadn't been there since she was a kid in the 1950s. She was so excited to be back at the Market! She had several bags with her but kept making

THREE HEADS ARE BETTER THAN ONE

Animal heads are mounted at three meat stands, boldly announcing what is sold there. The goat with its long vertical horns at Michael Turczyk's stand was a gift from a customer a few years back and the only one of the trio to have a name. "We call him 'Billy,'" says Turczyk. "Not the guy who gave it to me, the actual goat head!"

Two aisles over at A. A. Russ, the bison head is the most recent addition to the herd, only three years old, also a gift from a patron.

The most famous animal head is the Texas Longhorn mounted high on the corner of the stand once occupied by four generations of the Ehrnfelt family. "He's been here longer than anyone at the Market has been alive," says Brian Foster, who now occupies the stand. The long horizontal horns with turned-up tips are festooned at the holidays with ornaments, Santa hats, or candy canes. "People use it as a landmark all the time, a place to meet up," says Foster.

Above, from top : Matt Minyard of Edward J. Badstuber & Sons; The longhorn has looked out over the Market floor from F4 for a hundred years.

THE MAKING OF A MARKET SHOPPER

In May 2004, I escorted thirty high school students on a field trip to the West Side Market. None of them had ever set foot inside the building previously. I talked about the Market's history, ambiance, and culture and provided a primer on shopping the Market—how to manage huckstering, what questions to ask, and how to spot a bargain.

Before I sent the group out to shop, I finished my pep talk. "If a deal looks too good to be true, it might be and the only way you'll know is to look inside the bag before you leave the stand—right then and there. Once you're home, it's too late."

One young man returned with two mammoth honeydew melons. "They let me taste some, too," he said. As I looked at the soggy wet spot forming on one of the bags, I knew that he had been slipped a sorry excuse for a melon. I talked with him about his choices: return to the vendor or chalk it up as a lesson learned.

Within a few minutes, he returned with two fresh melons and a look of triumph. "I told the person at the stand that her sign read, 'two melons for two dollars.' It didn't say 'two rotten melons for two dollars.'" Good Market shoppers are always up for a challenge.

—Marilou Suszko

Right: Customers wonder about new and unusual fruits likely to be found at the Market

trips back to the car to lighten her load. I suggested she buy a cart. It's so much easier. To tell the truth, shopping here is like shopping at Marc's [an Ohio-based chain of discount closeout and grocery stores]—you can get caught up in buying more than you can carry."
—Annemarie Geffert, vendor, Annemarie's Dairy

"You have to experiment a little bit with different stands. We lay the meat out for you and you still pick what you want. It's not pre-wrapped; that's a concept that a lot of people don't understand anymore. When you shop the supermarket, you just throw stuff in your cart. There are eleven of us selling beef in this building. If you aren't happy with one, you have to try another."
—Steve Check, vendor, Steven Check Jr.

"Look and see how many vendors are down here trying to make a living! You have your choice of a bunch of different places to shop. Find the one you like—and go back every week."
—Larry Calabrese, former vendor

"I would suggest walking around first. Get your bearings, take a look and find a friendly face. Ask questions. Ask vendors which stands they buy from if you're looking for something else. We give people tips on how to cook and make things all the time."
—Diane Dever, vendor, Irene Dever

"Find someone you trust, someone who has been there quite a while and ask them where they go to buy their food. Vendors at the Market know what the others are doing and how they handle it. Stay with the same person and they will take good care of you."
—John Rolston, former vendor

"Don't be timid about asking for something. It doesn't hurt to ask questions. People always come up and say, 'I have a dumb question. I only need three slices of bacon.' They apologize for not ordering more. They feel like they have to buy more . . . not here."
—Tim Jeziorski, employee

HELPING YOURSELF
Picky about Picking

IT'S TEMPTING TO look at a neat pyramid of oranges and reach for a certain six—even if they're on the bottom. Further down the aisle, bins of brilliantly-colored bell peppers, arranged in stop light order (red, yellow, and green), beg to be inspected before being bagged. One stand over, an array of plump tomatoes are laid in tidy rows within easy reach, close enough for just one gentle squeeze. Produce vendors have always struggled with customers who want to help themselves, which can send an avalanche of fruits or vegetables tumbling onto the floor, leaving the product damaged, unsalable, and upsetting the entire appearance of the display.

A newspaper reporter in 1945 summed up what produce vendors of the day were thinking: "Today's satisfied customers won't handle and damage the merchandise tomorrow."[8] A satisfied customer is a trusting customer. Lasting relationships are built on fair treatment and personal service.

> "I started shopping at the Market regularly in 1988 and have established relationships with specific vendors inside and out. After he got to know me, Emery of Bacha Produce would always wait on me himself, giving me advice about what to buy.
>
> One day he was really busy and said, 'Jimmy, just leave your bag and your list. I'll take care of you.' Now that's what I do every week. Emery is not just the guy I get my celery from. We began by exchanging names but it has grown into much more. I know he bought a new house. We ask about each other's families. When his sister was sick, I visited her. I was at her funeral. It's the same with Diane Dever at the cheese and dairy stand. I can call in my order, even leave a phone message, and it will be ready for pick up the next day. It's like having a free personal shopper.
>
> I'm fifty-three and I live in Lakewood. Sure, it might be easier to get my food somewhere else. But it's the relationships that keep me coming back. I love the personal contact and the continuity of seeing the same people week after week."
> —Jim Metrisin

Above, from top: A sign above the arcade exit reminds shoppers that the Market management demands honesty; Jack and Jeanette Gentille wait to hand select tomato purchases for customers; Nate Anselmo arranges fresh corn at his stand

What initially draws customers to a stand is what former produce vendor Jack Gentille called "curb appeal." "If I had green peppers, red peppers went next to them; the long cukes would go next to the yellow peppers," he says. Colors, shape, and texture would play off one another and the display would draw the people in, hands poised to make their selections like they do in the grocery store. "Can't you read?" an exasperated Gentille would ask, pointing to the signs: "Please do not handle the merchandise. We are here to wait on you."

Gentille says he would have rather lost a customer, and probably did, than let them pick their own tomatoes and eggplant. He stood his ground for twenty-five years and still had customers standing five deep in the aisles on Saturdays.

"We handled the produce carefully so we could sell it in good condition," he explains. "If a customers sends it falling into the aisles, it bruises and breaks, the loss comes out of my pocket. It's always been about trusting us and for some people, that was just hard to do."

There are times when a shopper experiences the sting of being duped by a less than scrupulous vendor. It's not a Market memory anyone likes to recall, but it happens.

"If you've ever found a rotten tomato in the bottom of your bag, consider that your initiation to the West Side Market," says Robin Benzle, a local journalist and broadcaster who has not only written about the Market, but is a regular shopper. "One time, I went to a fairly new vendor to check them out and they had these big beautiful artichokes on display so I bought four," she explains. "I got home, opened the bag and had slimy artichokes. I got into the car, went back to the Market and raised hell with that vendor. Word spread like wildfire among the shoppers."

This kind of news circulates in the produce aisles; the offenders hate it, but reputable vendors hate it even more. "That's because people tell their friends they got bad produce at the Market," says Benzle. "There are a lot of good people who build their business on selling good produce and taking care of their customers and there are those who don't care if they get your business in the future. Find the first kind," she suggests.

> "It's true that sometimes the outside vendors put less than stellar produce in the bag. It should only happen once, because if somebody betrays your trust, tell them and make sure they understand you won't come back. My advice is to look inside [the bag] immediately. If you don't like what you see, say so. Don't walk away until you're happy. And the best thing is to establish a relationship, make a personal contact."
> —Lois Rose

> "Buyer beware! If it seems too good to be true, it's not a good buy. Half might only be usable."
> —Ricky Calabrese, vendor, Calabrese Produce

Above, from top: Emery Bacha and his sister Marie Smith at the family produce stand; Emery Bacha poses behind one of his signature products, green beans; Myrtle Chappell, known as the Horseradish Lady, ground the fresh root to order for lines of customers.

Nate Anselmo
Look, Touch, Taste

Nate Anselmo bent so many of the rules of doing business in the produce arcade during his years in business that it made him a Market legend. Hawking and calling out to the customers is prohibited, but it didn't stop him from delivering some famous chants like, "Ladies and gentlemen, this is not the Cleveland Museum of Art. Please look, touch, and take something home."

Handing out samples was against the rules in the produce arcade, but he would cut up fruit and entice customers to taste, offering chunks of pineapple or melon from the tip of his knife. It's how he earned the nickname, "Nate the Knife."

And if his customers wanted, he let them handpick their purchase, a practice that contradicted what other vendors were doing. "Pick what you want," he would say and grateful customers would pick and pass it to him to package. "Eventually, they would get to know me, get tired of picking and trust me to do it for them."

"My entire family were produce vendors at the Market," says Anselmo, the youngest of ten, who took his naps under the stand in the mid-1930s. "We all did business like this. To let a customer pick their own fruits in a place where most wouldn't allow it was kind of an adventure for them," says Anselmo. "Letting them do it in the first place meant they would come back." And they did until he closed the stand in 2000.

"This was the kind of work where it was easy to make people happy, you know, like giving a kid an orange or an apple," he says, "but first, you gotta like people."

Above, from top: Nate "The Knife" Anselmo trims head lettuce and pineapples for display; Various members of the Anselmo family

"*Some customers don't know about gravity.*"

—**Tom Boutrous, vendor, Boutrous Brothers Produce**

"*The produce arcade was so noisy with people yelling at you to try their green peppers, cabbage... whatever they had. If you touched the mountain of produce on display, you got yelled at!*"

—*Karen Stuart*

"*I used to sell little boxes of hot banana peppers for a buck. Once I had a guy coming up to the stand and he was switching them around between the boxes to get exactly the ones he wanted. I said, 'You know you're not buying a fur coat here; they're all banana peppers.' He started laughing and the next thing I knew he would leave his grocery list with us while he shopped inside and I would put together his order, plus the fruits he wanted from the vendor next to me. I had a customer for life*"

—*Jack Gentille, former vendor*

DEMOCRACY & DEMOGRAPHICS
Everybody's Food Store

ALL KINDS OF PEOPLE rub shoulders at the Market. That's part of what gives the place character. Neighbors, former high school buddies, and coworkers bump into each other. But it's just as likely that those in line together are from another part of town or even another continent, unlike each other in every obvious way. It's always been like that here.

"The West Side Market has never been gentrified or moved away from its original purpose in any way," observes public market expert David O'Neil. "People from all walks of life, income levels, and neighborhoods come together at the West Side Market to fill a common need and that is an equalizing experience. The makeup of the vendors however, has evolved with the times, and they carry products that today's consumers want and that reflect the tastes of new immigrant groups."

Generations of bargain hunters, bag toters, tomato squeezers, soup makers, chicken roasters, and pickle eaters have shopped the Market, reflecting how Americans define themselves: ethnic heritage, gender, age, and socioeconomic level. Traditionally, and to this day, newcomers—to the city and the country—shop side-by-side with those who have deep American and Ohio roots. The Market exemplifies the democratic spirit: classes and races mix freely and struggling immigrants determined to stretch every dollar purchase their food from the same vendors who supply some of Cleveland's wealthiest households. "You see the fur coats and the food stamp folks standing in line next to each other," says Gary Thomas, owner of the Ohio City Pasta stand. "Everyone feels safe, comfortable. And everybody's money is green."

For many, the chance to hear and speak their native language has always been part of the Market's appeal. German, Polish, Czech, Hungarian, Russian, Slovenian, Romanian, and Italian dominated exchanges through the

Above, from top: Young ladies make their selection in the produce arcade; A young visitor finds the perfect spot for a view of the crowd

LET'S TALK

Years ago, language barriers at the Market played out every day through hand gestures. Customers pointed to what they wanted, holding up fingers to indicate quantity. There were animated motions that indicated whether it should be ground, sliced, or chopped. Holding up a thumb and index finger was a measure of "this thick" or "this much." It was effective but lacked what many customers were looking for: a connection to their homeland and someone who spoke their language. A trip to the Market might fill that need in conversations among customers who shared a common tongue or with the many multi-lingual vendors and their employees. The ability to communicate with patrons in their own language contributed to the success of those stands.

"My mom Margaret Selezanu spoke some Hungarian…just enough and only at the Market. I picked up a few words in Hungarian from my mom but turns out they weren't very nice words."

—**Linda Selezanu Bistricky, former employee**

"*Wie geht's, ein Pfund* (German for 'Hello, One pound'). I would hear that a lot."

—**Bill Retzer, former employee**

"My dad used to work for me at the stand. He spoke Italian, which was good in helping our ethnic customers. Every once in a while, I would hear him say, 'Slow down. I can't understand you.' I find myself saying the same thing to some of my customers who speak English. We're speaking the same language but sometimes they just talk too fast."

—**Tony Pinzone, vendor, Pinzone Meats**

"My mom spoke with an accent but she never felt self-conscious about it or out of place at the Market."

—**Councilman Joe Cimperman**

"My grandfather (Arnold Sommer) spoke German, his parents came from Switzerland in 1889, and they spoke German at home. He only went to school through eighth grade, but always spoke perfect English, which always amazed me. I also spoke a bit of German, as I had taken two years of it in high school."

—**Chris Sommer Krisak, former employee**

---

mid-sixties. Now, although business is usually conducted in English, on a given day shoppers and merchants might break into Spanish, Arabic, or even Cambodian.

In similar fashion, the housedress and head scarf that defined female shoppers with Eastern European roots—once so much a part of the Market scene—has for the most part given way to more modern mainstream dress. But the Saturday crowd might still include women who stand out from the rest in their brightly-colored African head wraps, abayas (the head-to-toe black robes favored by some from the Middle East), and shalwar kameez (the loose pants and long tunics worn by both sexes in South and Central Asia).

> "In the mid to late fifties, when I was growing up we lived in Old Brooklyn. My mother would walk to the West Side Market and take the bus back, carrying all the bags. Even though it was hard work, she loved shopping there. Supermarkets were too antiseptic for her. She came to America in her thirties from a little village in western Ukraine and the Market reminded her of home. My mother liked the ambience, the mix of languages—she herself was also fluent in Polish, which some of the vendors spoke—and the fact that all the food wasn't wrapped and packaged. She felt comfortable there."
> —Andy Fedynsky

Shoppers' bags are stretched to the limit with bargains

THE MARKET HAS CHARACTER(S)
Oddballs, Eccentrics, & Lovable Folk

"**THE MARKET WAS** full of eccentrics," says Walter Ehrnfelt III, the fourth generation at the family-owned beef stand that operated for ninety-seven years. From childhood until he left the business to attend law school in 1974, Walter had the perfect vantage point for recognizing and getting to know the many Market personalities.

"The contrast of Market customers always interested me," says Ehrnfelt. "One minute we would be waiting on Jackie Mayer, the former Miss America from Sandusky, and the next minute wrapping up dog bones for the Dog Lady. She would come in late on Saturday with her three dogs, Nixon, Prosperity, and Depression, all twisted together on their leashes."

Dogs are prohibited in the Market, but the Dog Lady knew how to play the game, staying until Market management caught wind of her visit, then scooting out a nearby door before they could catch her.

Characters at the West Side Market were found on both sides of the counter. They could be customers, like the Mayor of the Market, who Annemarie Geffert would see regularly just outside her stand, Annemarie's Dairy:

> "He was gruff and had a heavy accent, but he was a fixture at the Market for the longest time. He used to get a cup of coffee from Frank's Bratwurst and just sit in that corner and watch everything that was going on while he drank it. He would come at 9 AM and leave at 2 PM. It was his job."

Walter Ehrnfelt's grandmother, Eleanore, a plucky redhead was a true original at the family stand from 1950 to the mid-1980s. Jim Petras, a former cooler boy for the Ehrnfelt family remembers her well:

> "Eleanore Ehrnfelt was the matriarch of the family and quite a character. She was a terror and spoke like a sailor. She was already in her seventies when I knew her but she still went to the Aragon Ballroom

Above, from top: Anthony "Banjo" Curiale waves from his stand, sporting his signature paper hat; Walter Ehrnfelt Jr. and his mother, the spunky and memorable Eleanore

with her boyfriend [Wheeler]. Many a Saturday customer suffered her wrath if she'd had too good a time on a Friday night. But she always came in religiously on Saturday morning and she had her following. Sometimes as people walked away from the stand, she'd make colorful, critical comments about them under her breath. She had the dirt on everybody and didn't hesitate to spread it around. Or someone would share news or gossip and then she would tell other customers. That was how things went viral before the Internet."

Reaching the status of "character" required having a colorful personality, quirky nature, endearing charm, a hint of delightfully offbeat behavior, and habits that ranged from just plain funny to wildly bizarre. For many who earned the reputation, the West Side Market served as a home and community, a comfortable place where they could easily be themselves.

Wally Ehrnfelt is quick to say that despite the odd qualities some customers displayed, even those bordering on the weird and wacky, most vendors at the Market treated the several oddballs like everyone else, never poking fun at them. "They would develop a comfort level with certain vendors," says Ehrnfelt.

One of the Ehrnfelt's regular customers was the Cat Lady. "No one knew much about her but she would come in tight dresses and spiked heels and she would buy every kidney we had in the case," recalls Walter. "It could have been twenty, thirty, sometimes forty pounds…all to feed her cats. No matter how strange anyone's behavior would seem we just went with it."

Tim Jeziorski has worked for a number of vendors and has befriended plenty of the Market's characters. "They are kind souls with unique personalities," he says. "The Market provides a special connection and a measure of familiarity for them."

Above: Fred Weigel (L) and unidentified man

"We had a customer named Beatrice. No matter what the weather she wore these big tent-like dresses tied at the waist with rope. Her dress and make-up were bizarre but we were taught to treat her kindly and with respect. Turns out she was stealing bread from us, stuffing loaves down the front of her dress. Nicky Roberto caught her but he didn't get mad or call the police. He just told her 'Beatrice, pay Angie for

Memories

"I had one regular customer who came dressed in military garb. He would always buy eggs and ask me to inspect them first. One time, he licked all the eggs. He obviously bought that dozen. What a character! He was high maintenance and would take up a lot of my time, but he was entertaining, not mean or aggressive, just unique."

—**Annemarie Geffert, vendor, Annemarie's Dairy**

"Fred Weigel was a tough character. One night at quitting time, one of the guys made a sculpture of his head out of pork fat, put Fred's glasses and fedora on it, stuck a lit cigarette in its mouth, and put it in the meat case for Fred to find. I don't know if Fred thought it was as funny as we did but I think he said it was good likeness."

—**Bill Retzer, former employee**

Del Russ at his lamb and goat meat stand, circa 1965

the bread you took.' And she did, reaching down into her cleavage to get the money. We still treated her nicely after that, but watched her more closely when she came."
—Beverly Tabacco, former employee

"Sour Belly George was a guy who loafed around the Market, did odd jobs, and was plastered all the time. One Saturday, he passed out and was taken to the emergency room. We were sure he ended up in the morgue that time.

When he showed up Monday looking for work, we were stunned. We told him we thought he was dead. Then he asked us if he could have the money we collected for funeral flowers."
—Charles "Bud" Leu Jr., former vendor

"I have a customer that calls himself 'The Pope.' He comes in and blesses me. He captivates the crowd in front of my counter. He hasn't shown up in a while. I'll have to call him and see where he is."
—Vince Bertonaschi, vendor, Vince's Meats

"Nicky Roberto was so handsome and quite the ladies man. He would come in on Monday mornings after a good weekend and head straight for the men's locker room to powder his face because he hadn't shaved. He was trying to cover his whiskers so nobody would know he hadn't been home since Saturday. Sometimes he fell asleep up there and didn't come down for a couple of hours."
—Beverly Tabacco, former employee

"Del Russ had a lot of Greek customers and during the holidays sold a lot of lamb. One Saturday, one of Russ's regular customers came in and bought three whole lambs for some big Greek celebration. The guy tucked a carcass under each arm and asked Del to help him carry the third to the car. It was really busy and Del couldn't leave the stand, so he took the third carcass and where they slit it along the stomach to clean out the entrails, Russ used that to put over the customer's head so he could carry all three out in one trip."
—Dennis Belovich, former employee

Many stands had a Saturday crew in order to keep up on busy weekends. "The intrigue of the Saturday crew was that they did something else during the week," explains Wally Ehrnfelt, "but would come down and work on Saturday. It wasn't because we paid them much. The stand would just turn into a huge work party."

Legendary among the crew was Walter Church, a truck driver during the week. "All you could do on Saturday was wait on people and nothing could stand in your way," says Ehrnfelt. "Church is slicing liver and his belt broke and his pants started falling down very slowly under his apron. He couldn't leave because we were so busy. So he kept spacing his feet further and further apart to keep his pants up. Finally, the pants came down and instead of stopping, he said, 'I'll get to that later.'"

Many vendors, workers, and customers were christened with nicknames. They could have been in place of given names that proved difficult to pronounce but it's more likely that they were inspired by a distinctive personality, personal quality, or occupation.

Broad, stocky, and often the last man standing in Felice's (a favorite vendor watering hole) at after work gatherings, it's not hard to imagine how Orlando Rivera earned the nickname Big O. He will go down in Market history for working in his tuxedo one Saturday in 1985, following after-prom festivities at St. Ignatius High School. A part-time Market employee since 1984, he says his ex-wife used to call the place his "mistress." "You're always running off to the Market on Saturdays," she would tell him. "You leave smiling and come home smiling."

Tony LaNasa was "Tony the Bag Man." Contrary to what one might think, LaNasa was actually an integral part of the Market in the early days and had an important part in just about every order. LaNasa sold bags, butcher wrap, and string to vendors and baskets to shoppers for fifty-one years, beginning in 1930. He started off in the alcove shared with the small grocery store just beyond the fish market inside the market house and eventually moved to a warehouse just off Market Square Park across the street.

Above: Orlando Rivera, or "Big O," has worked at the Market for more than twenty-five years

Memories

"I loved Eleanore Ehrnfelt. She taught me about food, life, and sex. And always reminded me that I should never eat ground beef unless it came from her stand."

—*Sandy Prince*

"Freddie Boehm would park his 1937 Packard on the sidewalk in front of the Market and walk in wearing a hat and a butcher's apron. No one ever bothered Freddie about parking on the sidewalk. He apparently was well-connected."

—*George A. Novak, former employee*

"I had one very eccentric customer. He bought cayenne pepper and put it in his socks in the winter to keep his feet warm."

—*Mary Cantillon, former vendor*

Produce vendor Lou Ralofsky was a victim of one of the only known violent attacks in the history of the West Side Market. It was a common everyday practice for vendors to have knives in their hands for trimming produce. According to various accounts of the event, Ralofsky was a kidder and teaser and provoked one of his employees, a serious drinker, to such a point that he stabbed his boss in the eye, leaving Ralofsky partially blind. Although he recovered and returned to work, he earned the legendary nickname One-Eyed Louie. It's a story that many of the old timers at the Market still recall.

"Another of our repeat customers was the Parrot Guy, a heavy drinker. He would come in dressed in a nice, neat nautical outfit with a parrot on his shoulder. He would always order a pound of ground chuck. When he would turn to leave, you could see that the parrot had pooped down his back."
—Wally Ehrnfelt, former vendor

"Mike Cafeteria. That's not a nickname. It's real. He sold fruit."
—Mike DiBlasio, former vendor

"Some of the butchers back in the 1960s used to put rose-colored bulbs in their cases to make the meat look pink. That was outlawed. My aunt would work for us on Fridays for a few hours and there was another vendor, an old timer, who used to grind up hearts and lungs and mix it into the ground meat to make it look fuller and redder. It would puff up and sink down. She christened him 'The Chemist.'"
—Ed Badstuber, former employee

"There was this girl from Serbia who worked at the Market and all she knew how to say was Ham and Eggs—hence her nickname."
—Chuck Maurath, former vendor

"My dad's nickname was Banjo. He started working at the Market in 1932 and he was about ten years old. He was washing windows for one of the vendors, Clayton Kuchle who told him his eyes were as big as banjos!"
—Karen Curiale Torreiter, employee

Above, from top: Tony Pinzone; Banjo Curiale

Memories

"*Silver Shoes worked over at Buechler Jaeger Meats in the early 1970s. He had a pretty flamboyant personality behind the stand. His signature fashion statement was a pair of work books sprayed with shiny metallic paint. There was also the Silver Fox, an older guy with some beautiful silver hair.*"

—**Tom Nagel, employee**

"*Tom Nagel used to call me Murray Hill [Cleveland's Italian neighborhood] because I was Italian.*"

—**Tony Pinzone, vendor, Pinzone Meats**

"*The Banana Lady would always come to our stand to get a glass of buttermilk to drink along with a banana. She seemed to be the poorest of the poorest with only one good tooth. We never charged her. Turns out she died very wealthy and left someone a pretty tidy estate. You never know.*"

—**Janet Penttila, former vendor**

Tom Nagel: The Nicknamer

Tom Nagel has worked at the West Side Market for forty-five years—mostly on Saturdays. It's hard to say whether this has been Nagel's hobby or second career, but if nothing else, it's been among the best times of his life. "I started as a cooler boy for Sam Santner in 1968. That day I made $12.50 and I thought I was a millionaire. My Cleveland Press paper route only paid $5.50 a week."

Nagel worked his way around the meat stands of the Market: from Santner to Ehrnfelt, then to Maurath, Krokey, Badstubers, and Jim's Meats. He honed skills in shooting the breeze and cutting, which means he not only knows what a "peeled knuckle" is (a primal cut of beef from the hind leg) but he can break it down into five unique value cuts and tell the customer how to prepare each one. But Nagel's most highly-developed skill is in creating nicknames for select shoppers, as well as colleagues. He acts as the unauthorized repository for scores of monikers bestowed on vendors, coworkers, and customers.

"You just see someone, you know they have a sense of humor, and it starts from there," he says of the process. "There's the lady who would always bring me photos of her daughter's dance recitals. That was Tap n' Jazz," says Nagel.

A customer who bore a striking resemblance to Billy Joel took on the singer's name. "I would say real loud, 'Hey! It's Billy Joel,' and everyone in line would turn to look." A woman with a thick accent would ask for marrowbones. "Mary Bones," says Nagel. One gentleman with the last name of Iwaskewych was "Alphabet Soup." "That guy read more comic books at the newsstand than anyone," recalls Nagel.

Tom Nagel has shared jokes, kind words, and nicknames for more than forty years

"We used to have a family of four guys who worked here and their father would come down to shop a lot," says Tom. "His name was Miles Mattern. I told him that we were going to switch to using the metric system at the Market so I was going to have to change his name to Kilometer. It stuck and years later his kids still call him Kilometer."

Nagel recognizes that there's a fine line between having fun with people and being mean-spirited. It's a skill like butchering meat with a sharp knife—one must be careful. "Sarcasm can work against you at the Market so you have to know how to make it work," says Nagel. "I can see it in their face when they are taking the kidding to heart so I pause. Then I smile at them and I can see that they get it."

For all he doles out in the way of nicknames, Nagel has yet to be blessed with one, "at least not that I'm aware of."

Memories

"There was this guy who worked at George Schwark's pork stand, who we used to call Ox Heart. He was big kid, over six feet tall and 250 pounds. His size equated to that of an ox."

—Tom Nagel, employee

"My mother Mary Gentille was called Red by her customers because of her flaming red hair."

—Maryann Gentille, former employee

"This guy we called 'Made in the Shade' worked at the Market. He always had some kind of big deal in the works that he would brag about but nothing ever panned out for him."

—Chuck Maurath, former vendor

IT'S PERSONAL
Kind Words, Conversations, & Customer Service

THE BUILDING IS beautiful. The selection of foods is amazing. The prices are fair and there are always bargains to be found. But the Market also offers something that can't be bought or packaged: face-to-face contact and all the particular and peculiar pleasures that come from forging friendships and interacting with fellow human beings.

Swapping opinions, cracking jokes, and good-natured teasing enliven otherwise ordinary encounters. Discussions about politics, sports, and family accomplishments, or the lack of them, help pass the day. Some stand owners and employees, like bartenders, do double duty as unofficial therapists, listening to customers' complaints and worries. Advice can be personal or culinary and it's given free of charge.

Shoppers buy from "their" vendors, merchants they know and trust, who reward these loyal regulars in a thousand small ways, from inquiring about their health and remembering what they like, to packing up the choicest pieces and maybe even a little something extra now and then. For those who work at the Market and those who come to buy, these connections are the heart and soul of what has kept the place going for a hundred years.

"I learned about how to get along with all kinds of people by working at the Market, and to treat everyone with kindness, compassion, and

respect. We often threw in a little extra if we knew people were having a hard time, maybe another donut if they came in with kids.

There was this one customer, she always bought two Italian twist breads. But she wanted us to go through them all to find the best ones. She'd spend ten minutes choosing and there'd be people waiting in line behind her. What I finally figured out was that she wanted them with the biggest widest ends because she could get an extra sandwich out of every loaf. So I started looking for those when the bread came in and setting them aside. I'd tell her 'I saved these specially for you' and that made her happy."
—Beverly Tabacco, former employee

"We lived down the street from the Market at 23rd and Bridge. I started working there as a cooler boy when I was twelve years old. Most of the kids who got those jobs were the children of the stand owners. I got lucky. My family belonged to St. Emeric's, the Hungarian church right behind the Market. Father John Monroe took me around and introduced me to all the vendors, telling them I was a good responsible kid. That got me in. It was 1953.

I remember my interview with Don Miller of Miller Meats. I was standing behind the counter telling him about my 'credentials'—I was a paper carrier. Someone came up and Miller's back was turned so he didn't see her. I told him, 'You've got a customer.' He took care of her and when he was done he said, 'You're hired.' I was surprised and asked him why. He told me it was because I already knew the customer always comes first."
—Joseph Trill Jr., former vendor

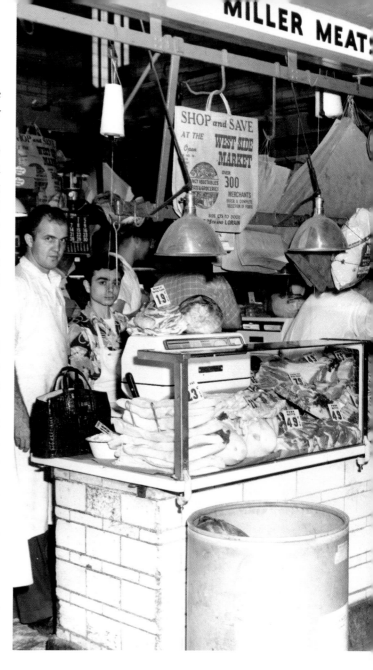

Above: Don Miller and his cooler boy Donny Bissell at the family pork stand, circa 1957
Opposite: Tom Sharp has worked behind the counter at Edward J. Badstuber & Sons for fifty-eight years

Memories

"My dad made the stuff we sold and my mom ran the stand. He didn't want to deal with customers, but she got along great with people. She gave away a lot of samples and if you came to buy just five pounds of something, you usually went away with much more. After I took over she stayed on another six years to help while the customers got know me, so they wouldn't be traumatized when she left."

—*Jerry Chucray, vendor, Czuchraj Meats*

"You build relationships even if it's for five minutes, with people on the other side of your counter."

—*Annemarie Geffert, vendor, Annemarie's Dairy*

"I communicate better across the counter than on the phone. It's like my little stage and I'm most comfortable in my own space. Sure, you see your share of angry people, but I like to think that I get most of them to smile before they leave."

—*Ed Meister, vendor, Meister Foods*

Robert E. Stumpf:
Kitchen Maid Meats

In the sixties, Robert E. Stumpf presided over an empire that included a meat-processing and sausage-making plant; Kitchen Maid Meats, a company with nine retail outlets around Cleveland, another in Akron, plus a stand at the Market; a catering operation; and gourmet foods division.

Although he was more boss than butcher, Stumpf continued to weigh sausage links and count change at the Market every Friday and Saturday. "Can't disappoint my old customers," Stumpf told a *Cleveland Press* reporter in 1963. "I've been waiting on them for years."[10]

He repeated this sentiment in a 1967 interview. "This has been a fine market ever since I helped my father there fifty years ago. I built my business by catering to the wants of old customers. Some of them wait for me to help them select their meat and advise them on its preparation."[11]

THANKS FOR THE "MEMORABILIA"

While food is the ultimate reward at the West Side Market, some vendors have handed out souvenirs or gifts to their customers especially around Christmas. Items included pins, buttons, potholders, thermometers, calendars, mugs, hats, and more. Of course, the stand owners' names were on the promotional giveaways. A marketing opportunity was never passed up.

"People began to expect to see something from us at Christmas," said former lunch meat vendor, Russ Schwark who used to give out adorable special die-cut, embossed calendars from Germany. Patrick Delaney, who operated the Euclid Sausage Shop at the Market, which he closed on New Year's Eve in 2008 was always giving "stuff" away.

"My wife almost threw me out of the house when two big boxes and the bill came for little plastic banks," he recalls. "We were closing and it was my last Christmas gift to customers. The Market is the best Chamber of Commerce that Cleveland has."

ⓜemories

"The customer is always right, even when they are wrong. People do not come here to listen to us complain. We are here to listen to them complain."

—**Tim Jeziorski, employee**

"I feel so privileged to have the West Side Market in my community. I go almost every Friday, around ten in the morning. If I miss a week, the next time I show up all my regular vendors want to know what happened. When they see me, they don't ask, 'What do you want?' they say 'How much' or 'How many?' I feel honored to know these people and do business with them."

—**Lois Rose**

Once a customer at the Market asked Bob Stumpf at Kitchen Maid Meats how much the broken hot dogs cost, compared to the whole ones. "Twenty-nine cents a pound," he replied, "versus fifty-nine cents for the whole." "Break me three pounds," said the man.[12]

THE CUSTOMER IS ALWAYS RIGHT: MOST OF THE TIME

In a place where the competition is just steps away, satisfying the demands of the customer is a priority, no matter how unusual or downright bizarre that request might be.

> "It was real busy, around Christmastime, and a middle-aged couple came to the stand. I had a twenty-five-pound boneless round on the block. They saw it and wanted it immediately. The whole thing. 'Just put it in here,' they said and they opened up an ugly green Naugahyde suitcase. No wrapping, no bagging, no nothing. They paid for it and left. They seemed perfectly normal but I never found out what they were going to do with it. That was around 1990. I never saw them before that day and haven't seen them since."
> **—Gordon Fernengel, vendor, Fernengel's**

Customers had ways of thinking that often didn't make sense to the vendor or employee waiting on them, but a happy customer was a satisfied customer and that was the ultimate goal. But the question remains: is the customer always right?

> "No. But they are always the customer."
> **—Jeff Campbell, vendor, Campbell's Popcorn Shop**

> "To a point they are. Let's face it, we make mistakes sometimes."
> **—Terry Leu, vendor, Rolston Poultry**

> "Mine were!"
> **—Larry Calabrese, former vendor**

> "No, but we let them think they were."
> **—Valeria Check, former vendor**

> "Of course, but not when they're wrong."
> **—Mary Pell, employee**

Lunch meat vendor Russ Schwark at his stand, 1960s

YOUNGER VISITORS, YOUNGER VOICES
From Toddlers to Teens

GOING TO THE MARKET is less chore and more play for those not in charge. Some kids are dragged along, but many more go willingly once they know this isn't a typical grocery store. There are new things and favorite things to devour, strange sights, and enough aromas to put noses on high alert. For children, who don't have to worry about getting everything on the list or the most bang for each buck, it can be an adventure, an education in 3-D, and a treasure trove of delicious indulgences. The sight of children in the Market is more than delightful, it suggests continuity—the next generation of Market shoppers getting off to an early start.

"In 1943, we lived on Courtland Avenue. I was six years old. Every other Saturday, mom, my sister Bev, and I would pile into Aunt Jean's car, with her two oldest children, Billy and Peachy. We were going to the West Side Market. Whoopee!

The market had a machine that spewed out fresh peanut butter—If you followed your nose you would soon find the fish market. Any kind you could imagine.

Our first stop would always be Lovaszy Hungarian Meat Stand. It is still there, but under a new name (Dohar). Mom would buy their cottage ham, rice sausage, blood sausage (my Dad's favorite), and also Hungarian fresh kielbasa. To this day I still purchase the rice sausage and it continues to be my favorite.

The best was Eva's Bakery—Mom would buy fresh warm rye bread and I remember eating it on the way home. Mom would also buy us another special treat—Lady Locks. They were big, flaky and very delicate, shaped like a cone, filled with a white sweet crème and sprinkled

Above, from top: A young customer inspects the fruit in the produce arcade; Diane Dever greets a young shopper at her stand and offers a taste of cheese
Opposite: Enjoying a fresh berry while mom places her order

with powdered sugar. They would be gently placed in a big white box and tied with string."
—Elaine Trizzino

Youngsters arrive with mothers and fathers, grandparents, aunts and uncles, teachers and chaperones. Viewing the place from their own unique perspective, it can seem like some real-life version of amusement park, classroom, and—thanks to the meat men—a house of horrors all rolled into one. Reactions range from amazement and giggles to shrieks of disgust. Impressions are vivid, even decades later.

"I was born in 1938. My mother was widowed in 1945, when she was twenty-one, and she moved us in with my grandparents in Ohio City. My grandma would take my sister and I with her to the West Side Market on Saturdays. We'd ride the streetcar from 44th to 25th and Lorain. It was a fun trip. She didn't have to drag me. I always wanted to go. I liked the noise, the smells, and the busyness. It was an adventure. I loved looking at the fish. It was like going to the zoo. The best part was all the free samples the vendors gave us. One guy would give us a slice of bologna, another a cookie. My favorite was a dab of freshly ground peanut butter on a little wooden spoon. We always left full. You know, it just occurred to me, maybe the reason grandma brought us along was so she wouldn't have to feed us lunch that day!"
—Jan Sustarsic

"As a little girl, I often accompanied my Nana to the West Side Market. Following her from the produce stands into the market building, we would always go through the same entrance—the one that funneled us right by the fish counter with all its smells and big fish that stared at me through the case. I would hold tightly to her with one hand and with the other, pinch my nose shut until we made it to the main market floor. To this day, if I walk through that particular entrance, I find myself catching my breath and remembering being eye to eye with all of the fish."
—Zoe Ann Komaransky

Memories

"In the late fifties, my grandpa would take me to the West Side Market. It was an all day trip back then—no super highways, just back roads with lots of conversation and anticipation of a day filled with mouthwatering delights."
—Debbie DeMaria

"When I was little my mom would drive to the Market and get me 'meat sticks.' It was great. I always knew what I was getting every Saturday morning and that made my weekends awesome. Even as I got older and my mom didn't have a car she would take us on the bus just to get produce and meat sticks. It was always worth the ride."
—Mary Gurley

"The market was where my mom went to socialize. She stopped and talked, and I'd stand there, bored silly, waiting for her to get done so I could go home and play."
—Theresa Kuehn

"When I was in high school, my photography class took a field trip to downtown Cleveland. What I remember most were the sights, smells, and sounds of the West Side Market.

From the moment we walked into the produce side I was in shock, not only from the different types of people around me, but the variety of fruits and vegetables. I had never seen many of them before—five different kinds of leafy greens (we had only iceberg and romaine in my small town near Hiram, Ohio) and potatoes—red potatoes, sweet potatoes, purple potatoes, fingerlings.

I never knew that places like this existed in Cleveland, or anywhere for that matter. There were meats I never dreamed of eating and cheeses made from the milk of sheep and goats. In the cases there were whole pigs next to hooves and snouts—we pressed our faces to the glass. The teacher bought smokies and passed them out like candy on the bus ride home."

—Kim Tilly

"When I was young, my mother took my sister and me to the Market. I carried as many heavy bags as I could to make my mom proud, while my little sister got to push the cart around, inevitably running into something and hopefully not someone. We always had our favorite stalls to visit. The 'nut guy' had a small stand in the corner; only one person could fit behind it. He would toast the nuts to order, then pass us the warm bag of goodies, and share stories with my mother about my grandmother and great-grandmother, both of whom he had known. My sister and I would spend what seemed like hours in front of the candy counter, clutching a single dollar in our hands, mulling over which candy we wanted, as if we had a life-and-death decision on our hands. I remember the flying saucers—two colored wafers forming a hollow collapsed sphere that contained a few grains of tasty sugary bits. When you ate it, the wafer part quickly dissolved, the same way a flying saucer quickly slips away into the night sky."

—Michael Walsh, chef

Above: Whole lamb and goat are frequent sightings on the Market floor
Opposite: Cheesy pizza bagels are a favorite "knosh and stroll" item

emories

"We had a field-trip to the West Side Market. It was a magical place to a child. The food, the vendors, and our first experience with homeless people—being told not to judge them but to put ourselves in their shoes. I went up to the balcony for the view of the Market in action—so much hustle and bustle lay out before our eyes. The overall vibe was entrancing. In a couple of weeks, I'll be showing my eleven-year-old nephew the Market. That's how old I was when I first saw it. I hope the experience stays with him the way it has stayed with me."

—**Jennifer Takacs**

"All seven of us kids came with my parents to shop at the Market. I was second oldest so I was supposed to help keep the little ones together, but I'd stop to stare into the cases and get separated from the group. I was fascinated by the random animal parts, the whole pigs and lambs, and the guys with sides of beef slung over their shoulders."

—**Sam McNulty, Market patron and Ohio City restaurateur**

BRATWURST, BUTTERMILK, & BROKEN COOKIES
Market Eats

THE MARKET IS a source of ingredients, food to chop and cook, slice, dice, sprinkle, and spread. But there is another category of things to buy that are ready right now, whenever that now moment arrives. These days the choice includes buttery Belgian waffles, Cambodian stuffed chicken wings, Scottish meat pies, a bag of caramel corn, fresh-squeezed vegetable juice with a shot of wheat grass, a foam-topped cappuccino—the list is luscious and long. It could be hunger that compels such purchases but it's just as likely a treat that's become a custom, a thing to do on every visit. For many, a trip to the Market just isn't—and wasn't—complete without these little indulgences.

> "How can I ever forget memories of going to the West Side Market when I was a kid...hanging on to my dad's pants while he drank a cup of buttermilk drawn from an urn sitting on the counter at Wendt's Dairy stand...We still shop there eighty years later, making sure we buy a bratwurst with sauerkraut."
> —Robert Borzak

> "Although I'm relatively new to the Market, pizza bagels started as a novelty that turned into a tradition for the past thirty years. Light and fluffy, not like a traditional bagel, it's saucy and cheesy. Grown men come to our stand and tell me how they used to come here as little kids. One man told me he lost his first tooth on a bagel and others said that their parents told them that if they were good at the market, they would get pizza bagels. And the pictures you see at the stand? [Frank Sinatra, Dean Martin, Luciano Pavarotti] Those are our boyfriends! And the guy with the cigar is Mr. Frickaccio!"
> —Terry Frick, vendor, Frickaccio's Pizza Market

"In the early 1970s, regardless of the weather, we would travel to shop the Market on Saturday. The parking lot would be so crowded my dad would often circle the lot just to find a spot. My mother had her favorite vendors and would refuse to buy from others. The 'Pickle Lady' always got our business and Dad and I would munch on smokies as we moved through the crowd. Sometimes, I would get to purchase penny candy and we always left with broken cookies from the cookie stand, which were cheaper than whole cookies."
—Lisa Michaels

"My son lives in New York City. He loves the Market and misses it. Whenever he comes home to visit he wants to go there and get a bratwurst from Frank's. Once, I made a sign that said, 'We miss you Steven.' I brought it to the stand, and a few others, and had them hold it up while I took photos. I sent the pictures to him."
—Lois Rose

"Dichotomy Corn rocks my socks. My husband Joel and I walk through the Market trying to find new faves and we always end up at Campbell's Popcorn Shop to get a bag of this sweet and salty goodness. It's our guilty pleasure—only $3.25—and our Saturday 'can't wait for lunch' food of choice. We promise ourselves just one handful and then break our promises each time."
—Jessica Heber Miller

"I have four boys, ages ten to sixteen. My wife and I take them to the West Side Market and it's kind of a ritual. We go to our favorite stands. We start at Vera's and get pretzel bread and little pizzas to get us started. Rita's Pickles next. Then the Cheese Shop (the selection is stunning) and the Candy Corner. Then it's Dohar's for sausage. We stay awhile to chat, then to the fish place, and finally Frank's Bratwurst. Sometimes, we'll sneak them into the Café and buy enough fries and drinks to justify taking up a table."
—Joe Eszterhas, screenwriter and author

Above, from top: A row of popcorn samples at Campbell's Popcorn Shop; Rita Graewe welcomed young visitors with a pickle

Memories

Jack Kahl, former Chairman and CEO of Manco Inc., wrote to Mayor White in 1997, advocating for the care and preservation of the West Side Market. Kahl talked about going to the Cleveland gem as a child with his mother and brother, and told the Mayor that he still went to the Market a couple of times a month to charge his batteries, and warm his heart, as well as fill his belly. And he had something particular to say about Frank's. *"I don't think there's a better bratwurst in the world than can be purchased in the Market on a hard roll with a little sauerkraut... and a smile from the wonderful lady that serves it to you. It's a lot more than a bratwurst, it's a brand."*

"My mother worked at the West Side Market as a waitress in the café from 1965 until 1970. She was twenty-nine, a single mom with five kids ranging from seven to one. I'm the fourth child. When she didn't have a baby-sitter and before we were old enough to go to school she'd take my little sister Monica and I [sic] with her to work. We hung out behind the counter and in the kitchen. We'd nap upstairs in the ladies locker room. I remember once we woke up and wandered into the men's side. There were urinals and we'd never seen anything like them. Monica thought they were special sinks for kids."

—Mary Hunter Masters

Shopping for food can work up an appetite. For more than seventy years shoppers have given tired feet a rest over a hot meal in the southeast corner of the Market. This corner has reinvented itself many times over in the last hundred years. Originally the space was a continuation of the Market, with four vendor stalls. The stalls were removed in the 1940s and the space reconfigured into a restaurant called Alexander's, with counters and booths.

The interior remained the same until 1971, when the space was converted into the West Side Market Cafeteria outfitted with orange and turquoise molded-plastic chairs and Formica-topped tables. However, even more of a difference was the presence of a worker nicknamed "Crabby Abbey," whose snappish attitude and unique style was as much of a draw as the daily special.

William "Gus" Glaros, owner of the cafeteria from 1971 until 2003, served up foods that echoed the European culture of the Market. "For the Greeks, I made lamb shanks; for the Germans, pork and 'kraut; beef goulash for the Hungarians; sauerkraut and kielbasa for everybody!" There was beef stew, chicken paprikash, homemade soups and chili, rice pudding, pies, and five daily specials. "I made everything from scratch and all the ingredients came from the vendors," he says, beef from Ehrnfelt's, pork from Fernengel's, chicken from Rolston's, and the produce from the best deals in the arcade.

The hours of the cafeteria were set to accommodate shoppers and Market workers, some of whom would arrive as early as 3:30 AM for breakfast. Glaros also kept the cafeteria open on Thursdays, just for the vendors and workers who came in that day to prepare for the weekend crowd.

The cafeteria was also the place for Market workers to stop at the end of the day for a beer and some talk before heading home. "This was the only place in the Market where the inside and outside vendors came together," recalls Glaros. "It was common ground. Lots of meetings were held here after hours, too."

Above, from top: Lunchtime rush at Alexander's, circa 1965; Kitchen and counter help at Alexander's, the first cafe at the Market

Mary Hunt: Hello, My Name is Crabby Abbey

Crabby Abbey reigned as the silver ponytailed, iron-fisted manager of the West Side Market Cafeteria for twenty-eight years, until the eatery was sold and restyled into the West Side Market Café in 2003. The cafeteria was the breakfast and lunch spot for shoppers and Market workers, serving up home cooking with a side of carefully crafted affronts courtesy of Abbey.

Crabby Abbey's given name was Mary Hunt, and she was a mouthy gal who picked up half of her nickname from the street she lived on—Abbey Avenue near the Market, and the other half from her typical mood. Sometimes she was called Gabby Abbey but only on days she felt exceptionally chatty.

Her boss, Bill "Gus" Glaros, owned the cafeteria from 1971 to 2003, and Crabby Abbey worked for him while she entertained and insulted customers. "They loved her," says Glaros who described the cafeteria as her stage and the customers her audience.

Crabby Abbey ruled over the hubbub of the cafeteria and according to Cleveland journalist and radio personality Robin Benzle, "she swore like a longshoreman, roared like a lion and was not afraid to toss out anyone she felt like." Benzle remembers an incident that was typical of how Abbey earned her name.

"Once during an election year [1980], Teddy Kennedy came to the Market with his entourage. One of his 'guys'

Bill "Gus" Glaros and the infamous Mary Hunt, aka Crabby Abbey

came in and said to Abbey, 'Mr. Kennedy wants a couple of hot dogs.' It bothered her that he thought he was too important to get his own hot dogs, so Abbey said, 'If he wants hot dogs, tell him to come and get them himself.' So he did."

"She always talked loud so everyone could hear her," Glaros remembers. "When someone would come to pay the bill and they would fumble around for the right change she would tell them, 'Take your time. We close at six,' or if a customer was leaving and would say to Abbey, 'Have a nice day,' she would say, 'Well, you're leaving so that's a start.' Abbey always had something to say to you in a funny way that would make you feel awkward."

Since the cafeteria had a continuous stream of activity, politicians frequently stopped in, especially during election years. "They would come in this door," Glaros says pointing to the entrance off Lorain Avenue, "and go out that door," nodding at the one leading into the Market. "They never stayed to eat."

Eventually, Glaros decided to leave the food operation. "You can only stand up so long in this business," says Glaros. In 2003, he sold the restaurant to Gus Mougianis, owner of the Mediterranean Import store and Jimmy Traynor, the Market cop.

Once again, the southeast corner was transformed, this time into the West Side Market Café. The new owners kept some of the original tables and polished the old glazed tiles to a bright white. To honor the long tradition of the corner spot, the new owners decorated the Café with Traynor's extensive collection of photos depicting the Market's history and cultural importance.

The cafeteria line and steam tables were replaced by a copper-topped bar, where patrons order wine and beers by the glass. The kitchen cooks up creative, contemporary fare that's served by waitresses with their own kind of attitude. Workers still gather at the end of the day for a drink, and the Cafe remains the only place in the Market where people can sit at a table to eat.

In another corner of the building, people prop themselves on the sparse counter space, lean against the wall, or sit on an overturned milk crate at Johnny Hot Dog. But most just take their order to go. The stand has been a traditional stop for generations of shoppers and workers.

In 1935, Anna Roth took over the stand renaming it after Johnny Dohanyos, a boy for whom she served as a guardian. Hot dogs were available every day the Market was open except on Fridays. A strict Catholic, Anna and therefore her customers observed the faith's abstinence rule.

The appellation Johnny Hot Dog stuck, both on the stand and for Dohanyos, who ran the stand after Roth. "Everywhere we would go, people would yell 'Hey, Johnny Hot Dog,'" said Dennis Belovich, a friend and one-time Market employee. "I guess his last name was just too hard to pronounce."

In 1978, produce vendor Nate Anselmo became the new owner of Johnny Hot Dog, and his wife Mary Ann ran the stand until 1999, keeping a photographic record of her customers. Signed snapshots of local celebrities and politicians and many more of Market workers are still affixed to the walls around the stand.

"We tweaked the recipe for the hot dogs, which were specially made for us by an outside producer, adding a little more garlic and some seasonings," she said. When that producer went out of business, the Anselmos found another maker to recreate the taste of the famous dogs.

Linda Bowling thinks she has watched at least a million of them brown on the grill in the forty-two years she's worked at the counter. She's seen a lot of customers who have grown up on Johnny Hot Dogs and many more Market merchants and their employees who had them for breakfast, topped off with the most popular condiments: chili and onions. Small and slender, Bowling used to eat a couple of hot dogs a week and admits, "I can't do that like I used to." But when people walk through the door of what is now one of the longest-operating stands in the Market, she knows what most customers will ask. "You're still here? I remember coming with my parents for a Johnny Hot Dog."

"Nothing has really changed," says Bowling, "other than the owners."

Above, from top: From left, Mary Ann Anselmo and Linda Bowling at Johnny Hot Dog, circa 1980; Pauline Badstuber orders her "breakfast" at the stand

(M)emories

"On Thursdays he [Johnny Dohanyos] would cut three hundred pounds of onions for the stand and not shed a tear."

—Dennis Belovich, former employee

"My father Nate Anselmo also owned Johnny Hot Dog at the Market for almost thirty years. My mother Mary Ann ran it. So she worked inside, he was outside at our family's produce stand. Dad's alarm would go off at 3, 3:30 in the morning Monday, Wednesday, Friday, and Saturday. If I was going to help, he'd wake me. We'd get to the Market extra early to open the hot dog stand so the coffee and donuts would be ready when the other vendors arrived. Mom came a little later. She made these great sandwiches—eggs, sausage, cheese, and a hash brown patty."

—Tony Anselmo, former employee

Above, from top: Customers line up for falafels; shoppers take a break for a bite outside; Ordering a brat, a favorite "to go" food for generations of shoppers

Husam "Sam" Zayed's first venture at the West Side Market was running the small grocery store, which was located in the room next to the fresh fish stand. It was 1987 and for the next seven years, the Palestinian immigrant struggled before he realized that shoppers were not purchasing items he stocked that they could find in supermarkets. Zayed decided to turn the space into a sandwich stand, selling his wife Maha's wonderful falafel. The new Market eatery offered soft round pita bread stuffed with deep-fried falafel patties from ground chick peas, onion, garlic, parsley, and Maha's special seasonings, along with tomato, lettuce, and tahini. After twenty years, the sizeable sandwiches are still among favorite Market eats, and Zayed notes that his long time customers now arrive with their children in tow.

Zayed says he's never done any marketing. But word-of-mouth and the smell of the falafel patties cooking in the deep fryer are best kind of advertising. "People see others around the Market eating the sandwich," he says. "I always hear them say, 'What's that? Where did you get that?'"

He also offers a money-back guarantee for meat-eaters who are skeptical of the vegetarian sandwich. In fact, Zayed tells them he'll give back double what they paid if the sandwich doesn't satisfy them. "I've never had to give anyone a nickel," he says.

It's a very common sight to see a line of people, old and young, in front of Frank's Bratwurst, waiting for what owner Ilse Sheppard calls their "nostalgia buy"—a "brat," a half pork, half veal sausage, with a distinct "snap" in each bite, courtesy of a special casing. Regulars order in brat-speak. "Gimme a Soft Yellow Horse," (soft roll, yellow mustard with horseradish) or "I'll have a Hard Brown Kraut," (hard roll, brown mustard with sauerkraut). There's the "Everything" (sauerkraut, ketchup, mustards, barbeque sauce, and horseradish), and if the order is to go, "Put some legs on it."

The stand was opened by Ilse's parents, Frank and Johanna Ratschki, who emigrated from Austria in 1962. "They fell in love with the Market," she says. "It reminded them of home." A mechanic by trade, Frank grilled and sold his first brat in 1970: chopped, no bun, on a paper plate for 45 cents; 10 cents more for kraut.

"He made $25 that first week and thought that was great," she remembers. The bun and condiments came a few years later. Since then, the menu has remained the same. When the company that supplied the bratwurst closed, another one had to be found that could reproduce not only the taste but the sound. "Gotta have the snap," says Ilse.

Today, Ilse works the stand with the help of her own family and serves four hundred pounds of brats each week. Most people discover how they like their bratwurst after a few visits, but Ilse suggests they try the sausage on a hard roll first because it "holds the brat better so it doesn't shoot out."

Hillary Clinton, Chevy Chase, and John Glenn have all had a Frank's brat; so have plenty of local dignitaries, including councilmen Jim Rokakis and Mike Polensek and television personality Robin Swoboda. Ilse tells a story that shows how far some people will go to keep the brats for themselves.

"We had a customer who ordered two hundred brats for her father's birthday party," says Ilse. "I cryovaced [plastic wrapped] them and got them all ready for her to take to him in San Francisco. When she got there he was so happy and excited that he put them in his freezer and didn't share them with anyone at the party."

Whether it's brats, falafels, hot dogs, smokies, popcorn, or a cup of buttermilk, Market eats are typically consumed on two feet, standing or walking through the Market. Lucky shoppers snag one of the few "bistro tables," otherwise known as the tops of trash cans positioned at the intersections of the aisles—no reservations required. On a nice day, the benches in the alley between the building and the arcade provide first-come seating. It may not be five-star dining but the experience can't be duplicated elsewhere.

Another area shoppers enjoy is located at the west end of the hall, where a trip up the staircase on the south side of the building leads to a balcony high above the Market floor. Out of the fray, visitors can gaze over the landscape of the hall. Photographers love the spot. The area also is the Market's ad hoc stage for performing musicians and singers. But for many, the most special

Memories

"The one aspect of trips to the West Side Market I never understood as a kid was the most ritualistic of them all…something my father took more seriously than any other part of the trip. Inside the Market is Frank's Bratwurst stand…my father religiously believed in stopping at this stand at 8 AM and getting a bratwurst. Among other many valuable life lessons, I know that one should always get a lot of sauerkraut and Stadium Mustard on their brat…For the better part of these years the very thought of sauerkraut grossed me out and the mustard wasn't really doing it for me either. My father did everything in his power to lead me to the right side. 'You're missing out,' he'd say. I don't remember when I finally saw the light but I am now completely with the program."

—*Matt Chester, excerpt from a college composition, "Bratwurst for Breakfast?"*

"I've traveled the world in search of exotic and interesting foods and lived in large cities with bustling international neighborhoods but nothing captivates me more than the experience of going to the West Side Market. Maha's Falafils are truly the very best I've ever had—the right texture and spice. They are tops in my book of falafel sandwiches."

—*Yvonne Maffei, author of the food blog* **My Halal Kitchen**

feature of the balcony is the deep tiled ledge that fronts the window. It's an excellent place to sit and the ideal spot for enjoying an impromptu feast.

"Early one wintry Saturday morning, I was perched happily in the balcony, in a spot carefully chosen so my feet could dangle in front of the nice, warm radiator, munching contentedly on my weekly bratwurst sandwich (hard roll with horseradish) from Frank's. I noticed there was a small knot of people in front of Kaufmann's poultry stand. They weren't just waiting to order. They were laughing excitedly and all eyes were on the guy behind the counter. He was holding up a chicken foot for all to see and was pulling on a tendon, which made the three toes wave up and down. Soon every passerby was stopping there, enjoying a serendipitous moment at the West Side Market—me, too."
—Gretchen Reynolds

"Every Saturday, starting when I was about five, my grandfather would pick me up and take me to the Market. We would first go directly to Leu's meats so grandpa could buy his smokies and chat. Then we would go to Johnny Hot Dog and buy one soda and two hotdogs to go. On the way out grandpa would buy a lottery ticket and ask me to kiss it. We'd then make the climb up to the balcony where we would have our picnic and people watch. It wasn't until after this ritual was complete that we actually started getting everything on the shopping list. I shop at the Market weekly and to this day I always begin with a Johnny Hot Dog, a lottery ticket, and a trip to the balcony. It's been forty-five years and grandpa is no longer with us, except when I sit down on that balcony every week."
—Cherie Duda

Above, from top: The balcony is the best seat in the house for eating and observing activity on the Market floor; Charles Leu at his lunch meat and sausage stand, circa 1955
Opposite: Extra help to push heavy carts comes in handy

MORE THAN A BAG OF GROCERIES
Routines, Rituals, & Recollections

FIRST TIMERS AT the West Side Market might think the appeal of the place is all in the food: freshly butchered meats, strings of sausages, and glistening fish; bags of noodles and nuts, jars of spices, and loaves of bread; trays of lemon bars or chocolaty fudge; bins of cherries, piles of fat tomatoes, and mounds of slender green beans. And it's true that the Market exists to sell food. But it's more than just a place to stock up on what goes in the refrigerator and on the table.

> "I once told a reporter that the West Side Market is the Wrigley Field of the grocery business. A lot of baseball fans, no matter where they live or what their team, want to make a trip to see a game at that ball park. It's a classic that hasn't changed. You can say the same about the Market and that's part of why people come. You have to honor that."
> —Patrick Delaney, former vendor

It's best to come armed with a finely-tuned grocery list and mark off each item purchased: eggs, milk, shrimp, cheese, onions, and carrots. But be prepared to leave with so much more—things that can't be eaten but can certainly be savored, like the start of a new shopping tradition with kids or a special place to stand and people watch while indulging in a kraut-covered bratwurst. It could be moment of fleeting friendship while the butcher wraps an order or the beginning of a beautiful relationship with the guy behind the counter that knows how to deliver a good joke or tosses an extra peach in the bag, just because. These are the kinds of memories that shoppers take home.

> "In the early 1960s, we would get up early on Saturday mornings, freezing cold, steamy hot, rain or shine, to go to the Market. My mom had one of those carts made of wire with wheels, and my sister and I just loved to pull it and watch it fill up with fresh meats, fruits, and vegetables.
>
> We always entered the building through the seafood store so Mom could check out the fish. In spite of the smell, we loved walking through there. Mom bought fresh fish to either bread or go into Hungarian fisherman's soup, a rich paprika broth with fish heads, chunks of fish, and roe.
>
> We bought all the meats first, heaviest items on the bottom of the cart. Kaufmann's was her usual stop for chicken and Lovaszy/Dohar for Hungarian sausage and smoked bacon. When we were done inside, we would head for fruits and veggies. Calabrese was the stand my mother favored. Funny, I pretty much shop the same stands. The Market not only creates memories but traditions. My mom shopped there, my husband and I shop there and my daughter as well."
> —Mary Nagy

"Back in the seventies, my neighbor Jean and I were single parents. We would bundle up our five sleepy children early Saturday mornings, no matter what the weather, and drive from Medina to the Market. Our trips weren't leisurely. We arrived before 7 AM and made our way around the produce vendors, looking and price shopping, before heading inside for meat, cheese, bread—and bacon, always from the Leu Brothers. We bought pastries and rolls and took them in the tiny cafeteria, parking the kids at a table and ordering coffee for us, milk for them. We cemented our friendship among those glazed brick walls. As we headed out to the parking lot, we bought our produce, then went home to put the fresh stuff away and be at work by 9 AM. There is comfort in such routines and we were surely aided by it. Nearly forty years later, I'm warmed by the memories."
—Linda Amstutz

"The first time I went to the West Side Market was during an annual sixth grade field trip for our school. We were about an hour away in Rock Creek, Ohio. I remember being in awe of the building and feeling a little overwhelmed as a kid from small town, USA. I live west of Toledo now and in recent years, my husband, children, and I visit the Market every time we are in the area. They love going to the Market. It is the hustle and bustle, all the different people to see, a nice leisurely day with the family and a lot of trips to the van to unload and go back in again! We even bring a blanket and napkins, shop our way around the Market, then go out to a shady spot and eat the lunch that we have purchased inside. It is a great time and a lot of great food. Something new to try every time! Thank you West Side Market for helping create wonderful memories for my family!"
—Kelli Alspaugh

 Memories

"My father and I would go to the Market early on Saturday morning. By ten we were almost finished shopping and headed to Johnny Hot Dog. I would have a hot dog and Coke. The grilled dogs were delicious and there were always people coming and going through the two doors to the street.

On a trip back to Cleveland, I took my two sons to the Market and we stopped at Johnny Hot Dog. The only thing that had changed was the menu. I had my boys stand in front of the Hall of Fame poster and snapped a photo of them. Hot dogs never go out of style."

—*Thomas Bacher*

"When I was a child in the 1960s, my dad would stop at the West Side Market every Friday evening on his way home from work at Meder Sheet Metal. He would bring cold cuts and bread from Vera's Bakery. The aroma was so wonderful! I always rushed to help him unpack his brown paper bags with the handles. It was such a treat to make a quick sandwich from the goodies he brought home."

—*Betty Hickle*

This is a place best enjoyed in the company of a husband or wife; aunts, uncles, and cousins; siblings; children or grandchildren; friends and neighbors; boyfriends and girlfriends. Most will find that they want to come back—again and again. Somewhere down the line they'll tell others about the Market. That's how an entirely new generation of memories and traditions begin.

Above: Shoppers crowd the aisles on a shopping day, circa 1950
Opposite: Explaining the fine points of selecting fresh meats

"I started taking my son Matthew when I carried him in a pack on my back. After he got older we both wore backpacks. When they were so full [of groceries] that we could hardly stand, it was time to go home. I carried on the habit of going very early. It was part of the Market experience. My son and I would always have a bratwurst. He's twenty-one and away at college now. When he comes home on break I can tempt him out of bed with a trip to market and the promise of a brat."
—Jerald Chester

"This is what the Market does for me: I am a child again, if only for a leisurely hour or two. My weekly pilgrimage to the West Side Market keeps me in touch with great memories of my Hungarian grandmothers. For twenty years, my wife and I have made the same journey with our own 'Market Monster' rolling cart. My trips are not for purchases alone. It's a personal time machine back into their world and my experiences of going there with them in the 1960s."
—Tom Sawyer

"I remember taking the bus to the West Side Market with my mom as a little boy and peering through the glass to see the amazing colors and foods that the vendors offered. Every single time we went to the

Market, we would finish the trip with a bratwurst on a bench outside. My mother passed away three years ago while I was training for my third deployment to Afghanistan. The Army is currently funding my Master's Degree and I chose to return home to attend Case Western Reserve University. I've been able to take my four-year-old son to the West Side Market for scavenger hunts regularly. In advance, we write up a long list of various vegetables, meats, and candies, along with quantities for each. He runs around filled with excitement every time he spots something from our list. He knows that I used to help my mom find foods at the Market and it makes me very happy to have the opportunity to share this amazing piece of Cleveland's (and my family's) history with him."

—Nathan Riedel

Notes

1. "Rules and Regulations Governing Municipal Markets," Department of Public Service, City of Cleveland, November 1, 1912. From the West Side Market file, Cleveland City Council Archives.

2. "Report of the Market Master," Division of Markets, Department of Public Service, City of Cleveland, November 1912. From the West Side Market file, Cleveland City Council Archives.

3. Charles Kamp, "Municipal Markets in Cleveland," Annals of the American Academy of Political and Social Science 50 (1913): 128–30.

4. *Cleveland Leader*, Feb. 18, 1914.

5. *Cleveland Press*, June 30, 1932

6. *Plain Dealer*, May 13, 1981.

7. Collection of Phyllis Richards Kyle, Ohio City, The West Side Market, Western Reserve Historical Society Archives.

8. *Cleveland News*, April 3, 1945.

9. *Crain's Cleveland Business*, Sept. 20, 1982.

10. *Cleveland Press*, Dec. 16, 1963.

11. *Cleveland Press*, July 28, 1967.

12. *Plain Dealer*, Dec. 9, 1991.

Above: The West Side Market, as it appears in 2012, still commands attention in this Ohio City neighborhood

Epilogue
The Closing

IT'S THE MORNING IN REVERSE, but at a slower tempo. There's less urgency to shutting down and everybody moves at a more leisurely pace. Activity dwindles gradually rather than coming to a halt all at once. The walkways inside the great Market hall and out in the produce arcades begin to empty but a few customers—the latecomers and dawdlers—linger. As some vendors remove products from their cases and counters, others are weighing out pounds of potatoes and pork chops for the stragglers. Another day in paradise is almost done.

A hush settles on the sprawling space. Brooms and buckets are hauled out. Slicers are wiped down. Many vendors drape sheets or tablecloths over their cases. Nobody knows exactly why. The theory most often proposed is that the practice shields freshly-polished glass fronts from fingerprints and splashes. Sounds logical, but it's not like anyone will be walking around touching the dis-

Memories

"As the end of the work day approached, the vendors would cut prices. The Ehrnfelts had a fresh meat stand near the one Dad worked for. About 6:30 on Saturday nights, a man named 'Duke,' who worked for Ehrnfelt, would wave a steak at Dad and say 'Hey, Novak! Twenty-five cents!' Sometimes Dad would buy it."

—*George A. Novak, former employee*

KEEPING COUNT

- 1 million visitors a year

- 5,220 shopping Saturdays and counting

- 27,000 sq. feet of interior floor space

- 100 vendors

- And countless stories— that's the West Side Market.

play cases or waving a mop in the air. There are those that suggest people started doing this during one of the renovations when conditions were especially dirty and dusty. But Peggy Penttila, who has been at the Market for much of her adult life, thinks it goes back even farther. In the old days, she explains, the refrigeration wasn't what it is now and the coverings helped keep the contents cool on warm evenings and protected foods like cheese and meat from light that could discolor them. Then there's this, heard from a few sources: that it's done to discourage what meat cutter Tom Nagel calls "prying eyes" and the temptation to engage in a bit of five-fingered discounting after hours. "Someone may see a nice ham or turkey that could…disappear." Of course, a few yards of fabric can't actually stop anyone from going behind the counter for a peak and grab. Necessary or not, draping the stands nightly has become routine.

One hundred years equals 20,800 shopping days, give or take a few for holidays and special occasions, each bracketed by a set list of chores for opening and closing that requires workers to arrive long before patrons and stay on after the last of them depart.

Memories

"My father Andrius Kuprevicius was born in Lithuania. He shopped at the West Side Market and when I was a little girl, in the late sixties, I'd go with him on Saturdays. There was a ritual to it and something we still occasionally did together even after I grew up. I just stood there and cried the first time I went by myself after he died. But now it's wonderful, giving me this sense of continuity. He liked to wander around inside, then buy produce. I do it the same way, starting with the fish and following the identical paths he did. He liked chatting with the vendors. I remember him laughing up a storm with Irene Dever. I have relationships like that, too. In my life, the West Side Market is so much more than just a place to buy food."

—Kristina Kuprevicius

Jeremiah Wiencek, who has family connections to the Market that date back to 1912, is counting cash and organizing receipts. He'll be busy for at least an hour after the official closing time. Gordon Fernengel is weighing plastic bags filled with coins on the scale that recently held a rack of baby back ribs. He's been doing it longer than he can remember; a pound of quarters is precisely $20.00. "It's a fast, easy way to know how much change you've got," he says, "and then it's sorted and ready for the next day." That's the kind of practical know-how that comes from being a seasoned pro.

People leave one by one. Echoing through the big hall are the final shouted "see ya's," and "good nights," punctuated by the clatter of handcarts rolling along the aisles, each loaded with products going back into the coolers downstairs. Some vendors still show no signs of being ready to wrap it up. A few are on the phone, placing orders or maybe just making plans with a wife or boyfriend. Lights go off at Reilly's, then Michelle's Bakery. At Kate's Seafood in the northwest corner, a man listens to a ball game on the radio while he hoses down the floor and washes the prep surfaces. Not far away, Michael Turczyk chats recipes with a chef from a neighborhood restaurant who has stopped by to pick up his order of lamb. Behind them, a helper scours the big butcher block with a stiff wire brush, the surface a landscape of dips and grooves, scrubbing off another micro-layer of wood along with bits of meat and fat.

It's louder and more frenzied among the oranges and spinach. Merchants shout out last-minute bargains to the few remaining people passing by, trying to lure them with incredible deals, so they won't have to cart unsold stuff to the basement. Savvy shoppers know this is the time to find great buys on fruits and vegetables that are teetering between ready and overripe. Mini motorized pallet movers are lined up in the alleyway behind the stands, ready to be loaded up with boxes and crates. Mounds of cardboard and spoiled product accumulate, awaiting the arrival of the trash collector.

Tommy Boutrous, who operates a produce stand with his brothers Chebel, Joe, and John, and their sister Rita, pauses as he packs up for the night and checks the time. He shrugs, a grin spreading across his handsome youthful face, and announces to no one in particular, "Just twelve hours till we're back to do it all over again."

Memories

"I was cleaning the counter and cases at Fernengel's late one afternoon and had accumulated a big wad of soggy paper towels, like a giant spit ball. I randomly lobbed it out of the stand and into the Market, not aiming for anything in particular. It landed square on top of Steve Check's bald head. I never saw it hit, because you can't even see his stand from where I was, but Mark Zarefoss and Jeff Schade were across from him and they said it was a great launch. They were practically rolling on the floor laughing."

—Michael Turczyk, vendor, Turczyk's

It's more a statement of fact than a complaint. Sure, he's eager to get home or go out. Who wouldn't be? And who wouldn't hate the thought of rolling out of bed before the sun's fully up? But ask anyone behind the counter if they like their job and they won't just say yes, but insist they can't imagine doing anything else. Those who've tried to give it a go behind a desk or in another, unrelated field admit to coming back. Nobody makes it sound like a walk in the park—they don't romanticize what goes on here—but at least it's never boring. There's no place like the Market and these men and women return to this life day after day, week after week, for decades.

It's a way to earn a living, but more than that, too. Working here means carrying on a tradition, being part of something bigger than just a paycheck. The West Side Market is Cleveland's Empire State Building, its Golden Gate Bridge, an iconic place where past and present literally and figuratively inhabit the same space, blending naturally and seamlessly to create a setting and an atmosphere that is unique and authentic.

Cleveland is not a glitzy, glamorous town. It isn't a place with a name and a mystique that lures travelers. This rust belt city is too real, too gritty, and too busy going about the daily business of being its Midwestern self, populated by mostly ordinary residents living regular lives. And that's where the Market fits into the cultural and social fabric. It was built for the people that live here, to make getting their daily bread—along with butter, beets, and beef—easier and better. And because that's still the primary purpose, it has developed the cachet that comes with longevity and consistency, qualities reinforced by the presence of vendors who recognize their customers and remember the parents and grandparents that brought them here when they were little. There's an inevitable tension between those who favor change and those that don't, but whether by intention or accident the two camps have achieved a sort of balance, accepting new ideas—not always, not swiftly, or even willingly—while holding fast to a sense of what matters and remaining reassuringly, resolutely the same.

America is still a relatively young country, charmed by the remnants of its own history. This hundred-year-old building, a hybrid of utility and grandeur, has endured and thrived. From the start it was

(M)emories

"Despite the popular and often repeated misconception, this was always a Market. The building has never been used for anything else. People often assume otherwise because of its grand proportions. The width and height are elegant, classical. The place has held up for a century with relatively little alteration. Now it has a history and people appreciate that. We are lucky to be able to do our shopping in such extraordinary surroundings. It is an event to be here and creates a special context for all the entrepreneurs that helps them sell their products."

—Paul Volpe, architect

designed to be a commercial space and a functional structure. But it was also a grand gesture, a spectacular architectural statement that spoke of permanence and prosperity, civic ideals, and community vitality. This combination has helped the West Side Market survive intact, while other, less-ambitious municipal markets, locally and around the country, were demolished or reinvented as purely tourist destinations.

There are loyal regulars who show up consistently and often, enthusiastic but occasional shoppers, once-a-year pilgrims, and sightseers. Fans travel from near and far, from cities and the suburbs. They are rich, poor, and in-between, white-collar professionals, dirt-under-their-fingernails working folks, retirees, and young families. Many residents have a sense of ownership and pride, claiming the Market as their own and showing it off to guests. Everyone who's ever spent time here has tales to tell. It might be dramatic—like getting their picture taken with a celebrity—or as small as a whiff of something wonderful that takes them back to childhood. Each memory is a piece of a jigsaw puzzle; put them together and they make a picture of Cleveland's West Side Market.

Food brought people to this area of Ohio City in 1840, when farmers sold their produce off the back of horse-drawn wagons. And it still does. In 2012, the Market is the centerpiece for a burgeoning culinary district. David O'Neil, a public market expert, believes its future is brighter than ever. "Retail has gotten so big, so nationalized. We've lost our Main Streets, our storefronts. The Market is really a collection of small neighborhood shops. It fills our hunger for community, an interest in buying food from people you know and a desire to support local businesses."

The few vendors and their employees who remain on this particular Friday night aren't pondering such lofty, forward-looking thoughts. They just want this day done. A uniformed security guard goes door to door—there are twenty-seven pairs in the building, plus eight sets in the produce arcades—carrying a clanking plastic milk crate filled with locks and lengths of metal chain that he uses to secure each one. His last stop, after everybody's gone, will be the loading dock. Then at last the West Side Market will be silent and still. Until tomorrow, when everyone returns and it begins all over again.

 Memories

"I believe Cleveland, like the rest of the nation, will see a renaissance in urban living, reversing the out-migration to the suburbs, and the West Side Market will have a renewed importance to new a generation of city residents."

—**Ted Sande, architect and historic preservationist**

"The Market is a beautiful place, but more importantly it's a beautiful experience, a physical and spiritual landmark, and an expression of how we see ourselves and our city."

—**Paul Volpe, architect**

SOURCES

Avery, Elroy McKendree. *A History of Cleveland and Its Environs: The Heart of New Connecticut.* Chicago & NY: Lewis Publishing Company, 1918.

Bremner, Robert. "The Civic Revival in Ohio." *American Journal of Economics and Sociology* 8, no. 1 (1948): 61–68.

———. "Reformed Businessman: Tom L. Johnson." *American Journal of Economics and Sociology* 8, no. 3 (1949): 299–309.

Bureau of the Census. "Municipal Markets in cities having a population of over 30,000: 1918." Washington, D.C.: U.S. Government Printing Office, 1919.

Condon, George. *West of the Cuyahoga.* Kent, OH: Kent State University Press, 2006.

———. *Cleveland: The Best Kept Secret.* Garden City, NY: Doubleday, 1967.

Cornell, Arnold. "Summer Prices in Mid-Winter: How Cleveland Does It." *Technical World Magazine* XXII, no. 1 (1914): 22–227.

Division of Architecture, City of Cleveland. "Historic West Side Market Revitalization: Masterplan Report," May 30, 1986.

Dyson, Carol and Floyd Mansberger. "Structural Glass: Its History, Manufacture, Repair and Replacement." *CRM (Cultural Resource Management): The Journal of Heritage Stewardship* 18, no. 8 (1995): 15–19.

Ganaccia, Donna. *We Are What We Eat: Ethnic Food and the Making of America.* Cambridge, MA: Harvard University Press, 1998.

George Evans & Associates. "West Side Market Improvement Project, Bid Package 'A' (mechanical, electrical, and service area improvements)." Cleveland, Ohio: George Evans & Associates, 1986.

Guastavino, Rafael IV. *The Architect and His Son: The Immigrant Journey of Rafael Guastavino.* Westminster, MD: Heritage Books, 2008.

Hopwood, E. C. "Newton D. Baker's Administration as Mayor of Cleveland and its Accomplishments." *National Municipal Review* 2, no. 3 (1913): 461–66.

Johanessen, Eric. *Cleveland Architecture, 1876–1976.* Cleveland, OH: Western Reserve Historical Society, 1979.

Kamp, Charles. "Municipal Markets in Cleveland." *Annals of the American Academy of Political and Social Science* 50 (1913): 128–130.

———. "The Management of a Municipal Market." *The American City* X (1914): 63–63.

Knepper, George W. *Ohio and Its People.* Kent, OH : The Kent State University Press, 1989.

Lewis, Joanne. *To Market, To Market: An Old-Fashioned Family Story.* Cleveland Heights, OH: Elandon Books, Inc., 1981.

Mayo, James. *The American Grocery Store: The Business Evolution of an Architectural Space.* Westport, CT: Greenwood Press, 1993.

———. "The American Public Market." *Journal of Architectural Education* 45, no. 1 (1991): 41–57.

Miller, Carol Poh and Robert Wheeler. *Cleveland: A Concise History, 1796–1990.* Bloomington, IN: Indiana University Press, 1990.

"New Market House for West Side." *The Ohio Architect and Builder* 8 (1906): 29–32.

Ochsendorf, John. *Guastavino Vaulting: The Art of Structural Tile*. NY: Princeton Architectural Press, 2010.

O'Neil, David. "What We Need to Learn from America's Classic Markets." Project for Public Spaces website, www.pps.org/articles/lessonsofclassicmarkets.

Parks, Janet and Alan Neuman. *The Old World Builds the New: The Guastavino Company and the Technology of the Catalan Vault, 1885–1962*. NY: Avery Architectural and Fine Arts Library and the Miriam and Ira D. Wallach Art Gallery, Columbia University in the City of New York, 1996.

Professional Service Industries, Inc., Herron Consultants Division. "Historic West Side Market Revitalization, 1986, Evaluation of Architectural Components, Masonry and Structural Steel Members Testing." April 22, 1987.

Tangires, Helen. "Feeding the Cities: Public Markets and Municipal Reform in the Progressive Era." *Prologue Magazine*. 29, no. 1 (1997): 17–26.

———. *Public Markets*. NY: W.W. Norton, 2008.

———. "Public Markets and the City: A Historical Perspective." Presentation, the 6th International Public Market Conference, October 30, 2005.

T. W. Grogan and Company. "Analysis and Appraisal of the West Side Market House for the City of Cleveland." Cleveland, OH, 1950.

U.S. Bureau of the Census. "Municipal Markets." *Municipal Journal and Public Works* XLVII, no. 10 (1919): 146–48.

Van Tassel, David, and John Grabowski, eds. *The Encyclopedia of Cleveland History*. Bloomington, IN: Indiana University Press, 1996.

Volpe, Paul et al. "Historic West Side Market Revitalization: Phase II-Exterior Restoration, Masonry Repairs, Window Replacement and Reroofing; Schematic Design Report." Cleveland, OH: Division of Architecture, 1987.

Wheeler, Robert A. *Pleasantly Situated on the West Side: A Catalogue of the Special Exhibition of the Ohio City Area of Cleveland…* Cleveland, OH: Western Reserve Historical Society, 1980.

Zuchelli, Hunter & Associates, Inc. "West Side Market: Preliminary Marketing and Merchandising Strategy Evaluation." Annapolis, Maryland: Zuchelli, Hunter & Associates, 1985.

ILLUSTRATION CREDITS

ii: Barney Taxel; iii: Shutterstock Images; v: Private Collection of Pat Deucher; Shutterstock Images; vi: Barney Taxel; vii: Barney Taxel; Shutterstock Images; ix: Shutterstock Images; xi: iStockphoto

Introduction

1: Private Collection of James Spangler; Shutterstock Images; 2: Barney Taxel; Private Collection of Linda Bistricky; Shutterstock Images; 3: Shutterstock Images; Cleveland Public Library Photograph Collection; 4: Barney Taxel; Private collection of Joe DeCaro; 5: Barney Taxel; 6: Barney Taxel; Shutterstock Images; 7: Shutterstock Images; Barney Taxel

Chapter 1

8: Barney Taxel; 9: Clockwise from top, Cleveland Public Library Photograph Collection; Private Collection of Karen Curiale Torreiter; Shutterstock Images; 10: Michael Schwartz Library, Cleveland State University; 11: The *Cleveland Press* Collection, Michael Schwartz Library, Cleveland State University; 12–13: Special Collections, Michael Schwartz Library, Cleveland State University; 15: Clockwise from top, Cleveland Public Library Photograph Collection; Special Collections, Michael Schwartz Library, Cleveland State University; 16: Courtesy the Western Reserve Historical Society; 17: Clockwise from top, Cleveland Public Library Photograph Collection; Special Collections, Michael Schwartz Library, Cleveland State University; 18: Courtesy the Western Reserve Historical Society; Background, Avery Architectural and Fine Arts Library, Columbia University; 19: Cleveland Public Library Photograph Collection; Courtesy the Western Reserve Historical Society; 20: The *Cleveland Press* Collection, Michael Schwartz Library, Cleveland State University; 22: Courtesy the Western Reserve Historical Society; 23: Clockwise from top, Private Collection of Gordon Fernengel; Courtesy the Western Reserve Historical Society; 24–27: Barney Taxel; 28: Clockwise from top, Private Collection of Jim Krestyan; Cleveland Public Library Photograph Collection; 29: Clockwise from top, Private Collection of Jim Krestyan; Private Collection of the West Side Market; Barney Taxel; 30: The *Cleveland Press* Collection, Michael Schwartz Library, Cleveland State University, Clayton Knipper photographer; 31–32: Barney Taxel; 33: Private Collection of Tim Jeziorski; 34: Clockwise from top, West Side Market, 1923, Photograph by Edd Ruggles, Image number 966579, Photo Studio Collection, The Cleveland Museum of Art Archive; The *Cleveland Press* Collection, Michael Schwartz Library, Cleveland State University, Paul Toppelstein photographer; Barney Taxel; 35: West Side Market, 1923, Photograph by Edd Ruggles, Image number 966578, Photo Studio Collection, The Cleveland Museum of Art Archive; 37: Private Collection of the West Side Market; 38: Clockwise from top, Cleveland Public Library Photograph Collection; Private Collection of Elaine Szilagyi; 39: The *Cleveland Press* Collection, Michael Schwartz Library, Cleveland State University, Tony Tomsic photographer; 40: Private Collection of Gary Fougerousse; Private Collection of Tim Jeziorski; 41: Cleveland Public Library Photograph Collection

Chapter 2

42: Barney Taxel; 43: Clockwise from top, Private Collection of Gordon Fernengel; Shutterstock Images; Special Collections, Michael Schwartz Library, Cleveland State University; 44: Shutterstock Images;

45: Clockwise from top, Private Collection of Tom Gillespie; The *Cleveland Press* Collection, Michael Schwartz Library, Cleveland State University; Private Collection of Charles "Bud" Leu Jr.; 46: Counterclockwise from top, Shutterstock Images; Private Collection of the Ehrnfelt Family; Private Collection of Karen Curiale Torreiter; Private Collection of Matt Minyard; 47: Photo courtesy of Terry Stevick; 48: Private Collection of Chuck Schilla Jr.; 49: Clockwise from top, Private Collection of Bill Rini; Shutterstock Images; 50: Top to bottom, Courtesy the Western Reserve Historical Society; Private Collection of the West Side Market; Private Collection of Charles "Bud" Leu Jr.; 51: Shutterstock Images; 52: Counterclockwise from top, Barney Taxel; Private Collection of the West Side Market; 53: Private Collection of the West Side Market; 54: Barney Taxel; 55: Clockwise from top, Private Collection of Bill Retzer; Private Collection of Karen Curiale Torreiter; 56: Private Collection of the Schwark Family; 57: Private Collection of Karen Curiale Torreiter; 58: From top, Private Collection of William Hildebrandt; Barney Taxel; 59: From top, Special Collections, Michael Schwartz Library, Cleveland State University; Barney Taxel; 60: Barney Taxel; 61: From top, Private Collection of Larry Vistein; Private Collection of the West Side Market; 62: Private Collection of Joe DeCaro; 63: From left to right, Courtesy of the *Cleveland Plain Dealer*; Veer; 64: From top, Courtesy the Western Reserve Historical Society; Special Collections, Michael Schwartz Library, Cleveland State University; 65: The *Cleveland Press* Collection, Michael Schwartz Library, Cleveland State University, Frank Aleksandrowicz photographer; 66: From top, iStockphoto; Private Collection of Roseann Anselmo DiBlasio; 67: From top, The *Cleveland Press* Collection, Michael Schwartz Library, Cleveland State University, Frank Aleksandrowicz photographer; Private Collection of Roseann Anselmo DiBlasio; 68: Private Collection of Anthony DiFranco; 69: Private Collection of John Rolston; 70: From top, Barney Taxel; Private Collection of the West Side Market; 71: iStockphoto; 72: Barney Taxel; 73: iStockphoto; 74: From top, Private Collection of the West Side Market; Private Collection of the Leu Family; 75: Private Collection of Tim Jeziorski; 76: The *Cleveland Press* Collection, Michael Schwartz Library, Cleveland State University; 77: Clockwise from top, Private Collection of Anthony Anselmo; Private Collection of Irene Dever; 78: iStockphoto; 79: Barney Taxel; 80: From top, Courtesy of Emile Chbeir, Johnny Hot Dog; Private Collection of the West Side Market; 81: iStockphoto; 82: Private Collection of Larry Schade; Background, Private Collection of Amy Freels; 83: Private Collection of Tina Swinehart; iStockphoto; 84: Barney Taxel; 85: Private Collection of the Little Sisters of the Poor, Cleveland; 86: From top, Private Collection of the Northeast Ohio Coalition for the Homeless; Private Collection of Karen Curiale; 87: Private Collection of Joe DeCaro; 88: From top, Barney Taxel; Private Collection of Bill Retzer; 89: Private Collection of Bill Retzer; 90: Private Collection of Becky (Stumpf) Fitch; 91: iStockphoto; 92: Private Collection of Tony Pinzone; 93: Private Collection of James Spangler; 95: Private Collection of Karen Curiale Torreiter; 97: Private Collection of the Penttila Family; 98: Private Collection of Irene Dever; 99: Barney Taxel; 100: Clockwise from top, Cleveland Public Library Photograph Collection; Private Collection of Roseann Anselmo DiBlasio; 101: From top, Private Collection of Larry Schade; Barney Taxel; 102–3: Barney Taxel; 104: Special Collections, Michael Schwartz Library, Cleveland State University, Tony Tomsic photographer; 105: Special Collections, Michael Schwartz Library, Cleveland State University, Bill Nehez, photographer

Chapter 3
106: Barney Taxel; 107: Clockwise from top, Mike Lembke, Taxel Image Group; Private Collection of the West Side Market; Shutterstock Images; 108: From top, Private Collection of William Hildebrandt; Private Collection of Bill Retzer; 109: From top, Private Collection of Linda Bistricky; Barney Taxel; 110: From top, Barney Taxel; Private Collection of Roseann Anselmo DiBlasio; 111: From top, Private Collection of Charles "Bud" Leu Jr.; Barney Taxel; 112: From top, Barney Taxel; Private Collection of Irene Dever;

113: Barney Taxel; 114: From top, Barney Taxel; The *Cleveland Press* Collection, Michael Schwartz Library, Cleveland State University, Glenn Zahn photographer; Barney Taxel; 115: From top, Barney Taxel; The *Cleveland Press* Collection, Michael Schwartz Library, Cleveland State University; 116–17: Barney Taxel; 118: From top, Barney Taxel; Private Collection of Elaine Szilagyi; 119: iStockphoto; 120: Private Collection of Linda Bistricky; 121: From top, Barney Taxel; Private Collection of William Hildebrandt; 122: From top, Private Collection of Matt Minyard; Private Collection of William Hildebrandt; 123: Barney Taxel; 124: Private Collection of the West Side Market; 125: Barney Taxel; 126: From top, The *Cleveland Press* Collection, Michael Schwartz Library, Cleveland State University, Bernie Noble photographer; Barney Taxel; 127: iStockphoto; 128: From top, Private Collection of Elaine Szilagyi; Barney Taxel; 129: Clockwise, The *Cleveland Press* Collection, Michael Schwartz Library, Cleveland State University, Tony Tomsic photographer; *Cleveland Plain Dealer*; 130: Private Collection of Elaine Szilagyi; 131: From top, The *Cleveland Press* Collection, Michael Schwartz Library, Cleveland State University; Barney Taxel; 132: From top, The *Cleveland Press* Collection, Michael Schwartz Library, Cleveland State University, Frank Reed photographer; Private Collection of Cleveland Produce Terminal; Private Collection of Cleveland Produce Terminal; 133: Barney Taxel; 134: From top, Private Collection of the Penttila Family; Private Collection of Larry Vistein; 135: Mike Lembke, Taxel Image Group; 136: From top, The *Cleveland Press* Collection, Michael Schwartz Library, Cleveland State University, Glenn Zahn photographer; The *Cleveland Press* Collection, Michael Schwartz Library, Cleveland State University, James Thomas photographer; 137: Barney Taxel; 138: From top, Barney Taxel; Private Collection of Roseann Anselmo DiBlasio; 139: Private Collection of the West Side Market; 140: From top, Private Collection of Beverly Tabacco; Private Collection of the Landmarks Commission Office; 141: From top, Private Collection of Tim Jeziorski; Private Collection of Chris Sommer Krisak; 142: From top, Private Collection of William R. Pawlowski; Private Collection of Beverly Tabacco; 143: Private Collection of William Hildebrandt; 144: Barney Taxel; 145: From top, Private Collection of Karen Curiale Torreiter; Private Collection of William R. Pawlowski; 146: From top, Private Collection of Miklos and Angela Szucs; Barney Taxel; 147: Barney Taxel; 148: From top, Barney Taxel; Private Collection of Gus Mougianis; 149: Clockwise, The *Cleveland Press* Collection, Michael Schwartz Library, Cleveland State University, Herman Seid photographer; Barney Taxel; 150: Barney Taxel; 151: iStockphoto

Chapter 4

152: Barney Taxel; 153: Clockwise, Private Collection of the West Side Market; Shutterstock Images; Private Collection of Charles "Bud" Leu Jr.; 154: Avery Architectural and Fine Arts Library, Columbia University; *Cleveland Plain Dealer*; 155: Private Collection of Elaine Szilagyi; 156: From top, Private Collection of Gordon Fernengel; Private Collection of William Hildebrandt; 157: From top, Private Collection of the Badstuber Family; *Cleveland Leader*; 159: From top, Courtesy the Western Reserve Historical Society; Private Collection of Victor Rini; Private Collection of the West Side Market; Private Collection of Bill Retzer; 160: From top, Private Collection of Pat Deucher; Private Collection of the West Side Market;
161: Private Collection of the West Side Market; Private Collection of Karen Curiale Torreiter;
162: Clockwise, Private Collection of the West Side Market; Barney Taxel; 163: The *Cleveland Press* Collection, Michael Schwartz Library, Cleveland State University, Tony Tomsic photographer; 164: From top, Private Collection of Gary Fougerousse; Private Collection of the West Side Market; 166: From top, Poster created for the Cleveland International Film Festival by The Adcom Group, photo by The Reuben Group; Private Collection of Elaine Szilagyi; 168: Barney Taxel; 169: From top, Cleveland Public Library Photograph Collection; Private Collection of Bill Retzer; 170: Private Collection of James Spangler;

171: From top, Barney Taxel; Private Collection of Gary Fougerousse; 172–75: Barney Taxel; 176: "Fruits and Vegetables" from *The Big Book of Daniel: Collected Poems*, ed. Maj Ragain (Bottom Dog Press 2011; http://smithdocs.net); Barney Taxel; 177: From top, The *Cleveland Press* Collection, Michael Schwartz Library, Cleveland State University, Tony Tomsic photographer; Private Collection of the West Side Market; 178: From top, Private Collection of John Rolston; Private Collection of the West Side Market; Private Collection of Irene Dever; 179: From top, Private Collection of James Traynor; Private Collection of Mary Masters; 180: From top, Private Collection of Tony Pinzone; Cleveland Public Library Photograph Collection; 181: From top, Private Collection of Ilse Sheppard; Private Collection of Elaine Szilagyi; 182: Private Collection of William R. Pawlowski; Barney Taxel; 183: From top, Private Collection of the City of Cleveland, Donn R. Nottage photographer; Barney Taxel; 184: From top, Genevieve Nisly Photography; Private Collection of Bill Retzer; 185: Private Collection of the Schwark Family; Private Collection of Roseann Anselmo DiBlasio; 186: From top, Private Collection of Jimmy Traynor; Barney Taxel; 187: Genevieve Nisly Photography

Chapter 5

188: Barney Taxel; 189: Clockwise, Barney Taxel; Private Collection of Elaine Szilagyi; Shutterstock Images; 190: From top, Private Collection of Roseann Anselmo DiBlasio; Barney Taxel; 191: From top, Private Collection of Gordon Fernengel; Private Collection of the Landmarks Commission Office; 193: From top, *Cleveland Plain Dealer*; Private Collection of Roseann Anselmo DiBlasio; *Cleveland Plain Dealer*; 194: From top, Private Collection of the West Side Market; Barney Taxel; 195: From top, Private Collection of George A. Novak; Private Collection of Beverly Tabacco; 196: From top, Private Collection of Elaine Szilagyi; The *Cleveland Press* Collection, Michael Schwartz Library, Cleveland State University; Barney Taxel; 197: From top, Barney Taxel; Special Collections, Michael Schwartz Library, Cleveland State University; 198: From top, Private Collection of Herbert Simpkins; Private Collection of the West Side Market; 199: From top, Private Collection of Elaine Szilagyi; Barney Taxel; 200–02: Barney Taxel; 203: From top, Cleveland Public Library Photograph Collection; Private Collection of Jack Gentille; Private Collection of Anthony Anselmo; 204: From top, Private Collection of Emery Bacha; The *Cleveland Press* Collection, Michael Schwartz Library, Cleveland State University, Tony Tomsic photographer; 205: From top, Private Collection of Anthony Anselmo; Private Collection of the West Side Market; 206–7: Barney Taxel; 208: From top, Private Collection of Rosie Leskovich; Private Collection of the Ehrnfelt Family; 209: Private Collection of the West Side Market; 210: Private Collection of Bill Retzer; 211: Barney Taxel; 212: From top, Private Collection of Tony Pinzone; Private Collection of Karen Curiale Torreiter; 213–14: Barney Taxel; 215: Private Collection of the West Side Market; 216: From top, Private Collection of Becky (Stumpf) Fitch; Barney Taxel; 217: Private Collection of the Schwark Family; 218: From top, Private Collection of Elaine Szilagyi; Private Collection of Irene Dever; 219–21: Barney Taxel; 222: From top, Barney Taxel; Private Collection of Bill Retzer; 223: Private Collection of James Traynor; 224: From top, Private Collection of William "Gus" Glaros; Barney Taxel; 225: From top, Private Collection of Anthony Anselmo; Private Collection of Bill Retzer; 226–27: Barney Taxel; 228: From top, Barney Taxel; Private Collection of Charles "Bud" Leu Jr.; 229–32: Barney Taxel

Epilogue

233: From top, Barney Taxel; Shutterstock Images; 234: From top, Barney Taxel; Shutterstock Images; 235: From top, Shutterstock Images; Barney Taxel; 236: Barney Taxel; 237: From top, Barney Taxel; Shutterstock Images